THE CRAFT OF LEGAL REASONING

THE POTOMAC SERIES

THE CRAFT OF LEGAL REASONING

Brian L. Porto
College of Saint Joseph

Under the general editorship of
Calvin C. Jillson
Southern Methodist University

Harcourt Brace College Publishers
Fort Worth Philadelphia San Diego New York Orlando Austin San Antonio
Toronto Montreal London Sydney Tokyo

Publisher: **Earl McPeek**
Executive Editor: **David Tatom**
Product Manager: **Steve Drummond**
Developmental Editor: **Pam Hatley**
Project Editor: **Matt Ball**
Art Director: **Brian Salisbury**
Production Manager: **Linda McMillan**

Text Design: **Linda Hines**

ISBN: 0-15-503696-3
Library of Congress Catalog Card Number: 97-61103

Address for orders:
Harcourt Brace College Publishers
6277 Sea Harbor Drive
Orlando, FL 32887-6777
1-800-782-4479

Address for editorial correspondence:
Harcourt Brace College Publishers
301 Commerce Street, Suite 3700
Fort Worth, TX 76102

Web site address:
http://www.hbcollege.com

Printed in the United States of America

7 8 9 0 1 2 3 4 5 6 066 9 8 7 6 5 4 3 2 1

For my mother, Ann Parlapiano Porto,
my first and best teacher

PREFACE

The Craft of Legal Reasoning is a text designed for advanced under-graduates, but beginning law students will also find it useful. The book results from my frustration at having to teach myself legal reasoning despite five years of graduate study in political science and three years of law school. It also results from my desire to spare today's students that same frustration by preparing them for case analysis through preliminary instruction in the legal method.

It may seem surprising that one who studied legal matters intensively during eight years of graduate and professional education claims to be self-taught in legal reasoning. This is not so surprising, though, when you stop to consider that during the 1970s, Ph.D. programs in political science were more interested in teaching their students how to use the quantitative techniques of behavioral science to explain and predict judicial decisions than how to reason through a maze of facts and legal principles to a sound conclusion.

That preference was understandable and defensible because, after all, political scientists—especially those who had earned Ph.D.'s in the 1960s and 1970s—were substantially more familiar with the quantitative methods of social science than the reasoning by analogy that lawyers use. Moreover, political scientists' aim in studying legal matters was not to retrace the steps of law school faculty whose law journal articles employed legal methodology almost exclusively and rarely cited social science studies to support their conclusions. Rather, political scientists were understandably eager to discover whether their statistical methods could explain the votes that appellate judges cast as the products of the judges' personal and professional backgrounds and public policy preferences. If so, political science would make a valuable contribution to the understanding of the judicial process that lawyers and law schools could not make.

Unfortunately, emphasizing ideology as the principal reason for judicial decisions and statistical analysis as the primary method of inquiry caused a corresponding de-emphasis upon teaching and learning legal reasoning. The result, in my case, was a new Ph.D. who began teaching constitutional law to undergraduates in 1979 without the firm grasp of legal reasoning necessary for that task.

Self-study narrowed that knowledge gap considerably by the autumn of 1984, when I entered law school. Absent that self-study, the introduction to law school would have been even more traumatic than it was, because law professors made no more concerted effort than the political scientists had to teach legal reasoning. That failure certainly did not result from unfamiliarity with the techniques of legal reasoning, because law professors use those techniques daily in their teaching and writing, frequently with remarkable skill. Rather, they assumed that (1) legal reasoning is simple enough, and (2) law students are capable enough so that direct classroom instruction in the legal method is unnecessary.[1] For example, one professor informed our class early in the first year of law school that he intended to teach "dancing, not walking." Mere dancing would have been fine; during the first year, though, it often seemed that professors were teaching pole-vaulting despite their students' inability to walk.

Similarly, professors who teach undergraduate law content courses sometimes require their students to "dance"—that is, analyze appellate opinions—before they are capable of "walking"—that is, reasoning by analogy. This book strives to teach infants in the law to "walk," in the hope that they will finish college and begin law school or graduate school ready to "dance." The book aims to prepare undergraduates for case analysis and debate by means of systematic instruction in the legal method. It will also assist first-year law students who did not study legal reasoning as undergraduates to catch up with their classmates who did study it.

Accordingly, Chapter One, titled "The Nature and Importance of Legal Reasoning," begins by explaining why legal reasoning is worth studying. Thereafter, Chapter One explains how the legal method works, using United States Supreme Court decisions on familiar subjects to illustrate the case-by-case development of legal principles.

---

[1] In fairness to law schools, I should note that they require first-year students to take a year-long course in legal writing and research wherein students perform writing exercises designed to teach legal reasoning. However, the legal writing and research course that I took did not explain or illustrate the reasoning process nearly as effectively as its importance demands. Among this book's purposes are to aid law students whose experiences were similar to mine and to give law schools a tool for teaching the legal method.

In so doing, Chapter One shows that both objective evidence and ideological preferences influence judicial decision making, especially in cases that involve controversial issues of constitutional law.

However, Chapter One also shows that typically, lawyers and judges use legal reasoning to resolve disputes that are important only to the named parties in a case. The discussion presents examples of such cases. Chapter One concludes with an illustrative case and discussion questions designed to facilitate a Socratic dialogue between professors and students concerning the case and the chapter.

Successive chapters apply the lessons learned in Chapter One to the four basic tasks that cases require lawyers and judges to perform. The four basic tasks include statutory construction, Chapter Two; constitutional interpretation, Chapter Three; common law decision making, Chapter Four; and administrative regulation, Chapter Five. Each of these chapters identifies the importance of its subject, explains in detail the reasoning process that occurs in a particular legal context by presenting numerous case examples, and concludes with an illustrative case and questions designed to provoke classroom discussion about the case and the chapter. Chapter Six reviews the legal method and the tasks it performs.

This book provides a framework for understanding judicial decisions. After reading and discussing its contents, students will proceed to case analysis familiar with legal language and the legal method. They will understand and be able to evaluate the legal principles, techniques of interpreting statutory and constitutional language, and philosophical debates between judges and justices that cases present. In law, as in life, careful instruction in walking must precede expectations of dancing.

ACKNOWLEDGMENTS

Numerous people helped to make this book possible, and I thank them sincerely. Three teachers are noteworthy. Stephen Wood sparked my interest in the law, Alan Engel made me appreciate its political context, and Patrick Baude showed me how a first-rate lawyer crafts an argument or an opinion.

Justice Denise Johnson of the Vermont Supreme Court, Judge William Garrard of the Indiana Court of Appeals, and Justice William Johnson of the New Hampshire Supreme Court demonstrated fine legal craftsmanship daily during my judicial clerkships in their offices. Students, past and present, have raised questions and made comments that inform this book.

Professors Herbert Waltzer and Augustus Jones of Miami University and David Schultz of the University of Wisconsin at River Falls offered insightful critiques during the early stages of this project. Harcourt Brace Senior Acquisitions Editor David Tatom believed in the project, and Developmental Editors Susan Petty and Pam Hatley brought it to fruition. Shirley Zybura typed the manuscript quickly, skillfully, and with unfailing good humor. Professors Gregory D. Russell, Washington State University; Susan Mezey, Loyola University of Chicago; James G. Dickson, Stephen F. Austin State University; Kenneth L. Deutsch, SUNY Geneseo; William M. Leiter, California State University, Long Beach; William Haltom, University of Puget Sound; and Priscilla H. Machado, United States Naval Academy provided encouraging reviews and helpful suggestions.

My wife, Sherrie Greeley, knew when I needed to leave the office and the library behind in favor of a hiking or cross-country ski trail. I am deeply indebted to her for that and for her continuing love and support.

Any remaining errors probably exist because I was daydreaming about hiking or skiing while working. I am responsible for them.

ABOUT THE AUTHOR

Brian L. Porto teaches courses in law and American politics at the College of St. Joseph in Rutland, Vermont, and the College for Life-long Learning, a division of the University System of New Hampshire. He holds a J.D. from Indiana University at Bloomington and a Ph.D. in political science from Miami University (Ohio). Dr. Porto has taught at Macalester College (Minnesota), at Norwich University (Vermont), and has worked as a lawyer in both state government and private practice. He is licensed to practice law in Vermont and Indiana. Dr. Porto's writings have appeared in *A.L.R. Fed.*, the *Commercial Law Journal*, the *Indiana Law Journal*, the *Journal of Law and Education*, the *New England Law Review*, the *Pace University Law Review*, and several edited volumes. Dr. Porto is a member of national and regional professional associations in both law and political science. He lives in Bethel, Vermont.

CONTENTS

Preface   vii

Chapter 1   The Nature and Importance of Legal
Reasoning   1

Why Legal Reasoning Is Worth Studying   2
Legal Reasoning Explained   7
Conclusion   19
Epilogue: Symbolic Speech and the First Amendment   20
Questions for Discussion   25

Chapter 2   Statutory Construction   27

Introduction   28
The Nature of Statutory Construction   28
The Techniques of Statutory Construction   32
  The Plain Meaning Rule   32
  Context   36
  Statutory Purpose   37
  Legislative History   40
  Presumptions and Canons of Statutory Construction   46
    Presumptions   46
    Canons   48
Conclusion   50
Epilogue: Construing the Federal Kidnapping Act   53
Questions for Discussion   56

Chapter 3   Constitutional Interpretation   59

Introduction   60
The Separation of Powers   60
Federalism   62
Civil Liberties   65
Interpreting Constitutional Language   68
  Introduction   68
  Methods of Constitutional Interpretation   68
    Historical   68
    Textual   73

Structural   75
Doctrinal   77
Prudential   80
Ethical   83
Evaluating Constitutional Opinions   87
Conclusion   88
Epilogue: The Constitutionality of a Veterans' Preference Law   88
Questions for Discussion   93

Chapter 4   Common-Law Decisionmaking   95

Introduction   96
The Common-Law Tradition   99
The Common Law in Action   109
Dangerous Products   109
Employer–Employee Relations   116
Conclusion   123
Epilogue: The Psychotherapist's Duty of Care   124
Questions for Discussion   127

Chapter 5   Administrative Regulation   129

Introduction   130
Agency Activities   131
Rule Making   131
Legislation   133
Assigning Responsibility for Rule Making   133
Developing a Draft Rule   133
Internal Review   134
External Review   134
Publication   134
Public Participation   135
Action on the Draft Rule   135
Congressional and Presidential Oversight   136
Congressional Oversight   136
Presidential Oversight   137
Rule Enforcement and Adjudication   139
Judicial Review of Agency Action   141
Conclusion   153
Epilogue: Passive Restraints Revisited   154
Questions for Discussion   158

Chapter 6 Summary and Conclusion 161
Summary 162
Conclusion 168

Appendix A American Courts: Organization
and Jurisdiction 171

Appendix B The Federal Appellate Circuits 175

Appendix C Finding Legal Sources 177

Index 185

CHAPTER 1

The Nature and Importance of Legal Reasoning

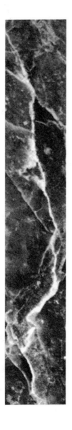

Why Legal Reasoning Is Worth Studying

Legal Reasoning Explained

Conclusion

Epilogue: Symbolic Speech and the First Amendment

Questions for Discussion

WHY LEGAL REASONING IS WORTH STUDYING

The study of law makes demands on students similar to the demands that the study of a language or a science makes. Law, like Russian or geology, requires you to master a unique body of rules and principles. Once you have done so, you can converse, conduct experiments properly or, if you are studying law, understand how lawyers and judges use legal reasoning to resolve disputes.

In learning law, as in learning Russian, you must grasp linguistic rules and vocabulary in order to converse in the new language. As a student of law, though, you learn the new language in order to understand how lawyers and judges use it to resolve disputes.

In learning law, as in learning science, you must familiarize yourself with a set of procedures developed during years of experimentation that professionals in your field use to answer challenging questions. There is a key difference though, between the scientist's procedures and the lawyer's procedures. The scientist's procedures examine reasonably predictable physical phenomena such as waves, photosynthesis, or erosion. The lawyer's procedures must operate in the unpredictable "laboratory" of human relations. People often act in a manner that is inconsistent with their words, and personal and business relationships can end quickly amidst anger and jealousy. As a result, you can gain insight into the legal method by studying the linguistic or the scientific method, but only by studying legal reasoning itself can you understand how lawyers and judges resolve cases.

Legal reasoning is the process by which lawyers argue and judges decide cases. One component of legal reasoning is **reasoning by analogy,** or, more simply put, reasoning by example. When lawyers and judges reason, they use rules and principles developed in earlier cases to decide current, similar cases. Frequently, when the facts of the present case are similar to those of the prior case, the court that decides the present case will apply to it the rule of law announced in the earlier case.

A second component of legal reasoning is **linguistic analysis,** which figures prominently in cases that require courts to determine the meaning and effect of statutory (see Chapter Two) or constitutional (see Chapter Three) language. This book uses the term linguistic analysis to refer not merely to close examinations of statutory or constitutional language, but, more broadly, to encompass all of the techniques that courts use to construe such language in order to resolve cases. In constitutional cases, those techniques are often more important to the outcome than reasoning by analogy because courts defer less often to prior decisions in constitutional cases than in other cases. Nevertheless, courts often resolve statutory and even constitutional cases by using reasoning by analogy and linguistic analysis together.

The third component of legal reasoning is judges' views about public-policy disputes and the role that courts should play in those disputes. These views often shape judges' attitudes toward prior cases and statutory or constitutional language and their decisions in particular cases. Thus, legal reasoning is a mixture of analogies, linguistic analyses, and **judicial discretion**. The interaction between the three components is the craft of legal reasoning. Section II will introduce you to this interaction, and subsequent chapters will explain it in detail.

It is worth making the effort necessary to understand legal reasoning. By doing so you can grasp the thinking that underlies prior court decisions and anticipate with reasonable accuracy the thinking that will drive future court decisions on the same subject and related subjects. You can also grasp the judicially created rules and standards, and the debates between judges and justices about legal philosophy and public policy, that are prominent in appellate-court opinions.

Furthermore, you will understand much about how the American political system responds to major public controversies. Judicial decisions increasingly address the most complex and divisive public-policy problems that confront Americans on the national, state and local levels. Those problems are complex and divisive because they present, in the words of noted legal scholar G. Edward White, "clashes between cherished values rather than between one desirable and one obnoxious set of attitudes."[1] A national-level example is *United States v. Eichman* (1990), in which the federal government asked the United States Supreme Court to decide whether a federal law that prohibited mutilating, defacing, defiling, burning, or trampling an American flag deprived one who did so of the freedom of expression

---

[1] G. Edward White, *The American Judicial Tradition* (New York: Oxford University Press, 1976), p. 374.

guaranteed by the First Amendment.[2] Justice William Brennan's majority opinion concluded that the flag law violated the First Amendment because it "suppresse[d] expression out of concern for its communicative impact," namely, damage to the flag's value as a national symbol.[3]

A state-level example is *Planned Parenthood of Southeastern Pennsylvania v. Casey*, 505 U.S. 833 (1992), wherein a family-planning organization asked the justices whether a state may, despite the constitutional guarantee of a right to abortion, restrict a woman's right to abortion services by requiring her to give informed consent to the procedure, wait twenty-four hours before having the abortion, inform her husband if she is married, and obtain the consent of one parent if she is a minor.[4] The Court, in a plurality opinion that Justices Anthony Kennedy, Sandra Day O'Connor, and David Souter authored jointly, reaffirmed its decision in *Roe v. Wade*, 410 U.S. 113 (1973) that "before [her fetus is viable, that is, able to survive outside the womb] a woman has a right to terminate her pregnancy,"[5] but upheld all but the spousal-notification provision of the Pennsylvania law because only that provision placed an unconstitutional **undue burden** in the path of a woman who sought a legal abortion.[6]

A local-level example is *County of Allegheny v. American Civil Liberties Union* (1989), in which a county government asked the High Court to decide whether, despite the First Amendment guarantee of separation between church and state, it could display on public property a Chanukah menorah or a nativity scene depicting the birth of Christ to celebrate those religious holidays.[7] Justice Harry Blackmun, writing for the majority, reiterated the "long-standing constitutional principle that government may not engage in a practice that has the effect of promoting or endorsing religious beliefs."[8] He then concluded that the nativity scene had precisely that effect because its presence conveys "an indisputably religious message: Glory to God for the birth of Jesus."[9] However, the menorah did not endorse religious beliefs

[2] 496 U.S. 310.
[3] 496 U.S. at 317.
[4] 505 U.S. 833.
[5] 505 U.S. at 870.
[6] 505 U.S. at 893–894.
[7] 492 U.S. 573.
[8] 492 U.S. at 621.
[9] *Id.* at 598.

because: (1) the menorah's message is not exclusively religious since Chanukah, which it symbolizes, has "secular dimensions,"[10] and (2) in this case, the menorah stood "next to a Christmas tree and a sign saluting liberty," which are secular symbols.[11]

Certainly, some of the divisive public controversies that judges face are plainly "political" conflicts, such as whether the president possesses the authority to send military assistance to foreign governments[12] or terminate treaties with other countries.[13] Increasingly, though, judicial decisions also address intensely personal matters of life and death. For example, in *International Union, U.A.W. v. Johnson Controls, Inc.* (1991), employees of Johnson Controls asked the Supreme Court to decide whether that company could bar a female employee who was able to bear children (i.e., could not show medically documented infertility) from certain jobs for fear that those jobs might expose her to lead that could harm any fetus she might conceive.[14] The Court, speaking through Justice Blackmun, held that the company's policy violated Title VII of the Civil Rights Act of 1964,[15] which prohibits sex discrimination in employment. That is because the policy: (1) "requires only a female employee to produce proof that she is not capable of reproducing,"[16] despite evidence that lead adversely affects the male reproductive system too, and (2) permits an employer rather than an employee to decide "whether [her] reproductive role is more important to herself and her family than her economic role."[17] Justice Blackmun noted that when Congress enacted Title VII, it intended to leave that choice between one's reproductive and economic roles, respectively, to the individual employee.

In *Cruzan v. Director, Missouri Department of Health* (1990), the parents of a woman who was in a persistent vegetative state asked the justices whether the United States Constitution protected a **right to die** that entitled them to discontinue nutrition and hydration for their daughter.[18] Chief Justice William Rehnquist, writing for the

---

[10] *Id.* at 614.
[11] *Id.*
[12] *Crockett v. Reagan*, 558 F. Supp. 893 (D.D.C. 1982).
[13] *Goldwater v. Carter*, 444 U.S. 996 (1979).
[14] 499 U.S. 187.
[15] Title VII of the Civil Rights Act of 1964 begins at 42 U.S.C., section 2000.
[16] 499 U.S. at 198.
[17] *Id.* at 211.
[18] 497 U.S. 261.

majority, concluded that Missouri acted constitutionally in requiring that "evidence of the incompetent's wishes as to the withdrawal of treatment be proved by clear and convincing evidence," which Ms. Cruzan's parents were unable to do.[19] In other words, the Constitution permits a state to require a guardian to demonstrate clearly that her ward, if competent, would wish to discontinue nutrition and hydration.

However, the study of legal reasoning would be worthwhile even if courts did not decide the major public controversies of the day. Indeed, most courts do not face cases as politically significant as *Goldwater v. Carter* or as emotionally wrenching as *Cruzan v. Director.* Those courts nevertheless bear watching because, on a daily basis, they resolve disputes that are important to the parties. They also enforce social norms, which are rules of behavior designed to promote peaceful and orderly personal and business relationships. Ordinary citizens are most likely to become involved in disputes of this nature.

The following cases, decided during the late 1980s by the New Hampshire Supreme Court and the Indiana Court of Appeals, respectively, illustrate how courts resolve disputes and enforce norms.[20] In *New Hampshire Donuts, Inc. v. Skipitaris* (1987), the court affirmed the trial judge's decision ordering Skipitaris to remove a portion of his pizza restaurant because it substantially reduced the visibility of the donut shop next door to the restaurant.[21] Skipitaris constructed his restaurant in violation of a clause in the donut shop's lease, which Skipitaris knew about, and which prohibited improvements to the restaurant that would restrict the visibility of the donut shop.[22] The New Hampshire Supreme Court's decision settled the dispute between the parties and enforced a social norm in favor of honoring contractual terms. It also enforced social norms against rewarding those who knowingly violate contracts, then seek to invalidate them, and those who operate their businesses so as to injure other business owners.

[19] *Id.* at 280.
[20] I helped research and draft the court's opinion in these cases while working as a law clerk to Associate Justice William R. Johnson of the New Hampshire Supreme Court in 1987 and 1988 and to Judge William I. Garrard of the Indiana Court of Appeals in 1988 and 1989.
[21] 129 N.H. 774, 533 A. 2d 351.
[22] The clause contained a *restrictive covenant,* which is a provision in a deed or lease of property that prohibits certain uses of that property.

In *Isom v. Isom* (1989), the Indiana Court of Appeals affirmed a lower court decision modifying a child-custody agreement.[23] The lower court granted the father's request to transfer custody of his five-year-old daughter from her mother to him because there had been changes in the mother's life, in particular a worsening psychological disorder, that were sufficiently substantial and continuous to justify modifying the original custody award. Besides resolving a dispute between the parents, the court enforced the social norm and legal rule that courts should base child-custody decisions on the best interests of the child, which, in this instance, dictated that the father should have custody.

In *State v. Sullivan* (1988), the New Hampshire Supreme Court affirmed Sullivan's first-degree murder conviction, concluding that there was sufficient evidence of premeditation to support that charge.[24] Sullivan shot the victim twice, firing the second shot from close range after pursuing the victim from the kitchen into the living room of the victim's house. The court enforced the social norm and legal rule that first-degree, or premeditated, murder is a more serious offense than murder without premeditation; hence, before the state can punish a person for first-degree murder, it must show, beyond a reasonable doubt, sufficient evidence of premeditation.

The previous discussion teaches that legal reasoning is too important for lawyers and judges to monopolize it; as undergraduates, the future linguist and the future scientist should learn its basics alongside the future lawyer. That lesson informs and guides the discussions that follow, in this chapter and succeeding chapters.

LEGAL REASONING EXPLAINED

In order to illustrate how legal reasoning works, it is helpful to turn to cases concerning the constitutionality of laws that regulate reproductive freedom. You are likely to have studied or be studying constitutional law, and to be familiar with the legal and public-policy debates surrounding this issue. The aftermath of the Supreme Court's decision in *Griswold v. Connecticut* (1965) illustrates the progression

[23] 538 N.E. 2d 261.
[24] 131 N.H. 209, 551 A. 2d 519.

of legal reasoning. In *Griswold*, the Court held that the Constitution contains a guarantee of privacy that protects the right of married couples to use contraceptive devices, and bars states from preventing married couples from using them.[25] Justice William O. Douglas, writing for the majority, reasoned that the First, Third, Fourth, Fifth, and Ninth Amendments to the Constitution created a "zone of privacy"[26] that includes the marital relationship and protects it against overly broad laws that would "allow the police to search the sacred precincts of marital bedrooms for telltale signs [of contraceptive use]."[27] Subsequently, in *Eisenstadt v. Baird* (1972),[28] the Court broadened the right of privacy announced in *Griswold* when it held, in Justice Brennan's words, that "if the right of privacy means anything, it is the right of the individual, married or single, to be free from unwanted governmental intrusion into matters so fundamentally affecting a person as the decision whether to bear or beget a child."[29] Brennan relied on the **equal-protection clause** of the Fourteenth Amendment, which requires government to treat similarly situated persons similarly, to extend the **right of privacy** from protecting the use of contraceptives by married couples to protecting the distribution of contraceptives to individuals, married or unmarried. The majority reasoned by analogy that the circumstances in *Eisenstadt* were similar enough to those in *Griswold* that the *Griswold* rule should apply in *Eisenstadt* too.

The extension of privacy protection to unmarried persons in *Eisenstadt* illustrates that legal reasoning frequently includes **deductive reasoning** as well as reasoning by analogy. Deductive reasoning proceeds from the general to the specific. It uses a general principle or rule of law as the basis for deciding a specific case that presents a new set of facts to which no court has yet applied that principle or rule. The noted legal scholar and former attorney general of the United States, Edward Levi describes this as a three-step process; first, "similarity is seen between cases; next the rule of law inherent in the first case is announced; then the rule of law is made applicable to the second

[25] 381 U.S. 479.
[26] *Id.* at 485.
[27] *Id.*
[28] 405 U.S. 438.
[29] 405 U.S. 438, 453 (1972).

case."[30] Identifying the similarity between cases, and announcing the rule of law contained in the first case is reasoning by analogy. Applying that rule of law to the second case is deductive reasoning.

When the Supreme Court decided *Eisenstadt,* then, even though the majority opinion relied on **equal-protection analysis** and avoided mentioning the right of privacy explicitly, it expanded the legal rule of *Griswold* to cover the somewhat different, but analogous, facts that *Eisenstadt* presented. In step one, the Court, reasoning by analogy, decided that *Eisenstadt,* like *Griswold,* concerned governmental intrusion into an individual's choice to prevent conception. In step two, based on that analogy, it determined that the right of privacy that controlled in *Griswold* should also control in *Eisenstadt.* In step three, the Court reasoned deductively and applied to unmarried persons the personal autonomy concerning contraception that, previously, only married couples enjoyed.

The example above illustrates that legal reasoning necessarily involves attention to prior decisions, or *stare decisis.* Nonetheless, it also illustrates that although lawyers and judges carefully consider and commonly use prior decisions in current cases, they are not slaves to those decisions. The Supreme Court was free to extend the protection for married couples announced in *Griswold* to unmarried persons in *Eisenstadt,* but it did not have to do so. Had the majority believed that the constitutional right of privacy only protected the reproductive choices of married couples, it would presumably have distinguished the facts of *Eisenstadt* from those of *Griswold* and declined to expand *Griswold* in *Eisenstadt. Stare decisis* is a guide, not a requirement.

The comments of Connecticut Superior Court Judge Robert Satter illustrate this point. Judge Satter observes:

> *When a clearly worded statute or my analysis of authoritative precedents points toward only one result, I decide that way. It is my duty to do so, not only as a trial judge who will otherwise be reversed by an appeals court, but also as a principled judge whose individual notions of fairness must give way to the law.*[31]

---

[30] Edward H. Levi, *An Introduction to Legal Reasoning* (Chicago: University of Chicago Press, 1949), pp. 1–2.

[31] Robert Satter, *Doing Justice: A Trial Judge at Work* (New York: Simon & Schuster, 1990), p. 64.

However, he also notes:

> *When I discern a certain tensile tolerance in the law to meet the peculiar demands of the case before me, or I discover competing legal principles of equal validity, then I can legitimately bring into play my personal values, my own sense of justice. Such opportunities arise in only a few cases a year; but they are the cases that really matter.*[32]

There are several reasons why *stare decisis* is prominent in American law. First, lawyers and judges possess limited amounts of time and energy; therefore, they seek to avoid "reinventing the wheel" by finding and using, whenever possible, shortcuts that speed decision making. Famed legal scholar Karl Llewellyn observes, in this regard, that "both inertia and convenience speak for building further on what you have already built."[33] For example, a busy judge who must decide whether a particular search and seizure was constitutional lacks time to research the history of the Fourth Amendment and to read all the decisions courts have handed down on that subject. Therefore, she will most likely study recent search-and-seizure decisions of the Supreme Court, of her own court, and—if she is a state trial judge—of her state's supreme court. Typically, the judge's research will reveal one or more cases that contain facts strikingly similar to those of the present case. The judge will select the precedent that, in her view, best resolved the issue in the past, and will apply that precedent (or precedents) to the present case.

A second reason why *stare decisis* is prominent is the powerful human desire for stability and predictability in law. As a consequence of that desire, legislators rarely change statutory provisions that establish, for example, the elements of a valid will or the requirements for setting up a corporation. Frequent changes in those provisions would likely discourage personal and commercial transactions by upsetting the plans and expectations of individuals, businesses, and institutions. For similar reasons, individuals, businesses, and institutions expect current judicial decisions to reflect the legal rules announced and the outcomes reached in prior cases or, at least, those rules and outcomes with which they agree.

---

[32] *Id.*, p. 76.
[33] Karl Llewellyn, *The Bramble Bush* (Dobbs Ferry, NY: Oceana, 1930), pp. 64–65.

Finally, *stare decisis* is prominent because judges typically lack both an electoral mandate (all federal and many state judges are appointed) and the power to implement their decisions by appropriating funds or dispatching troops. Therefore, they are eager to, in Professor G. Edward White's words, "deflect fears of judicial tyranny," and wish to give their decisions the appearance of being the inevitable results of neutral principles and flawless logic in order to ensure public support and compliance.[34] One way to attain that goal is to link the result reached in the present case to familiar, popular precedents.

Unfortunately, as Professor White notes, some judges, especially during the nineteenth century, followed *stare decisis* so rigidly that they promoted a conception of judges as "passive oracles making already existing truths intelligible,"[35] and of judicial opinions as "mere declarations of the state of the law."[36] Despite this judicial self-image, lawyers still scrutinized court opinions, especially appellate opinions, because the legal community had long recognized that those opinions, according to Professor White, "expressed political and social points of view and . . . advanced theories of governmental relations," frequently in language that was "transparently opinionated."[37] However, this self-image caused courts to follow outmoded precedents and antiquated interpretations of statutory language on the grounds that doing so enhanced the predictability of the law and restricted the judiciary to its proper function, which was to find the law, not make it.

Today, *stare decisis* remains prominent, but because judges no longer regard themselves as "passive oracles," it does not prevent them from being flexible or creative when those qualities are necessary. In reality, *stare decisis* never entirely prevented creativity and flexibility because legal reasoning features what Professor Lief Carter terms "fact freedom."[38]

Fact freedom is the discretion of a judge in the case at hand to assign a different degree of importance to a particular fact than the

[34] White, *The American Judicial Tradition*, pp. 148–149.
[35] *Id.*
[36] *Id.*
[37] *Id.*
[38] Lief Carter, *Reason in Law*, third edition (New York: HarperCollins, 1988), p. 31.

judge in a prior, similar case assigned to the same or a similar fact. Although *stare decisis* counsels the judge to look to prior cases for facts similar to those in the present case, there is no rule that tells the judge how to determine which facts in the prior case are similar to those at hand, or whether the similarities are sufficient to justify applying the rule in the earlier case to the present dispute. The judge faced with case "C," after carefully reviewing the facts, may choose precedent "A" instead of precedent "B" to guide his decision. Whether the judge chooses "A" or "B," he remains faithful to *stare decisis* but nonetheless reaches a different conclusion by selecting "A" rather than "B," after deciding that the facts of "A" more closely approximate those of the present case than the facts of "B". Fact freedom thus means that although judges are obliged to follow precedent, they are not obliged to follow any particular precedent.

Another reason why *stare decisis* does not prevent flexibility or creativity is that no two cases are identical. This means that no particular precedent will ever be so similar to the case at hand as to compel a judge to follow it. As a result, the judge in today's case must always ask: "What do the prevailing legal rules and precedents mean *as applied to the problem before me?*" [39] In some cases, when change results in a whole new category of legal dispute, the answer will be that those rules and precedents are meaningless, and the judge must create new law in order to adequately address a new problem. Professor Carter comments that, in those instances, "Judicial wisdom lies in knowing when to acknowledge the presence of uncertainty and the necessity for choice that enables law to change for the better." [40]

Judge Patricia Wald of the United States Court of Appeals for the District of Columbia Circuit expressed the same sentiments in different words when she wrote several years ago, "Of course, we judges are bound by precedent, but the most difficult cases are unprecedented." [41]

In the unprecedented cases, judges seek analogous cases for guidance, but they are hard to find and, even when they exist, are unlikely to yield a rule that judges can easily apply to the case at hand. When deciding unprecedented cases, judges analogize their conclusions to prior cases as much as possible, but the new rules they create are

[39] *Id.*, p. 8.
[40] *Id.*, p. 44.
[41] Patricia Wald, "Thoughts on Decisionmaking," *West Virginia Law Review* 87 (Fall 1984), p. 11.

largely the products of inductive, not deductive reasoning. **Inductive reasoning** proceeds from the specific to the general, using the particular set of facts presented by a novel case to construct a new legal rule or principle.

Griswold v. Connecticut, introduced earlier, illustrates both an unprecedented case and inductive reasoning. In *Griswold,* Connecticut prosecuted the executive and medical directors, respectively, of the State's Planned Parenthood League for distributing contraceptive information and devices to married couples. The Supreme Court used those facts to articulate a previously unrecognized right of marital privacy that protects the choice of whether or not to have children. When possible, the Court majority analogized the right of marital privacy to a specific "zone of privacy" that the Court had recognized in earlier cases as being constitutionally protected.[42] Nevertheless, there was no previously announced constitutional principle concerning marital privacy from which to reason deductively. Therefore, the justices had to create that principle by reasoning inductively. Specifically, they interpreted several constitutional provisions to protect a newly announced right of personal privacy for married couples concerning contraception. Subsequently, in *Eisenstadt v. Baird,* they reasoned deductively in order to expand the constitutional protection announced in *Griswold* to protect individuals, whether married or unmarried.

A third and final reason why *stare decisis* does not stifle flexibility and creativity is that judges are imperfect human beings who must make difficult choices in a field in which there are no absolutely correct answers and no empirically testable hypotheses. Under those conditions, judges, sometimes consciously, other times unconsciously, will insert their biases, frustrations, fears, aspirations, and public-policy preferences into their decisions. Recognizing this, Judge Wald writes, "The cumulative knowledge, experience and internal bents that are in us are bound to influence our notions of how a case should be decided."[43]

Thus, even if lawyers, judges, and the American people desired a legal system featuring fixed, unchanging rules, they would be regularly disappointed because law is not a science. Therefore, the uncertainties of human discretion will always shape law, at least in part.

[42] 381 U.S. at 485.
[43] Wald, "Thoughts on Decisionmaking," p. 12.

Some recent and not-so-recent Supreme Court decisions illustrate fact freedom, the differences between cases, and the influence of judges' values on their decisions. Two vivid illustrations are *McCollum v. Board of Education* (1948)[44] and *Zorach v. Clausen* (1952).[45] In *McCollum*, the Court held that a religious instruction program in Champaign, Illinois, in which religious-school instructors conducted voluntary religion classes for public school students in public school buildings violated the First Amendment's command of **separation between church and state.** Justice Hugo Black, writing for the majority, said:

> *Here not only are the State's tax-supported public school buildings used for the dissemination of religious beliefs. The State also affords sectarian groups an invaluable aid in that it helps to provide pupils for their religious classes through use of the State's public school machinery. This is not separation of Church and State.*[46]

In *Zorach*, the Court held that New York City's "released-time" program, wherein public schools released students for one hour per week to the church of their parents' choice for religious instruction was constitutionally permissible. Justice Douglas stated in his majority opinion that:

> *When the state encourages religious instruction or cooperates with religious authorities by adjusting the schedule of public events to sectarian needs, it follows the best of our traditions. For it then respects the religious nature of our people and accommodates the public service to their spiritual needs.*[47]

The Court's decision in *Zorach* demonstrates the power of fact freedom. In *Zorach*, the Court could have applied to the New York City program the principle it appeared to announce in *McCollum*. That principle was that when public schools shorten the school day in order to make their students available for religious education, they aid religion in violation of the **establishment clause** of the First Amendment, which requires governmental institutions to be neutral toward religion. In *McCollum*, Justice Black's majority opinion described that arrangement as "a utilization of the tax-established

---

[44] 333 U.S. 203.
[45] 343 U.S. 306.
[46] 333 U.S. at 212.
[47] 343 U.S. at 313–314.

and tax-supported public school system to aid religious groups to spread their faith."[48] Zorach's lawyer, whose client challenged the New York City released-time program, argued that the Court should decide *Zorach* in the same way that it had decided *McCollum* because, in both instances, a school district, an instrument of the state, placed its stamp of approval on a religious education program. Clausen's lawyer, representing New York City school authorities, countered that the New York City program, by releasing students to churches for religious education instead of permitting religious instruction in public schools, was different enough from the program challenged in *McCollum* that the *McCollum* rule should not control in *Zorach*.

Apparently, Clausen's lawyer was more persuasive because the Court distinguished *McCollum* from *Zorach*, that is, rejected *McCollum* as a precedent in *Zorach*. The Court concluded that shortening the public school day for some students in order to make them available for religious education was an acceptable accommodation between church and state so long as the religious education occurred off public school grounds, which it did in New York City. In contrast, the Champaign, Illinois, program took place on public school grounds which, in the Court's view, amounted to unconstitutional assistance by the school district to the participating churches. Justice Douglas emphasized that distinction in his majority opinion in *Zorach*. He wrote:

In the McCollum *case the classrooms were used for religious instruction and the force of the public school was used to promote that instruction. Here, the public schools do no more than accommodate their schedules to a program of outside religious instruction.*[49]

The public outcry that followed *McCollum* may also have influenced the outcome of *Zorach*. Protestant and Catholic religious leaders attacked the Supreme Court after *McCollum* for hostility to religion, and for having established a "creed" of secularism in the United States. Many Americans in those years viewed secularism as being dangerously close to the atheism of our chief Cold War rival, the Soviet Union, so the charges leveled at the Court were not ones that the justices could easily ignore.[50] Nevertheless, it is impossible to be

[48] 333 U.S. at 210.
[49] 343 U.S. at 315.
[50] See Gerald T. Dunne, *Hugo Black and the Judicial Revolution* (New York: Simon & Schuster, 1977), p.268; and Leo Pfeffer, *Religious Freedom* (Skokie, IL: National Textbook Co., 1977), p.75.

certain whether or to what degree public anger about *McCollum* affected the Supreme Court's decision in *Zorach*.

Thus, because *McCollum* and *Zorach* presented slightly different facts, fact freedom and the justices' particular views about church-state relations combined to produce rather different results in the two cases, even though one might reasonably have expected the same result in both cases. When the Court distinguished *McCollum* from *Zorach*, it limited the power of *McCollum* as a precedent to circumstances in which religious teachers conduct religious education on public school grounds. As long as religious education occurs only on church property, even if done in cooperation with a public school district, *Zorach*, not *McCollum*, provides the governing legal standard.

Both school districts and churches had every reason to obey the Court's order restricting religious education to church grounds, and no reason to disobey. Consequently, school districts outside of New York City adopted the released-time program, and the *Zorach* decision, instead of being merely an exception to the *McCollum* rule, became the rule. It is debatable whether one result is wiser public policy than the other, or whether both results are wise, but there is no question that, together, *McCollum* and *Zorach* illustrate the power of fact freedom and judicial discretion to ensure flexibility and creativity in American law.

Two abortion cases also illustrate legal flexibility. In *Roe v. Wade*, cited earlier, the Supreme Court articulated its now famous **trimester analysis** with the aim of balancing a woman's privacy interest in choosing to terminate an unwanted pregnancy and a state's interest in protecting both maternal and fetal life. The Court divided a pregnancy into trimesters of three months duration and held that during the first, the woman's right to an abortion supersedes the state's interest in protecting life. During the second trimester, the mother's right remains most important, but the state is entitled to impose restrictions related to protecting maternal health. Those include requirements concerning the qualifications of the person who performs the abortion and the facility in which it is performed. During the third trimester, the state's interest in protecting life is sufficiently great that it can prohibit abortions.

Critics, including several justices, charged that *Roe's* trimester analysis: (1) was rigid and inconsistent with a Constitution that expresses general principles, (2) permitted almost no regulation of abortion during the first trimester despite the state's interests in protecting and preserving human life, and (3) failed to take into account advances in obstetrics that would likely cause viability to occur earlier in pregnancy in the future and make obsolete *Roe's* assumption that viability occurs in the twenty-fourth week of pregnancy.[51]

In *Planned Parenthood of Southeastern Pennsylvania v. Casey*, introduced earlier, Justices Souter, Kennedy, and O'Connor, none of whom was a member of the Court that decided *Roe*, reiterated those critiques when they affirmed the basic principle of *Roe*—that a woman possesses a constitutionally protected privacy right to terminate a pregnancy—but rejected trimester analysis in favor of viability as the point at which a state can prohibit abortion. They wrote that:

> *A logical reading of the central holding in* Roe *itself, and a necessary reconciliation of the liberty of the woman and the interest of the State in promoting prenatal life, require, in our view, that we abandon the trimester framework as a rigid prohibition on all previability regulation aimed at the protection of fetal life.*[52]

Thus, *Roe* and *Casey* illustrate the capacity of law to reflect new societal conditions, including advancements in medicine and personnel changes on the Supreme Court, without destroying long-standing legal arrangements upon which Americans have come to rely.[53] Since *Casey*, the Constitution still protects a woman's right to obtain an abortion, but it also protects a state's right to impose previability

---

[51] See, e.g., Justice O'Connor's dissent in *Akron v. Akron Center for Reproductive Health*, 462 U.S. 416 (1983), and Chief Justice Rehnquist's majority opinion in *Webster v. Reproductive Health Services*, 492 U.S. 490 (1989).

[52] 505 U.S. at 873.

[53] It may be easier for the Supreme Court to adapt its constitutional jurisprudence to changing medical conditions than to changing societal conditions. A case in point is *Bowers v. Hardwick*, 478 U.S. 186 (1986), wherein the Court held that the right to privacy it announced in *Griswold*, and extended in *Eisenstadt* and *Roe*, does not protect sodomy between consenting adult homosexuals. The Court distinguished the earlier cases from *Bowers* because the former concerned procreation, which the latter did not. The Court also rejected plaintiff Michael Hardwick's contention that the earlier cases extended a broad protection to the consensual sexual activities of adult heterosexuals, a protection that Hardwick believed the Constitution also grants to analogous homosexual activities.

restrictions on abortion, provided those restrictions do not place an undue burden on the right itself.[54]

McCollum, Zorach, Roe, and *Casey* illustrate the role of law in attempting to reconcile established legal principles, such as the separation of church and state or the state's power to protect individual and public health, with the changing facts of cases and changing societal attitudes toward religion, sex, and participation by women in social and economic life. In fulfilling this role, our legal system tries to balance American society's competing needs for continuity and change. Chief Justice Arthur Vanderbilt of the New Jersey Supreme Court eloquently explained the importance of striking that balance in a dissent he wrote in 1950:

> *The doctrine of* stare decisis *tends to produce certainty in our law, but it is important to realize that certainty per se is but a means to an end, and not an end in itself. Certainty is desirable only insofar as it operates to produce the maximum good and the minimum harm and thereby to advance justice.*[55]

He therefore concluded:

> *When it appears that the evil resulting from a continuation of the accepted rule must be productive of greater mischief to the community than can possibly ensue from disregarding the previous adjudications of the subject, courts have frequently and wisely departed from precedent.*[56]

For this reason, Judge Frank M. Coffin of the United States Court of Appeals for the First Circuit, writing thirty years after Chief Justice Vanderbilt, observed that judging involves temporarily choosing among competing principles rather than declaring the law for all

---

[54]Besides illustrating law's capacity for flexibility, the joint opinion by Justices Souter, Kennedy, and O'Connor in *Casey* illustrates that factors other than personal policy preferences influence judicial decisions. Among those are collegial interaction, judges' views about the importance of continuity in the law, and judges' concern for the institutional health of the courts. Despite their reservations about the wisdom of *Roe,* Justices Souter, Kennedy, and O'Connor voted to affirm its core principle in *Casey* because American women rely on that principle, and the three justices did not wish to destroy that reliance or public goodwill toward the Court by overturning *Roe.*

[55]*Fox v. Snow,* 6 N.J. 12 (1950), cited in Carter, *Reason in Law,* p. 163.

[56]*Id.,* cited in Carter, p. 164.

time.[57] The lawyer's task, then, is to convince the judge to choose the principle that results in the decision most favorable to her client.

CONCLUSION

Legal reasoning is a unique method of dispute resolution. It is part science, part art. Like science, it follows prescribed rules and procedures and strives to proceed rationally to a conclusion based on careful observation and thoughtful weighing of evidence. Like art, it is, at least in part, the product of discretionary choices that reflect the hopes, fears, and preferences of its practitioners.

Judges make choices because no two cases are identical, and judges are imperfect human beings prone to inject into decisions their views of how society should work. Because no two cases are identical, a judge, in order to resolve the current case, must sometimes select a guiding principle, as Judge Satter noted, from among "competing legal principles of equal validity."[58] Chapters Two and Three, respectively, will demonstrate that judicial choice-making also occurs because judging often requires interpreting the applicability of statutory or constitutional language to problems that the author of that language could not possibly have anticipated.

Because it may reflect personal policy preferences, a judge's choice in a controversial case is likely to anger persons whose preferences conflict with the judge's views. Such critics may charge that the judge has exceeded the proper bounds of judicial power and become a "superlegislator" determined to impose on society a particular view of how it should function. Sometimes the critics will be right; sometimes they will be wrong. Whether right or wrong, their criticisms reflect the fact that judging requires human beings of limited wisdom and energy to make difficult choices about human relationships of infinite variety and complexity. Those choices will result from subjective preferences as well as from objective evidence.

The more that judicial choices appear to result from subjective preferences, the more likely the critics are to be numerous and loud.

[57] Frank M. Coffin, *The Ways of a Judge: Reflections from the Federal Appellate Bench* (Boston: Houghton Mifflin 1980), p. 246.
[58] Satter, *Doing Justice*, p. 76.

Americans do not expect judges to refuse to decide political questions, but they do expect judges not to decide such questions in what
Professor White terms "too openly partisan a fashion."[59] According
to Professor White:

> *Judges cannot become so isolated from contemporary conditions that their
> views are obsolescent. . . . On the other hand, they cannot reveal by their
> opinions too passionate a concern with partisan issues or too strong an
> interest in passing on orthodox political questions. . . . Paradoxically, the ef-
> fectiveness of an appellate judicial decision is related to its ability to tran-
> scend mere partisanship; and yet the more effective a decision, the wider
> its political impact.*[60]

The chapters that follow illustrate the interaction between objective evidence and subjective preferences, as lawyers and judges use
legal reasoning to perform four distinct functions: **statutory construction, constitutional interpretation, common-law decision making, and administrative regulation.** Chapters Two
through Five will discuss those functions in turn. Each function is
important enough to warrant its own chapter, but that does not
mean courts necessarily perform only one function per case. For example, statutory construction is often an integral part of administrative cases, and constitutional interpretation may occur alongside
statutory construction when a plaintiff presents both constitutional
and statutory claims in a single case. In reading the following chapters and the illustrative case that concludes this chapter, try to distinguish the legal reasons from the policy reasons for particular
judicial choices, and decide for yourself whether, together, they justify the court's decision.

EPILOGUE: SYMBOLIC SPEECH AND THE FIRST AMENDMENT

The following case and discussion questions give you an opportunity to practice legal reasoning for yourself. In this case, three Iowa

[59] White, *The American Judicial Tradition,* p.371.
[60] *Id.*

schoolchildren asked the United States Supreme Court to decide whether the **freedom of speech** that the First Amendment guarantees protects their right to wear black armbands in a public school as a means of protesting America's military involvement in Vietnam. When reading the case, try to identify examples of reasoning by analogy, deductive reasoning, *stare decisis,* and fact freedom in the majority and dissenting opinions. After reading the case, ask yourself how this decision might influence court decisions concerning more recent examples of political protest, such as burning the American flag.

Tinker v. Des Moines Independent Community School District *393 U.S. 503 (1969)*

Mr. JUSTICE FORTAS delivered the opinion of the Court.

Petitioner John F. Tinker, fifteen years old, and petitioner Christopher Eckhardt, sixteen years old, attended high schools in Des Moines, Iowa. Petitioner Mary Beth Tinker, John's sister, was a thirteen-year-old student in junior high school.

In December 1965, a group of adults and students in Des Moines held a meeting in the Eckhardt home. The group determined to publicize their objections to the hostilities in Vietnam and their support for a truce by wearing black armbands during the holiday season and by fasting on December 16 and New Year's Eve. Petitioners and their parents had previously engaged in similar activities, and they decided to participate in the program.

The principals of the Des Moines schools became aware of the plan to wear armbands. On December 14, 1965, they met and adopted a policy that any student wearing an armband to school would be asked to remove it, and if he refused he would be suspended until he returned without the armband. Petitioners were aware of the regulation that the school authorities adopted.

On December 16, Mary Beth and Christopher wore black armbands to their schools. John Tinker wore his armband the next day. They were all sent home and suspended from school until they would come back without their armbands. They did not return to school until after the planned period for wearing armbands had expired—that is, until after New Year's Day.

This complaint was filed in the United States District Court by petitioners, through their fathers, under Section 1983 of Title 42 of the United States Code. The District Court dismissed the complaint. It upheld the constitutionality of the school authorities' action on the ground that it was reasonable in order to prevent disturbance of school discipline.

[Editor's Note: On appeal, the Court of Appeals for the Eighth Circuit affirmed the District Court's decision.]

I.

The District Court recognized that the wearing of an armband for the purpose of expressing certain views is the type of symbolic act that is within the Free Speech Clause of the First Amendment. See *West Virginia v. Barnette*, 319 U.S. 624 (1943); *Stromberg v. California*, 283 U.S. 359 (1931). Cf. *Thornhill v. Alabama*, 310 U.S. 88 (1940); *Edwards v. South Carolina*, 372 U.S. 229 (1963); *Brown v. Louisiana*, 383 U.S. 131 (1966). As we shall discuss, the wearing of armbands in the circumstances of this case was entirely divorced from actually or potentially disruptive conduct by those participating in it. It was closely akin to "pure speech" which, we have repeatedly held, is entitled to comprehensive protection under the First Amendment. Cf. *Cox v. Louisiana*, 379 U.S. 536, 555 (1965); *Adderly v. Florida*, 385 U.S. 39 (1966).

First Amendment rights, applied in light of the special characteristics of the school environment, are available to teachers and students. It can hardly be argued that either students or teachers shed their constitutional rights to freedom of speech or expression at the schoolhouse gate. This has been the unmistakable holding of this Court for almost fifty years [citations omitted].

In *West Virginia v. Barnette*, this Court held that under the First Amendment, the student in public school may not be compelled to salute the flag. Speaking through Mr. Justice Jackson, the Court said:

> *The Fourteenth Amendment, as now applied to the States, protects the citizen against the State itself and all of its creatures—Boards of Education not excepted. These have, of course, important, delicate, and highly discretionary functions, but none that they may not perform within the limits of the Bill of Rights. That they are educating the young for citizenship is reason for scrupulous protection of Constitutional freedoms of the individual, if we are not to strangle the free mind at its source and teach youth to discount important principles of our government as mere platitudes.*

On the other hand, the Court has repeatedly emphasized the need for affirming the comprehensive authority of the States and of school officials, consistent with fundamental constitutional safeguards, to prescribe and control conduct in the schools. [citations omitted]. Our problem lies in the area where students in the exercise of First Amendment rights collide with the rules of the school authorities.

II.

[T]he school authorities did not purport to prohibit the wearing of all symbols of political or controversial significance. The record shows that students in some of the schools wore buttons relating to national political campaigns, and some even wore the Iron Cross, traditionally a symbol of Nazism. The order prohibiting the wearing of armbands did not extend to these. Instead, a particular symbol—black armbands worn to exhibit opposition to this Nation's involvement in Vietnam—was singled out for prohibition. Clearly, the prohibition of expression of one particular opinion, at least without evidence that it is necessary to avoid material and substantial interference with schoolwork or discipline, is not constitutionally permissible.

In our system, state-operated schools may not be enclaves of totalitarianism. School officials do not possess absolute authority over their students. Students in school as well as out of school are "persons" under our Constitution. They are possessed of fundamental rights which the State must respect, just as they themselves must respect their obligations to the State. In our system, students may not be regarded as closed-circuit recipients of only that which the State chooses to communicate. They may not be confined to the expression of those sentiments that are officially approved. . . .

As we have discussed, the record does not demonstrate any facts which might reasonably have led school authorities to forecast substantial disruption of or material interference with school activities, and no disturbances or disorders on the school premises in fact occurred. These petitioners merely went about their ordained rounds in school. Their deviation consisted only in wearing on their sleeve a band of black cloth, not more than two inches wide. They wore it to exhibit their disapproval of the Vietnam hostilities and their advocacy of a truce, to make their views known, and, by their example, to influence others to adopt them. They neither interrupted school activities nor sought to intrude in the school affairs or the lives of others. They caused discussion outside of the classrooms, but no interference with work and no disorder. In the circumstances, our Constitution does not permit officials of the State to deny their form of expression.

We reverse and remand for further proceedings consistent with this opinion.

Reversed and remanded.

Mr. JUSTICE BLACK, dissenting.

The Court's holding in this case ushers in what I deem to be an entirely new era in which the power to control pupils by the elected "officials of state-supported public schools . . ." in the United States is in ultimate effect transferred to the Supreme Court. . . .

While the record does not show that any of these armband students shouted, used profane language, or were violent in any manner, detailed testimony by some of them shows their armbands caused comments, warnings by other students, the poking of fun at them, and a warning by an older football player that other, nonprotesting students had better let them alone. There is also evidence that a teacher of mathematics had his lesson period practically "wrecked" chiefly by disputes with Mary Beth Tinker, who wore her armband for her "demonstration." Even a casual reading of the record shows that this armband did divert students' minds from their regular lessons, and that talk, comments, etc., made John Tinker "self-conscious" in attending school with his armband. While the absence of obscene remarks or boisterous and loud disorder perhaps justifies the Court's statement that the few armband students did not actually "disrupt" the classwork, I think the record overwhelmingly shows that the armbands did exactly what the elected school officials and principals foresaw they would, that is, took the students' minds off their classwork and diverted them to thoughts about the highly emotional subject of the Vietnam war. And I repeat that if the time has come when pupils of state-supported schools, kindergartens, grammar schools, or high schools, can defy and flout orders of school officials to keep their minds on their own schoolwork, it is the beginning of a new revolutionary era of permissiveness in this country fostered by the judiciary. The next logical step, it appears to me, would be to hold unconstitutional laws that bar pupils under twenty-one or eighteen from voting, or from being elected members of the boards of education.

It is no answer to say that the particular students here have not yet reached such high points in their demands to attend classes in order to exercise their political pressures. Turned loose with lawsuits for damages and injunctions against their teachers as they are here, it is nothing but wishful thinking to imagine that young, immature students will not soon believe it is their right to control the schools rather than the right of the States that collect the taxes to hire the teachers for the benefit of the pupils. This case, therefore, wholly without constitutional reasons in my judgment, subjects all the public schools in the country to the whims and caprices of their loudest-mouthed, but maybe not their brightest, students. I, for one, am not fully persuaded that school pupils are wise enough, even with this Court's expert help from Washington, to run the 23,390 public school systems in our fifty states. I wish, therefore, wholly to disclaim any purpose on my part to hold that the Federal Constitution compels the teachers, parents, and elected school officials to surrender control of the American public school system to public school students. I dissent.

 ## QUESTIONS FOR DISCUSSION

1. Why did the school district suspend the protesting students from attending classes?

2. What condition did the school district impose on the protesting students that would allow them to return to school? Did the students comply?

3. In what court did the students first file suit, and how did that court decide the case? What were the grounds for that decision?

4. Why does the First Amendment protect the wearing of an armband even though it is not "speech," that is, oral or written communication? What analogy does the Court draw in reasoning that the First Amendment protects the wearing of an armband?

5. Why, according to the Court, must schools give "scrupulous protection" to their students' freedom of expression?

6. Does the Court respect *stare decisis* in concluding that a student's wearing of a black armband is constitutionally protected expression? How does the Court majority use *stare decisis* in its opinion?

7. Is the students' freedom of expression the only right or value involved in this case? If not, what values besides freedom of expression are competing here for the Court's attention and protection?

8. Under what circumstances do you think the Court majority would have decided this case in favor of the competing values instead of freedom of expression?

9. What justification did school authorities cite for prohibiting the wearing of the armbands? What facts caused the Supreme Court majority to reject the justification that school authorities cited for banning the armbands?

10. What facts caused Justice Black to accept the justification that school authorities cited for banning the armbands?

11. What, if any, personal values of the justices does the majority opinion reflect? What, if any, personal values does Justice Black's dissent reflect?

12. Who do you think reached the correct result in this case, the majority or Justice Black? Why?

CHAPTER 2

Statutory Construction

Introduction

The Nature of Statutory Construction

The Techniques of Statutory Construction

Conclusion

Epilogue: Construing the Federal Kidnapping Act

Questions for Discussion

INTRODUCTION

One major change that has occurred in American law during the twentieth century is that statutes enacted by Congress and the state legislatures have replaced judicial decisions, or common law, as the primary source of law. This change began at the turn of the century, when the Progressive movement spearheaded the enactment of state and federal regulatory statutes designed to ensure that American business produced safe products and protected the health and welfare of its workers.

After World War II, the trend in favor of statutes accelerated. New problems emerged, and Congress and the state legislatures—in response to these problems—added staff, lengthened and increased the frequency of their sessions, and, most importantly, enacted more statutes. This trend has continued to the present day.

One consequence of this "orgy of statute making" is that individuals and institutions unhappy about the effects of particular statutes on their family relationships and business plans increasingly ask judges to determine what those statutes mean.[1] Therefore, judicial decisions about the meanings of statutes dramatically affect the lives of individuals, families, and institutions every day. Consequently, it is extremely important to understand the process by which judges decide what statutes mean. That process features a **linguistic analysis** of statutory language known as **statutory construction**.

THE NATURE OF STATUTORY CONSTRUCTION

When parties to a case ask a judge to determine the meaning of all or part of a statute, the judge faces two related but distinct responsibilities. The first responsibility is to read the challenged statute carefully to determine not only what it means but whether and how

[1] Guido Calabresi, *A Common Law for the Age of Statutes* (Cambridge: Harvard University Press, 1982), p.1; see also Grant Gilmore, *The Ages of American Law* (New Haven: Yale University Press, 1977), p. 95.

it relates to the present controversy. This is the "cognitive" part of statutory construction.[2]

The second responsibility weighs heavily on the judge when the statute does not resolve the case at hand. This "creative" part of statutory construction involves either stretching the meaning of the statute so that it resolves the present case or designing a rule, independent of the statute, that resolves the case.[3]

The principal reason why "creative" statutory construction is an awesome responsibility is that it contradicts a cornerstone of the American constitutional structure, the doctrine of **legislative supremacy**. Legislative supremacy does not mean that the legislative branch of government exercises exclusive lawmaking authority. It means, instead, that legislative lawmaking power is greater than executive or judicial lawmaking power because it derives from the will of popular majorities.[4] Judges should therefore seek, whenever possible, to determine what the legislature intended when it enacted a particular statute and to apply the legislature's intent to the facts of the present case. In other words, cognition should occur before creation, and creation is justified only when cognition cannot yield a solution to the case.

Creation is often necessary, though. That is because there are limitations built into the legislative process that prevent the enactment of statutes that are clear, precise, and always applicable to current controversies. One such limitation is that legislators who enact a statute today cannot foresee every change in public values or every advance in technology that will affect the statute in the future. Therefore, legislators cannot anticipate all of the cases in which tomorrow's litigants will seek to apply the statute. As a result, judges frequently conclude, after examining statutory language, that the legislature expressed no intent concerning a problem at hand because it did not envision that problem when drafting the statute.

Another limitation in the legislative process is the need for compromise between competing economic, geographic, ethnic, religious, and ideological interests within the legislature. A rural legislator may vote in favor of increased subsidies for urban mass transit as part of

---

[2] F. Reed Dickerson, *The Interpretation and Application of Statutes* (Boston: Little, Brown, 1975), p. 18.

[3] *Id.*

[4] Dickerson, *The Interpretation and Application of Statutes*, p. 7.

an agreement to help an urban colleague in return for his vote in favor of her bill to increase subsidies to dairy farmers.

Under such circumstances, it is unlikely that every member of the majority that enacts a particular statute agrees about what goals the statute should accomplish or what means it should use to realize those goals. In fact, the less clear the statute is about its goals and the means of achieving them, the greater may be its prospects for enactment. That is because it is easier for legislators to support a bill whose impact is unclear than one whose impact is clearly harmful to an important constituency. Thus, clarity is a frequent casualty of the need for compromise in the legislative process.

Finite vision and the pressure for compromise often produce statutes that are vague and/or ambiguous. People use those two terms synonymously in everyday speech, but *vagueness* and *ambiguity* actually have different meanings. A vague statute or statutory provision is unclear because its language is overly general. An ambiguous statute or provision is unclear because it can have two or more possible meanings.

To begin with a simple example, a city ordinance that states "No vehicles may be taken into city-owned parks" is vague. That is because the reader cannot possibly know whether the ordinance bars from city parks all means of personal transportation other than walking, running, or swimming, or merely some of those means. It is unclear whether the ordinance bans placement within a park of a military jeep, no longer in operating condition, as part of a war memorial. It is equally unclear whether the ordinance bans motorized toy airplanes, or even motorized wheelchairs, from city parks.[5]

A city ordinance that states "Sleeping is prohibited in city-owned parks" is ambiguous because the reader can reasonably interpret it to have several different meanings. One such meaning prohibits all sleeping in city parks, including the office worker's lunchtime dozing and the toddler's late-afternoon nap. Another meaning prohibits sleeping overnight in city-owned parks. Still another meaning permits a scout troop to camp overnight in a city park, but prohibits homeless persons from taking up residence there.

Even when a statute is neither vague nor ambiguous, it may well be a patchwork quilt of unconnected provisions stitched together by

[5] D. Neil MacCormick and Robert S. Summers, *Interpreting Statutes: A Comparative Study* (Brookfield, VT: Dartmouth Publishing Co., 1991), p. 409.

political compromises and lacking any unifying motivation or overriding aim. In such instances, even if the language of the statute appears to apply to the case at hand, a judge will hesitate to apply the statute to conditions the legislature did not envision. This would be especially true if doing so would cause an unwarranted hardship to an individual or the community. In that case, a judge would likely undertake the creative role in order to avoid imposing the hardship.

There are many case examples that show how challenging statutory construction can be as a result of legislators' limited ability to anticipate the future. One example is *Baker v. Jacobs*, (1891) in which Baker gave cigars to jurors after they returned a verdict in his favor at trial.[6] The Vermont Supreme Court faced the question of whether Baker's action violated a Vermont statute stating that "if a party obtaining a verdict in his favor, shall during the term of the court in which such verdict is obtained, give to any of the jurors in the cause, knowing him to be such, any victuals or drink," the court must set the verdict aside, and order a new trial.[7]

In construing the statute, the justices followed the rule of an earlier case, *Ryegate v. Wardsboro* (1858),[8] which counseled them to "look to the whole and every part of a statute, and the apparent intention derived from the whole" in order to "ascertain the true meaning of the legislature, though the meaning so ascertained conflict with the literal sense of the word."[9] They inferred from the statute's evident policy against currying jurors' favor by treating them to pleasures of the taste buds that the prohibition against "victuals or drink" should extend to cigars. They thus added cigars to the list of gifts to jurors that the statute prohibited.

Another example is *Riggs v. Palmer* (1889), in which Palmer, who stood to inherit a large sum of money under his grandfather's will, murdered his grandfather, Riggs, yet contended that he was entitled to his inheritance because Riggs had intended to leave it to him and had executed a valid will.[10] The legislature had not addressed this circumstance, but the court nonetheless voided Palmer's inheritance. The court reasoned that if Riggs had discovered Palmer's intentions prior to his death, Riggs would have disinherited Palmer.

[6] 64 Vt. 197.
[7] *Id.* at 199.
[8] 30 Vt. 746.
[9] *Id.* at 749.
[10] 115 N.Y. 506.

The court also inferred that the legislature had not wished to enact a policy that rewarded one who murdered his benefactor in order to hasten receipt of an inheritance.

In reaching that conclusion, the *Riggs* court expressly rejected the rule of *Owens v. Owens*, (1888), a North Carolina case that Palmer cited, wherein the court permitted a widow to receive the statutorily mandated share of her late husband's estate even though she had facilitated his murder.[11] Instead, the *Riggs* court followed "fundamental maxims of the common law" that "[n]o one shall be permitted to profit by his own fraud, or to take advantage of his own wrong, . . . or to acquire property by his own crime."[12] Like the Vermont court in *Baker v. Jacobs*, the New York court in *Riggs v. Palmer* refused to read a statute literally when the result of doing so would be a morally offensive public policy.

Modern judges face the same sorts of problems applying statutory language to the conditions at hand that the *Baker* and *Riggs* courts faced. The tension between honoring legislative supremacy and resolving the case before the court is as real today as it was a hundred years ago. However, modern judges more often encounter that tension in cases in which the parties ask the court to choose between opposite and passionately held political, social, or economic values in rendering its decision. In such cases, the choice the court makes and the reasoning that produces that choice are certain to be controversial. Section III analyzes the techniques that judges use to construe statutes, demonstrates why the exercise of discretion is inherent in those techniques, and presents examples of creative, sometimes controversial, statutory construction.

TECHNIQUES OF STATUTORY CONSTRUCTION

The Plain-Meaning Rule

Statutory construction typically begins, but rarely ends, with the **plain-meaning rule**.[13] The plain-meaning rule dictates that "[w]here

[11] 100 N.C. 240, 6 S.E. 794.
[12] 115 N.Y. at 510.
[13] Patricia M. Wald, "Some Observations on the Use of Legislative History in the 1981 Supreme Court Term," *Iowa Law Review* 68 (1983), p. 197.

the language [of a statute] is plain and admits of no more than one meaning, the duty of interpretation does not arise and the rules which are to aid doubtful meanings need no discussion."[14] Therefore, if the meaning of a statute is clear, judges should apply that meaning to the case(s) at hand, and not interpret the statute. In such instances, cognition is sufficient for statutory construction.

Few would disagree with such an eminently sensible notion. However, statutory language is rarely so plain as to "admit of no more than one meaning." In statutes, as in everyday life, the meaning of a word can change depending on the circumstances in which one uses it. Justice Oliver Wendell Holmes Jr. expressed this thought eloquently when he wrote, "A word is not a crystal, transparent and unchanged, it is the skin of a living thought and may vary greatly in color and context according to the circumstances and time in which it is used."[15] A generation later, Justice Felix Frankfurter expressed a similar view when he wrote, "The notion that because the words of a statute are plain, its meaning is also plain, is merely a pernicious over-simplification."[16]

The comments of Justices Holmes and Frankfurter, respectively, reflect the rarity of cases in which a court can confidently conclude that a statute possesses a single, clear meaning. Not surprisingly, then, what might be called the "reverse plain-meaning" rule, which states that whenever statutory language is unclear, courts should consult sources outside the statutory text, has become more important to statutory construction than the original rule.

Nevertheless, statutory construction should, and typically does, begin with a careful examination of the text in order to determine whether the words convey a meaning that is clear. Most judges respect legislative supremacy and are eager to construe statutes in such a way as to implement the expressed desires of the legislative majority. They also want to encourage legislators to draft statutes carefully, and showing legislators that courts read statutes closely is an excellent means of achieving that goal. Therefore, the most powerful argument that a lawyer can make in a statutory case is one that demonstrates that the legislature expressed its intent in plain, ordinary language when it drafted the statute in question.

[14] *Id.*
[15] *Towne v. Eisner*, 245 U.S. 418, 425 (1918).
[16] *United States v. Mania*, 317 U.S. 424, 431 (1943).

Even when it is unclear what the language of a statute means, it may be clear from reading the text what that language does not mean. For example, suppose a court concludes that the purpose of the ordinance banning "vehicles" from city parks is to ensure that parks will be quiet, safe havens offering relief from the noise and bustle of the city. Few would agree that this conclusion justifies construing the prohibition on "vehicles" to ban rock 'n' roll concerts in city parks. No matter how loud its music, a rock band is not a "vehicle," hence, this ordinance cannot reasonably be read to bar rock concerts in city parks.

Thus, in the case of the proposed rock concert, the argument based on the ordinary meaning of the ordinance would likely convince the court that the ordinance does not permit the city to ban rock concerts in its parks.[17] Would that same argument be convincing if the city seeks to prohibit horseback riding in city parks on the ground that horses are "vehicles" that threaten the serenity and safety of park users? If you find the horseback riding ban a "closer call" than the ban on rock concerts, you understand why judges frequently look beyond the text of a statute in order to determine what it means and how to apply it. In the horseback riding example, the city council's intent concerning the meaning of the term "vehicle" within the scope of the ordinance is much less clear than it is in the rock concert example. Even knowing that the council's purpose in banning vehicles from the parks is to promote quiet and safe enjoyment of parks does not inform a court whether the council wished to prohibit both motorized and nonmotorized forms of transportation there. Thus, in order to resolve the horseback-riding case, the court is likely to exercise its creative function and decide, without guidance from the legislature, whether the ban on vehicles in city parks applies to horseback riding.

There may be no judge in America who opposes that creative function more than current Supreme Court Justice Antonin Scalia, whom President Reagan appointed to the High Court in 1986. Indeed, Justice Scalia refuses to consult sources other than the statutory text, except for related statutes, and insists on construing statutes according to the plain meanings their texts convey. He often consults dictionaries for the meanings of statutory terms; alternatively, he examines "internal context," namely, the words and phrases that

[17] MacCormick and Summers, *Interpreting Statutes,* p. 436.

surround disputed language in a statute, in order to decipher its meaning.[18]

If a statutory text is unclear, Justice Scalia permits federal agencies to enforce reasonable interpretations of the statute because he assumes, in such circumstances, that Congress intends those agencies to exercise discretion in implementing statutory language. His colleagues, however, consult nontextual sources such as **statutory purpose** and **legislative history** (to be discussed below) when the text is unclear. Justice Scalia rejects that approach because he believes that it permits judges to substitute their own policy preferences for those of the legislators who drafted the statute.

The best evidence of Justice Scalia's commitment to text-based statutory construction is that even when he agrees with the Court majority's construction of a statute, he does not join its opinion but prefers instead to write a separate, **concurring opinion** that supports the majority's conclusion but criticizes its reasoning, particularly its reliance on nontextual sources of statutory meaning. In one case in which he did this, for example, Justice Scalia scolded the majority for devoting "[a]pproximately four-fifths of its substantive analysis . . . to examining the evolution of [a statutory provision at issue]," including the subcommittee, committee, and conference committee reports, and the "so-called floor debates" concerning that provision.[19] He advised that:

> [t]he meaning of terms on the statute books ought to be determined, not on the basis of which meaning can be shown to have been understood by a larger handful of the Members of Congress; but rather on the basis of which meaning is (1) most in accord with context and ordinary usage, and thus most likely to have been understood by the whole Congress which voted on the words of the statute (not to mention the citizens subject to it), and (2) most compatible with the surrounding body of law into which the provision must be integrated. . . .[20]

He then added that those factors alone, and not "any of the historical and legislative material discussed by the Court, or all of it combined," should determine the outcomes of statutory cases.[21]

[18] David A. Schultz and Christopher E. Smith, *The Jurisprudential Vision of Justice Antonin Scalia* (Lanham, MD: Rowman and Littlefield, 1996), p. 70.

[19] *Green v. Bock Laundry Machine Company*, 490 U.S. 504, 527–528 (1989).

[20] *Id.* at 528.

[21] *Id.*

Justice Scalia's approach to statutory construction may be simpler than his colleagues' approach, but it is equally subject to discretion. For example, Justice Scalia's reliance on dictionaries is highly discretionary because he chooses the dictionary to consult, and if, as often happens, it contains several meanings for a single word, he chooses the meaning to apply in the case at hand. Moreover, Justice Scalia has not identified the rule(s) he uses to decide when statutory language is clear enough that the plain-meaning rule applies, or when to consult a dictionary in order to determine the meaning of that language. Thus, Justice Scalia's method for construing statutes appears to be just as prone to "judicial lawmaking" as are his colleagues' exercises in creative statutory construction.

Context

Justice Scalia notwithstanding, most judges look beyond the text to determine the meaning of vague or ambiguous statutory language. In such cases, they typically begin by examining the statutory **context.** At this point, they are still performing the cognitive function. A statute's context consists of related statutes and case law as well as the information, values, and assumptions that the statute's drafters and audience share. All of those items help to give meaning to statutory provisions that might otherwise be vague or ambiguous. Context is also useful when the literal meaning of the statutory language does not resolve the case at hand. An examination of context may reveal that the statute has a purpose broader than its literal meaning, and that the broader purpose applies to the present case.

A simple example will illustrate context. Assume that your sister has asked you to watch her young children while she attends a meeting. Before leaving, your sister asked you to "play a game with the children." She did not specify what games are acceptable, but you nevertheless know that craps and blackjack are unacceptable. The context, including the information and values that you, your sister, and the larger society share about child rearing, dictates the acceptable games. Therefore, your sister need not give you precise instructions in order to ensure you will do as she wishes.[22] This example illustrates that communication is invariably a combination of express

[22] This example is adapted from one presented in Dickerson, *The Interpretation and Application of Statutes*, pp. 111–112.

and implied meanings. Context enables speaker and listener to communicate despite the implied elements.

Baker v. Jacobs and *Riggs v. Palmer,* discussed earlier, show the importance of context in statutory construction. In *Baker,* the court construed the statutory prohibition on giving "victuals or drink" to jurors to include cigars because it understood the implied meaning of the statute as prohibiting all gifts designed to appeal to a juror's taste buds, and cigars fit within that category. In *Riggs,* the court construed the relevant statute to bar recovery under a will by one who murdered his benefactor. The court reasonably inferred that despite its silence on the subject, the legislature shared the court's wish not to honor the inheritance of one who murdered his benefactor in order to collect sooner than he otherwise would have.

Statutory Purpose

Context helps judges to determine the "ultimate purpose" of statutes whose provisions are vague and/or ambiguous. By determining a statute's purpose, judges can then decide whether or not that statute governs the case at hand, and if so how it resolves that case. When judges attempt to discover the ultimate purpose of a statute, they ask themselves, "What problem does this statute try to solve? Is the case before me an example of such a problem?" and "If so, how does this statute tell me to solve it?"[23]

Determining *the* purpose of a statute is not an easy task. A statute commonly possesses more than one purpose, and the respective purposes may conflict with each other. For example, a statute designed to protect workers might also aim to assist union, at the expense of nonunion, employment; similarly, a statute designed to protect the environment might also aim to protect eastern coal producers.[24] Thus, there will most likely be ample room for the exercise of judicial creativity in answering the three questions posed above. Cognition often gives way to creation here.

Technological change frequently gives rise to a judicial search for statutory purpose. *Commonwealth v. Tilley* (1940) illustrates this

[23] Lief Carter, *Reason in Law,* third edition (New York: HarperCollins, 1987), p. 58.

[24] Cass R. Sunstein, "Interpreting Statutes in the Regulatory State," *Harvard Law Review* 103 (1989), pp. 405–505.

point.[25] A Massachusetts statute, enacted in 1853, made it a felony to knowingly possess "an engine, machine, tool or implement adapted and designed for cutting through, forcing or breaking open a building, room, vault, safe or other depository, in order to steal therefrom money or other property."[26] In *Tilley*, the Massachusetts Supreme Judicial Court held that the above statute applied to a defendant who knowingly possessed, with criminal intent, keys to the trunk locks of automobiles belonging to salespersons who carried goods in their cars and stored the goods there while calling on customers.

The Court concluded that the purpose of the 1853 law was to punish the knowing possession of instruments that would provide unauthorized access to a locked place of safekeeping, for the purpose of stealing its contents. Thus, the Court's construction of the statute turned not on the legislature's *intent* in 1853 as to what instruments were prohibited, but instead, on the *ultimate purpose* of the statute, which remained as relevant in 1940 as it had been in 1853. In relying on statutory purpose to resolve *Commonwealth*, the court followed the rule it had established in earlier cases, namely:

> *Statutes framed in general terms commonly look to the future and may include conditions as they arise from time to time not even known at the time of enactment, provided they are fairly within the sweep and the meaning of the words and falling within their obvious scope and purpose.*[27]

Changing public values may also generate a search for statutory purpose. A good example of this is the case of *Bob Jones University v. United States* (1983).[28] The issue in *Bob Jones* was the legality of a decision by the Internal Revenue Service (IRS) in 1970 to revoke the tax-exempt status of the university, a private institution "[d]edicated to the teaching and propagation of . . . fundamentalist Christian religious beliefs."[29] The IRS's decision resulted from the university's rule that prohibited interracial dating and marriage by its students and denied admission to applicants who were partners in interracial marriages or were known to advocate interracial dating or marriage.

[25] 306 Mass. 412, 28 N.E.2d. 245.
[26] James Willard Hurst, *Dealing with Statutes* (New York: Columbia University Press, 1982), p. 35.
[27] 28 N.E.2d at 247.
[28] 461 U.S. 574.
[29] 461 U.S. at 580.

The university lost its tax-exempt status under the Internal Revenue Code,[30] and contributions to it were no longer tax deductible after 1970.[31] The university challenged the authority of the IRS to change its interpretation of the tax code in this way.

The Supreme Court majority upheld the decision of IRS because it concluded that Congress's purpose in enacting sections 501(c)(3), under which the university had been tax-exempt, and 170, under which contributions to it had been tax-deductible, was to assist "charitable" organizations. Chief Justice Warren Burger, writing for the majority, noted that in several nineteenth-century decisions, the Court defined "charitable" organizations as private institutions that perform useful public functions "consistent with local laws and public policy."[32]

In 1954, when Congress enacted section 501(c)(3), state laws requiring racial discrimination were common in the United States. In those circumstances, a private university that discriminated on the basis of race could still be a "charitable" institution worthy of tax-exempt status because that practice was consistent with local laws and public policy. That was no longer true, however; today, "racial discrimination in education violates deeply and widely accepted views of elementary justice."[33] Therefore, the chief justice concluded that there was "no question that the interpretation of 170 and 501(c)(3) announced by the IRS in 1970 was correct."[34] Bob Jones University is not a "charitable" organization by contemporary standards, and Congress gave the IRS authority to make rules interpreting the language of the tax code, including the word "charitable."

In reaching that conclusion, Chief Justice Burger rejected the university's argument that neither section 501(c)(3) nor section 170 contained language requiring the university to satisfy the Court's traditional definition of a "charitable" organization in order to qualify for tax-exempt status. He observed that in 1857, in *Brown v. Duchesne* (1857),[35] the Court articulated the rule of statutory construction that "in interpreting a statute, [it will] not look merely to a particular

[30] IRS Code §501(c)(3).
[31] IRS Code §170.
[32] 461 U.S. at 588.
[33] 461 U.S. at 592.
[34] 461 U.S. at 595.
[35] 60 U.S. (19 Howard) 183.

clause in which general words may be used, but will take in connection with it the whole statute . . . and the objects and policy of
the law. . . ." [36] Therefore, it must examine section 501(c)(3) "within
the framework of the Internal Revenue Code and against the background of the congressional purposes." This examination yielded,
according to the Court,

> *unmistakable evidence that, underlying all relevant parts of the Code, is*
> *the intent that entitlement to tax exemption depends on meeting certain*
> *common law standards of charity—namely, that an institution seeking*
> *tax-exempt status must serve a public purpose and not be contrary to es-*
> *tablished public policy."* [37]

Bob Jones University failed to satisfy that standard because its prohibitions against interracial dating and marriage were contrary to
established public policies against racial discrimination.

　　Commonwealth v. Tilley and *Bob Jones University v. United States* illustrate how reliance on statutory purpose enables judges to achieve
their desired results when the statutory text does not contemplate
such results. The *Commonwealth* court rejected the literal meaning of
a statute, which prohibited possession of tools used for breaking and
entering, in favor of a broader construction that prohibited possession of keys that would facilitate *unforced,* but nevertheless *unauthorized* access to automobile trunks. The court molded the statute to fit
the court's aim of keeping Massachusetts's criminal law current
with technological developments. Similarly, the *Bob Jones* court rejected the literal meaning of the federal tax code, which does not
require tax-exempt institutions to meet the traditional legal definition of a "charity," and substituted a broader construction that denies tax-exempt status to institutions that engage in conduct, such
as racial discrimination, that violates public policies that the Court
and American society favor.

Legislative History

In order to identify statutory purpose, judges frequently examine
the legislative history of a statute. That is, they carefully review the

[36] 461 U.S. at 586.
[37] *Id.*

origins of a statute by examining debate transcripts, witness testimony at hearings, its author's comments, and reports filed by legislative committees that have considered and support the legislation. The justices of the United States Supreme Court regularly consult a wide range of legislative materials during such examinations.[38] That does not necessarily mean, though, that the High Court majority will reach the correct conclusion about the statute's purpose or how it should apply to the case at hand. Nor does it necessarily mean that the justices' respective political philosophies will not influence the conclusion they reach. Legislative history is a highly imperfect tool for uncovering the legislature's aims, hence, there is ample room for judges to interpret that history and apply it to the case at hand in accordance with their public-policy goals. Nothing prevents a judge from assigning greater weight to some pieces of historical evidence than to others merely because the favored evidence is consistent with the judge's view of the correct result in the case at hand. That is why one judge characterized the use of legislative history as being similar to "looking over a crowd and picking out your friends."[39]

Legislative history is imperfect principally because legislatures are interested in enacting or defeating bills, not in explaining why they did so. Consequently, they may purposely keep debate to a minimum or leave key provisions vague or unsettled in order to build majority support for a bill. Such vagueness and restricted debate may increase the chances for passage, but they also make the judge's task of reconstructing legislative history difficult and cause the judge's interpretation of that history to be highly subjective.

Another reason why legislative history is imperfect is that legislatures fail to record, or record inadequately, much important discussion about a bill, leaving only fragments preserved for examination. Ironically, some of the least organized and thoughtful portions of the legislative process in Congress, such as public hearings and floor debates, are available in printed form for courts to use. Some of the most important proceedings—such as the "markup" sessions in which committee members revise statutory language in an effort to build majority support and the conference committee sessions wherein members of both legislative houses try to produce a mutually satisfactory bill—are not available on tape or in print for courts to use.

[38] Wald, "Some Observations on the Use of Legislative History," p. 214.
[39] Id.

The most outspoken contemporary critic of legislative history is Justice Antonin Scalia, whom this chapter introduced earlier. Justice Scalia opposes courts' use of legislative history to search for the meaning of statutory language because he believes that such searches uncover only that which a judge chooses to find.[40] For example, in one case he observed that courts use committee reports, a prominent source of legislative history, "when it is convenient, and ignore them when it is not."[41] In that same case, he recalled Justice Robert Jackson's characterization of legislative history in 1953 as "psychoanalysis of Congress" and a "weird endeavor,"[42] and he described committee reports as "unreliable . . . not only as a genuine indicator of congressional intent but as a safe predictor of judicial construction."[43] Justice Scalia advised that instead of relying on legislative history, "we should try to give the [statutory] text its fair meaning, whatever various [legislative] committees might have had to say—thereby affirming the proposition that we are a [g]overnment of laws, not of committee reports."[44]

Nevertheless, most judges believe that legislative history can be a helpful tool in individual cases, and they rely on several different sources. The most reliable sources are committee reports that, at least in the United States Congress, committees produce after reporting out a bill favorably to the full House or Senate. These reports are reliable because they are likely to reveal what the bill's author(s) and strongest proponents think it means and intend for it to accomplish. Courts give particular weight to reports by conference committees, which contain the compromise language to which the conferees agreed. Within conference committee reports, statements of "floor managers," legislators assigned to guide bills to passage in each house, are especially weighty in the minds of judges.

Despite their relative reliability, conference reports have limitations. They often fail to explain why the conferees from one house followed the wishes of the conferees from the other house regarding

[40] William D. Popkin, "An Internal Critique Of Justice Scalia's Theory of Statutory Interpretation," *Minnesota Law Review* 76 (May 1992), p. 1136.
[41] *Wisconsin Public Intervenor v. Mortier,* 501 U.S. 597, 617(1991).
[42] *Id.* at 622, quoting *United States v. Public Utilities Commission of California,* 345 U.S. 295, 319 (1953).
[43] *Wisconsin Public Intervenor v. Mortier,* 501 U.S. at 617.
[44] *Id.* at 621.

particular provisions of the bill. Sometimes they interpret the legislation in a way that no other record of the legislative process can verify. Finally, they are silent about matters on which the conferees agreed not to legislate in order to achieve a workable compromise.

Courts typically regard records of floor debates as less reliable than committee reports in revealing legislative intent. That is because floor debates contain not only the comments of a bill's author(s) and floor manager, but also the comments of legislators who played only minor roles in the bill's journey to passage. Courts often assign significant weight to the statements of authors and floor managers, but rarely give much importance to the statements of minor participants in the legislative process.

Like floor debate, committee hearings vary in usefulness as sources of legislative history. The testimony of a witness who is more interested in promoting her own political philosophy, or the philosophy of some segment of the committee membership, is unlikely to merit much judicial attention. In contrast, the hearing testimony of executive-branch officials or nongovernmental experts such as academics and consultants often contains the best explanation of the flaws in existing legislation or of the problem that proposed legislation aims to solve.

A rather unreliable source of legislative history is legislative action that occurs after the legislature enacts a bill. Suppose, for example, that a state court construes the "no sleeping in the park" ordinance discussed earlier to prohibit all sleeping overnight in city parks. Thereafter, the city council amends the ordinance to prohibit taking up residence in a park but to allow camping outings with permission of the parks commissioner. A court that construes the amended ordinance should not assume that the council intended in the original statute to prohibit residency but permit camping in city parks. Quite possibly, when drafting the original ordinance, the council failed to consider that a total prohibition on sleeping in city parks outlaws both park uses it approves of (e.g., camping) and uses of which it disapproves (e.g., residency).

Legislative inaction after a bill becomes law is even less reliable as an indicator of intent than postenactment legislative action. Suppose that after the court construes the "no sleeping" ordinance to prohibit both residing and camping in city parks, the city council does nothing. Scout troops appeal the court's decision to a higher court, claiming that the city council did not intend to ban camping in city parks. If the appellate court concludes that the council's inaction means that council members agree with the lower court's construction of the statute, the appellate judges will have relied on the weakest form of legislative history. It is just as likely that the press of more important business or a lack of public interest in camping in city parks were reason(s) why the council did not amend the ordinance after the lower court's decision. Therefore, the appellate court would be vulnerable to the criticism that it used legislative history to mask the real reason for its decision, namely, its conclusion that the ordinance prohibits all sleeping overnight in city parks.

Thus, judges can use legislative history to support almost any conclusion they might favor in a particular case. Indeed, sometimes the majority and the dissenters on an appellate court will use the same legislative history to support opposite conclusions in a particular case. A good example of that is *North Haven Board of Education v. Bell* (1982).[45]

In *North Haven*, the United States Supreme Court considered the validity of regulations that the federal Department of Education wrote to enforce Title IX of the Education Amendments of 1972.[46] Title IX states that: "No person in the United States shall, on the basis of sex, be excluded from participation in, be denied the benefits of, or be subjected to discrimination under any educational program or activity receiving Federal financial assistance."[47] It also authorizes each federal agency that awards funds to educational programs to write regulations to ensure that the schools and colleges that receive those funds obey the prohibition against sex discrimination. Any recipient that discriminates on the basis of sex risks losing its federal funds.

In 1975, the former Department of Health, Education and Welfare (HEW) adopted regulations governing the operation of federally funded education programs. HEW interpreted the word *person* in Title IX to include both employees *and* students. Therefore, it wrote regulations that prohibited sex discrimination in employment practices ranging from job classifications to pregnancy leave. Two

[45] 456 U.S. 512.
[46] 20 U.S.C. sections 1681–1688.
[47] 20 U.S.C. section 1681.

Connecticut school boards challenged the employment-practices regulations on the ground that Congress intended the word *person* in Title IX to mean only students. According to the school boards, HEW only possessed authority to enact regulations prohibiting sex discrimination against students.

The Supreme Court, with Justice Blackmun writing for the majority, concluded that Congress intended Title IX to apply also to employees of educational institutions. He first examined the text of Title IX and reasoned that because it "neither expressly nor impliedly excludes employees from its reach," the Court should construe it broadly, as "Congress easily could have substituted 'student' or 'beneficiary' for the word 'person' if it had wished to restrict the scope of [the statute]."[48] However, "because Title IX does not expressly include or exclude employees from its scope," Justice Blackmun turned his attention to legislative history for evidence of Congressional intent regarding the applicability of Title IX to employees of educational institutions.[49] He cited the comments of the Senate sponsor of Title IX, which indicated that it would apply to "faculty employment;" the conference committee report, which deleted language from the House bill stating that Title IX would apply to students only; and Congress's refusal to amend Title IX to exclude employment practices from coverage as evidence that Congress intended Title IX to apply to students and employees.

However, Justice Lewis Powell, in a dissent in which Chief Justice Burger and Justice William Rehnquist joined, concluded that Congress did not intend Title IX to apply to employees of educational institutions. He observed that a "natural reading" of Title IX reveals that only one who is enrolled in an educational program can be "excluded from participation in" or be "denied the benefits of" that program because of sex discrimination.[50] Therefore, he claimed, Title IX applied only to students. Justice Powell added that legislative history did not support the majority's construction of Title IX. Interestingly, he relied on the same Senate sponsor's comment that the statute that was the model for Title IX prohibited discrimination only against "beneficiaries" of federal programs, and the same conference report

[48] 456 U.S. at 521.
[49] *Id.*
[50] *Id.* at 540.

that the majority cited, along with the context that related statutes provided, to conclude that Congress intended Title IX to prohibit sex discrimination against students only.

Presumptions and Canons of Statutory Construction

Sometimes courts reject legislative history in favor of one or more **presumptions** or **canons** of statutory construction that they consider to be especially important in the case at hand. Presumptions and canons are general guides designed to assist courts in construing statutory language that is vague or ambiguous or that may produce absurd or unfair results when courts read it literally. Like legislative history, they clarify statutory language and suggest how a statute applies to a particular case.

1. Presumptions

The presumptions that courts use in construing statutes are general statements of probability about what the legislature intended when it enacted the statute in question. The presumptions that courts use most often follow.

1. The legislature intended to use ordinary English words in their ordinary senses.
2. The legislature intended the statute to be prospective (that is, to apply only to events that occur *after* the statute becomes law), not retrospective.
3. The legislature did not intend an absurd or manifestly unjust result.
4. The legislature intended to enact a constitutionally valid statute.

In *Nix v. Hedden* (1893), the United States Supreme Court used the presumption in favor of construing words according to their ordinary meanings.[51] The case featured a tariff statute wherein Congress set different rates for imported fruits and vegetables, respectively. The statute did not define *fruits* or *vegetables*, and a question arose as to whether tomatoes were to be considered fruits or vegetables. The

[51] 149 U.S. 304.

answer would have financial consequences for Nix, whom Hedden, the customs collector for the Port of New York, had ordered to pay a vegetable tariff on imported tomatoes. Nix paid the tariff under protest, then sued Hedden to recover the amount of the tariff, claiming that it did not apply to tomatoes because they were fruit. Justice Horace Gray, writing for a unanimous Court, observed that because there was no evidence that the words *fruit* and *vegetables* had any special meaning in commerce, "they must receive their ordinary meaning."[52] According to that ordinary meaning, vegetables were "usually served at dinner in, with or after the soup, fish or meats which constitute the principal part of the repast, and not, like fruits generally, as dessert."[53] Therefore, tomatoes were considered vegetables, and Hedden properly applied the tariff to them.

Presumptions are rebuttable, though. For example, the Supreme Court will not presume that a statute that would permit government to intrude into private matters such as religious practices, childbearing, and child rearing is constitutional. When construing such a statute, instead of presuming constitutionality, the Court requires supporters to show a compelling reason why the Court should uphold it. That is because a long line of decisions that protects personal freedoms overrides the presumption of constitutionality when those decisions and that presumption conflict.

Sometimes, the Court will reject a presumption in one case, then follow it in another, although the two cases raise similar legal issues. That happens when the later case is factually distinguishable from the earlier case, thereby justifying a different result. For example, in *Griswold v. Connecticut, Eisenstadt v. Baird,* and *Roe v. Wade,* discussed in Chapter One, the Supreme Court rejected the presumption of constitutionality and required supporters of the statutes in question to show compelling justifications for prohibiting contraception and abortion, respectively. However, in *Maher v. Roe* (1977),[54] the statute at issue denied public funds for poor women to use to pay for abortions they otherwise could not afford. The Court presumed the statute was constitutional and did not require its supporters to show a compelling reason for limiting abortion to those who could pay for it. The majority rejected the presumption favoring constitutionality

---

[52] 149 U.S. at 306.
[53] *Id.* at 307.
[54] 432 U.S. 464.

in *Roe* but followed it in *Maher* because the justices concluded that the Constitution permits abortion but does not require government to make it affordable to all who seek it. Justice Powell, writing for the majority, concluded that the statute at issue in *Maher* was "different in kind from the laws invalidated in our previous abortion decisions" because it "imposed no restriction on access to abortions that was not already there."[55] That is, women who were unable to pay for abortions before that statute became law remained unable to do so after it became law.

Canons

The canons of statutory construction, like presumptions, are probability statements that judges devise as to what the legislature intended when it wrote certain language. They aim to guide judges in determining the meaning of statutory language and its relevance to the present case.

It is impossible in the space available here to discuss, or even list, all of the canons that courts have devised during more than two hundred years of construing statutes. Among those that courts cite most frequently are the following.

1. *Ejusdem generis* ("of the same kind, class, or nature"). When several words follow an enumeration, construe the general words as applying only to persons and things of the same general kind or class specifically mentioned. For example, if the city park ordinance discussed earlier said: "It shall be unlawful to operate an automobile, truck, jeep, or other vehicle in city parks," this canon suggests that the ordinance does not prohibit riding horseback in city parks because horses are not within the class enumerated, namely, motorized vehicles.

2. *Expressio unius est, exclusio alterius* ("the expression of one thing excludes another"): For example, if the city park ordinance said: "It shall be unlawful to operate a motorized vehicle in city parks," this canon suggests that the ordinance does not prohibit riding horseback in city parks because riding horseback is outside the category of activity that the ordinance expressly prohibits, namely, operating a motorized vehicle.

[55] 432 U.S. at 474.

3. *Noscitur a sociis* ("it is known from its associates"): This means that one should read statutory words in context with neighboring words in that statute. For example, suppose that the ordinance prohibiting "vehicles" in city parks also prohibits dogs in the parks unless their owners are equipped to clean up after them. A court, citing this canon, could conclude, in light of the ordinance's concern for keeping parks both clean and uncongested, that the prohibited class, "vehicles," includes horses because they contribute to unsanitary conditions and congestion.

4. *In pari materia* ("upon the same matter or subject"): Suppose now that there are two statutes regulating city parks. One statute prohibits dogs in parks unless their owners are equipped to clean up after them. The other statute prohibits vehicles in the parks. The court could conclude that the two statutes address the same set of problems and, therefore, that it is proper to read them together. A likely result would be prohibition of horseback riding in city parks on the grounds that it would contribute to unsanitary conditions and congestion.

Legal scholars have criticized the canons for many years for appearing to constrain judicial discretion without really doing so.[56] Karl Llewellyn observed in 1950 that for each canon there is a countervailing canon that suggests the opposite result.[57] For example, courts should construe statutes *in pari materia* together. Nevertheless, another canon states that a statute is not *in pari materia* if its purpose is distinct or if there is evidence that the legislature intended the statute to have a different purpose than previous statutes.[58]

Similarly, *expressio unius est, exclusio alterius* states that the expression of one thing excludes another. Another canon, however, states that the expression of one thing does not exclude another when the

---

[56] The Honorable Richard A. Posner, "Statutory Interpretation—In the Classroom and in the Courtroom," *University of Chicago Law Review* 50 (1983), p. 805.

[57] Karl Llewellyn, "Remarks on the Theory of Appellate Decision and the Rules or Canons about How Statutes Are to Be Construed," *Vanderbilt Law Review* 3 (1950), p.401. The appendix to this article contains an exhaustive list of the canons of statutory construction.

[58] *Id.* at 402.

things expressed are expressed merely by way of example.[59] In other words, just because the statute expressly prohibits "cars and trucks" or "motorized vehicles" from city parks does not necessarily mean that it permits horses in the parks. "Cars and trucks" or "motorized vehicles" may be an example, but not an exhaustive list, of the means of transportation prohibited in the parks.

More recently, Judge Richard Posner of the United States Court of Appeals for the Seventh Circuit described the canons as "vacuous and inconsistent," and therefore incapable of constraining judicial discretion.[60] According to Judge Posner, the canons enable a judge to create the impression that statutory construction is mechanical and certain instead of creative and uncertain. They may thus conceal the extent to which a judicial decision makes new law.[61]

Professor Lief Carter perhaps best summarized the shortcomings of the canons when he noted that "[c]anons don't give *the* answer, they justify *an* answer." [62] Therefore, "[t]he judge who, for whatever reason, reaches any conclusion can find a canon to defend it." [63]

Despite their shortcomings, the canons remain popular with judges. They appear as frequently in judicial opinions today as they did years ago.[64] For that reason, students should learn to identify the canons that courts most commonly cite in opinions. Most importantly, students should learn to assess whether any canon cited in an opinion justifies a conclusion that is defensible on legal and policy grounds or, instead, merely props up shaky reasoning.

CONCLUSION

When construing statutes, judges are neither subject to powerful constraints upon their exercise of discretion, nor free to read their personal policy preferences into the legislature's words. Constraints exist, but there is ample room for judicial discretion too.

[59] *Id.* at 405.
[60] Posner, "Statutory Interpretation," p. 816.
[61] *Id.* at 816–817.
[62] Carter, *Reason in Law,* p. 76.
[63] *Id.* at 77.
[64] Posner, "Statutory Interpretation," p. 805.

Statutory language sometimes provides a constraint. The ordinance banning "vehicles" from city parks does not also ban rock concerts, even if both vehicles and rock concerts arguably disrupt the serenity of park users.

Context also often provides a constraint. Context may take the form of a related statute. Courts are unlikely to interpret the ordinance banning vehicles from city parks as also banning inoperable military jeeps or tanks if another ordinance authorizes the display of such machinery on city property. Context may also take the form of shared assumptions and values. Few courts or individuals today would question the wisdom of the decision in *Riggs v. Palmer* to bar inheritance by one who murdered his benefactor. The widely shared value that a wrongdoer should not profit from misdeeds constrained the exercise of judicial discretion in that case.

Institutional factors can also constrain judicial discretion. A trial-court judge is unlikely to construe a statute in a way that is certain to cause an appellate court to reverse her decision. In the appellate court, the need to obtain a majority for any decision may well constrain judicial discretion in construing statutes. In both trial and appellate courts, the threat of public noncompliance with a particular statutory construction can be a significant constraint on discretion.

Congress can constrain judicial discretion by enacting legislation that reverses a Supreme Court decision in a statutory case. A good example is the Civil Rights Restoration Act of 1988, which reversed the High Court's decision in *Grove City College v. Bell* (1984).[65] *Grove City*, like the *North Haven* case discussed earlier, required the Court to construe Title IX of the Education Amendments of 1972. The issue in *Grove City* was whether that statute's prohibition against sex discrimination in "any education program or activity receiving Federal financial assistance" applied to an entire school, college, or university, even if only one of its departments or programs received federal funds. The Court construed "program or activity" narrowly, and concluded that Title IX only affects departments and programs that receive federal funds, not entire institutions. That conclusion was controversial on college campuses because it limited the impact of Title IX there; for example, it placed virtually all athletic departments

[65] The Civil Rights Restoration Act is located at 20 U.S.C. section 1687. *Grove City College v. Bell* is located at 465 U.S. 555.

beyond the reach of Title IX. Colleges could continue to offer substantially greater athletic opportunities for male students than for female students, and many did so until Congress overturned *Grove City* by enacting the Civil Rights Restoration Act. The Civil Rights Restoration Act states that in Title IX, "program or activity" means "all of the operations of a college, university, or other postsecondary institution . . . any part of which is extended Federal financial assistance."[66] Thus, Congress made sure that the Supreme Court would adhere to Congress's construction of Title IX in the future.

Nevertheless, many cases give judges ample opportunity to be creative in construing statutes. The limitations inherent in the legislative process, and the vague and/or ambiguous language that results, make judicial creativity inevitable and even necessary if law is to govern human affairs fairly and rationally. *Nix v. Hedden* demonstrates that statutory language can be disputed even when its subject, fruits and vegetables, is decidedly mundane. *Grove City College v. Bell* shows that statutory language is almost certain to be disputed when its subject is controversial. Technological change and changes in public values also necessitate judicial creativity if the law is to keep pace with social realities, as *Commonwealth v. Tilley* and *Bob Jones University v. United States* illustrate. Sometimes, as in *North Haven Board of Education v. Bell* and *Maher v. Roe*, judges must choose, in the course of construing a statute, between deeply held values such as gender equity and local control of public education, or the individual's right to terminate a pregnancy and the state's right to protect life. In such cases, their decisions may spawn allegations that they have taken over the legislative function and rewritten the statutes in question to reflect their own values.

Thus, statutory construction is an awesome responsibility. It frequently requires the exercise of considerable judgment about details that legislators have not resolved or even anticipated. It also requires cautious wisdom in consulting materials outside the statutory text. Like the architect designing an addition to a Victorian house, a judge must modernize the style enough to serve current needs without destroying the original concept as its creator viewed it.[67] For the

[66] 20 U.S.C. section 1687(2)(A).
[67] For an earlier use of the architectural analogy, see Dickerson, *The Interpretation and Application of Statutes*, p. 248.

judge, as for the architect, achieving that balance is the challenge that makes the effort worthwhile.

EPILOGUE: CONSTRUING THE FEDERAL KIDNAPPING ACT

The case printed below illustrates the ambiguity that results from legislators' inability to anticipate all of the circumstances to which a statute might apply. The United States Court of Appeals for the Fourth Circuit (MD, VA, WV, NC, and SC) must decide whether the provision in the Federal Kidnapping Act [a.k.a. the Lindbergh Act] that exempts from punishment parents who abduct their minor children applies to a biological parent after a court has terminated her parental rights. When reading the case, try to identify the techniques of statutory construction that are evident in the majority opinion and the dissent, respectively. After reading the case, ask yourself whether the majority's or the dissent's construction of the word *parent* is more compatible with Congress's probable intent when it passed the statute.

United States v. Sheek
990 F.2d 150 (4th Cir. 1993)

MORGAN, District Judge:

Grace Ann Sheek was indicted . . . on three counts relating to the August 1991 kidnapping of her two natural children, Amanda and Michael York, and their subsequent transportation across state lines. The district court dismissed the three counts applicable to Sheek upon the grounds that she was exempted from liability by virtue of her status as the parent of the two children. The United States appeals the dismissal.

I.

There is no dispute that Sheek is the biological mother of the two children. In November of 1987, the South Carolina Department of Social Services (SCDSS) removed the children from the custody of the Defendant and placed them in the care of . . . licensed foster parents. In November of 1989, a South Carolina family court issued an Order wherein the parental rights of the Defendant were permanently terminated. The government alleges that [Sheek] travelled from Missouri to South Carolina in August of 1991 and abducted the children through the use of force, violence and intimidation. . . .

The district court dismissed the indictment as to Sheek because the federal statute excluded "parents" from criminal liability.

II.

The statute at issue is the Federal Kidnapping Act [hereinafter the "Act"]. In pertinent part it reads:

> *Whoever unlawfully . . . abducts or carries away and holds for ransom or reward or otherwise any person,* except in the case of a minor by the parent thereof, *when . . . the person is willfully transported in inter-state or foreign commerce . . . shall be punished by imprisonment for any term of years or for life.*

As originally enacted, the statute was worded to impose criminal liability only for kidnappings which were committed for "ransom or reward." There was no explicit reference to a kidnapping by a parent. The Act was first amended in 1934 to expand liability to kidnappings "for ransom or reward *or otherwise . . . except in the case of a minor by a parent.*" An amendment passed in 1990 also addressed "parents."

> *If . . . the victim of an offense under this section has not attained the age of eighteen years; and . . . the offender . . . has attained such age; and . . . is not (I)* a parent; *the sentence under this section for such offense shall be subject to [statutorily prescribed enhancement of sentence under the Federal Sentencing Guidelines].*

Noting that the term "parent" is not defined, the government argues that it is ambiguous as used in the statute. In support of this contention, the government points to the 1990 amendment in which Congress found it necessary to expressly exempt parents from enhanced sentencing provisions. The argument is made that if "parents" could not be liable under the general provisions of the statute, it would be unnecessary to exempt "parents" from the sentencing provision. Thus, the government asserts that biological parents who have had their parental rights permanently terminated are a type of parent who should not be considered "parents" under the general exemption to the Act.

Statutory construction must begin with the language of the statute and the court should not look beyond that language unless there is ambiguity or unless the statute as literally read would contravene the unambiguously expressed legislative intent gleaned from the statute's legislative history. *Russello v. United States*, 464 U.S. 16, 20–28 (1983). Even if the result appears to be anomalous or absurd in a particular case, the court may not disregard unambiguous language. *United States v. Harvey*, 814 F.2d 905, 917 (4th Cir. 1987).

In its suggestion that this Court must read into the statute congressional intent not to exempt a biological parent whose rights have been permanently terminated, the government faces three persuasive counterarguments:

(1) [T]his Court finds no basis for contracting the definition [of "parent"] to exclude one who begets the child. A state court, pursuant to its authority to oversee domestic relations matters, may terminate parental rights, but it may not alter the identity of a biological parent.

(2) The government has not persuaded this Court that some "anomalous result" would occur if a biological mother is found to be a parent under the circumstances of this case.

(3) It is a fundamental rule of criminal statutory construction that statutes are to be strictly construed and should not be interpreted to extend criminal liability beyond that which Congress has "plainly and unmistakably" proscribed. *Dunn v. United States*, 442 U.S. 100, 112–13 (1979). The accused lacks fair notice of criminal liability when it is based on some "unforeseeable judicial construction of the statute." *Marks v. United States*, 430 U.S. 188 (1977). Thus, "ambiguities in criminal statutes must be resolved in favor of lenity for the accused." *United States v. Headspeth*, 852 F.2d 753 (4th Cir. 1988). This rule alone prevents this Court from carving out of the parental exemption to the Lindbergh Act those biological parents who have been the subject of a termination decree at the hands of a state court.

III.

The parental exemption from criminal liability under the Lindbergh Act should apply to the biological parent of the child kidnapped. For the foregoing reasons, the dismissal of the indictment by the district court is

AFFIRMED.

K. K. HALL, Circuit Judge, dissenting:

Grace Ann Sheek was not embroiled in a custody battle with Amanda's or Michael's father(s) or with some other third party. In August 1991, Sheek had no greater legal claim on the children than I did. Nevertheless, under the banners of plain meaning and lenity, the majority holds that this stranger may abduct two children without transgressing the Lindbergh Act. I cannot accept such an anomalous result, and I dissent.

The legislative history of the Lindbergh Act may be scant, but what is available does not support the interpretation of the parental-exemption provision adopted by the majority. Congressman Dyer's explanation—that the original statute was not intended to include any "parent . . . taking possession of his or her own child, even though the order of the court was violated and it was a technical kidnapping"—clearly indicates an intent to keep federal law out of the realm of divorce and custody disputes between parents with existing legal ties to the child. The 1934 amendment merely clarified this. See *Crandon v. United States*, 494 U.S. 152, 157–58 (1990). Grace Ann Sheek, however, was not on the losing end of a custody decree vis-à-vis the children's father(s); the state court irrevocably rendered her a legal stranger to the child. Her crime was no "technical violation."

> *A criminal law is not to be read expansively to include what is not plainly embraced within the language of the statute, since the purpose fairly to apprise men of the boundaries of the prohibited action would then be defeated; but there is no canon against using common sense in reading a criminal law, so that strained and technical constructions do not defeat its purpose by creating exceptions from or loopholes in it* (Kordel v. United States, 355 U.S. 345, 349–50 [1948]).

The Lindbergh Act enables the vast resources of the federal government to be mobilized against the heinous crime of kidnapping. See *Chatwin v. United States*, 326 U.S. 455, 462–63 (1946). Now, at least in Maryland, the Virginias and the Carolinas, the federal government has been rendered powerless to punish abductions of children by persons who have forfeited the right to be called a parent.

I would reverse and remand with directions to reinstate the indictment.

 ## QUESTIONS FOR DISCUSSION

1. What was the defendant's legal status regarding her children in August, 1991 when she abducted them from a foster home?

2. On what grounds did the district court dismiss the federal kidnapping indictment against the defendant?

3. What does the Federal Kidnapping Act provide regarding parents who abduct their minor children?

4. Did the Fourth Circuit majority conclude that the defendant was a "parent" within the meaning of the Lindbergh Act?

5. What techniques of statutory construction did the majority use in determining whether the defendant was a "parent" within the meaning of the Lindbergh Act?

6. How does the majority opinion reflect Judge Posner's view, cited earlier, that the canons of statutory construction continue to influence judicial opinions?

7. What is the reasoning underlying the canon that the majority relies on in this case?

8. How does reliance on that canon affect the majority's conclusion in this case?

9. How does Judge Hall's dissent disagree with the majority's construction of "parent" within the meaning of the Lindbergh Act?

10. What does the disagreement concerning the proper construction of "parent" demonstrate about the plain-meaning rule?

11. Why does Judge Hall argue that in following the canon that advises reading criminal statutes narrowly, the majority has violated the presumption against absurd results? What does this disagreement demonstrate about canons and presumptions of statutory construction?

12. Who do you think construed the Federal Kidnapping Act correctly, the majority or Judge Hall? Why?

CHAPTER 3

Constitutional Interpretation

Introduction

The Separation of Powers

Federalism

Civil Liberties

Interpreting Constitutional Language

Conclusion

Epilogue: The Constitutionality of a Veterans' Preference Law

Questions for Discussion

INTRODUCTION

In constitutional cases, parties ask courts to resolve disputes that turn on the interpretation of a particular clause or word in the federal Constitution. Like statutory construction, **constitutional interpretation** features the linguistic analysis component of legal reasoning; however, in constitutional cases, courts focus that linguistic analysis on constitutional rather than statutory provisions. Section IV of this chapter will discuss each of the methods of constitutional interpretation that courts use.

An appellate court may exercise the power of **judicial review** in constitutional cases, invalidating a legislative, executive, or lower-court decision that conflicts with its interpretation of constitutional language. Judicial review is controversial because it can nullify a statute that represents the majority will of the people's elected representatives. For example, in *United States v. Eichman,* cited in Chapter One, the Supreme Court invalidated, as a violation of the **freedom of speech,** the Flag Protection Act of 1989, which prohibited the desecration of an American flag.[1] *Eichman* restricts the power of the majority to govern a country whose founding principles include representative democracy premised on majority rule. However, *Eichman* honors another founding principle of American democracy, namely, respect for the rights of numerical minorities.

Judicial review is also controversial because it determines the balance of power between the branches of the federal government **(separation of powers)**, between the federal government and the states **(federalism)**, and between government and individuals **(civil liberties)**. Before returning, in Section IV, to the debate surrounding judicial review, it is necessary to discuss, in Sections II and III, the categories of cases in which the debate occurs.

THE SEPARATION OF POWERS

Courts interpret the Constitution to determine the limits of the power that each branch of the federal government possesses. The separation of powers is a core principle of the Constitution.

[1] 18 U.S.C. section 700.

The framers built that principle into the Constitution because they were dissatisfied with the **Articles of Confederation** wherein the Continental Congress was simultaneously legislature, executive, and judiciary. That was an impossible burden that the Continental Congress could not satisfy.[2]

The framers also wanted the branches to be able to check each other's power so that no single branch would become too powerful. Their greatest fears were that legislative majorities who represented debtors would enact policies harmful to the creditor minority and that the country would destroy itself in class warfare. They believed that only a "balanced government" in which each social class was represented and possessed a check on the others would prevent national political suicide.[3]

The separation of powers principle works by first assigning to each branch a crucial function and then placing each branch beyond the direct control of the other two.[4] This arrangement prevents one branch from forcing its will on the others and from acting effectively without their concurrence.[5] Thus, the branches are simultaneously separate from and dependent on each other.

An example of their interdependence is that the Constitution assigns legislative power to the Congress but also assigns power to the president to veto legislation; hence, Congress and the president share the legislative power. An example of their separateness is that Article I, section 8 assigns to the Congress exclusive power to levy taxes and appropriate money, while Article II, section 2, clause 1 assigns to the president exclusive power to grant pardons.

The simultaneous separateness and interdependence of the branches leads to conflicts about whether particular governmental actions exceed the powers that the Constitution grants to a particular branch. The Supreme Court has decided many such cases.

---

[2] Louis Fisher, *Constitutional Conflicts between Congress and the President,* third edition (Lawrence, KS: University Press of Kansas, 1991), p. 9.

[3] Merrill Jensen, *The Making of the American Constitution* (Melbourne, FL: Krieger Pub. Co., 1979), p. 8.

[4] The Hon. Richard A. Posner, "The Separation of Powers" in *Politics and the Constitution: The Nature and Extent of Interpretation* (Washington, DC: The National Legal Center for the Public Interest and the American Studies Center, 1990), p.42.

[5] *Id.*

In *Watkins v. United States* (1957), the Court concluded that Congress's investigatory power does not entitle it to expose for the sake of exposure.[6] Congressional investigations must relate to the larger purpose of enacting legislation, and must not violate a witness's privacy or freedoms of speech, press, religion, or assembly.

In *United States v. Nixon* (1974), the Court held that the president possesses a constitutionally protected privilege of confidentiality that results from the need to protect national security.[7] The Court also ruled, however, that this privilege is not so broad as to entitle the president to withhold evidence in a criminal trial. The justices rejected President Nixon's theory that all presidential conversations with staff members are confidential and ordered him to release tape recordings of Oval Office conversations to the prosecution.

In *Baker v. Carr* (1962), the majority held that courts could decide cases in which plaintiffs claim that the systems by which their state legislators draw district boundaries overrepresent rural residents and underrepresent urbanites in violation of the **equal protection clause** of the Fourteenth Amendment.[8] Before *Baker,* the Court had ruled that this was a political question best left to the elected branches of government to resolve.[9] The justices rejected that view in *Baker* on the ground that the rural representatives who controlled state legislatures would not voluntarily redraw district lines because that would destroy their power. In *Baker, Watkins,* and *Nixon,* the Supreme Court fulfilled the Constitution's promise of limited but effective government by clarifying the parameters of legislative, executive, and judicial power, respectively.

FEDERALISM

Courts must also decide whether the federal government or a state has exceeded its constitutional authority relative to the other. **Federalism** is another core principle of the Constitution.

American federalism resulted from a compromise at the Constitutional Convention. Ardent Nationalists wanted to reduce the states

---

[6] 354 U.S. 178.
[7] 418 U.S. 683.
[8] 369 U.S. 186.
[9] See *Colegrove v. Green,* 328 U.S. 549 (1946).

to mere administrative units designed to carry out the policies of a strong national government. Equally ardent proponents of state power wanted to increase the power of the national government but retain the principle of state supremacy that underlay the Articles of Confederation. Both sides agreed to significantly increase the power of the federal government but retain the states as sovereign, if inferior, political entities.[10]

Their compromise spawned a continuing debate about the proper contours of federalism. At the center of that debate is the Tenth Amendment, which states that "[t]he powers not delegated to the United States by the Constitution, nor prohibited by it to the States, are reserved to the States respectively, or to the people."

Proponents of an activist federal government ("Nationalists") argue that the above language merely means that the states retain those powers that have neither been expressly delegated to nor judicially interpreted as belonging to the federal government.[11] This view leaves little independent authority to the states because the Supreme Court has interpreted federal power broadly for more than fifty years. Nationalists argue that a broad interpretation of federal power is consistent with the Constitution's assignment to Congress of power to "provide for the general welfare"[12] and to "make all laws which shall be necessary and proper" for carrying out its express powers.[13] The broad interpretation reflects the desire of the American people in 1789 for a strong national government that would accomplish the ambitious goals listed in the **Preamble** to the Constitution.[14]

Proponents of less federal power and more state independence ("States' Rights Theorists") counter that the states, not the people, are the source of the Constitution, and that the states ceded only limited authority to the federal government in the Constitution.[15]

[10] Jensen, *The Making of the American Constitution,* pp. 51–52.

[11] See *United States v. Darby,* 312 U.S. 100 (1941); dissenting opinion by Justice Stone in *United States v. Butler,* 297 U.S. 1 (1936).

[12] Article I, section 8, clause 1.

[13] Article I, section 8, clause 18.

[14] The goals listed in the Preamble are to "form a more perfect union, establish justice, insure domestic tranquility, provide for the common defense, promote the general welfare, and secure the blessings of liberty to ourselves and our posterity. . . ."

[15] J. W. Peltason, *Understanding the Constitution,* thirteenth edition (Fort Worth: Harcourt Brace College Publishers, 1994). p. 19.

Accordingly, the federal government's delegated powers do not curtail full use by the states of their reserved powers, but the states' reserved powers restrict the scope of the federal government's delegated powers.[16] Therefore, courts should resolve doubt about whether the Constitution has delegated a particular power to the federal government or reserved it to the states in favor of the states. Since the late 1930s, however, the Supreme Court has almost always resolved such doubt in favor of the federal government.

For example, in *South Dakota v. Dole (1987)*, the justices concluded that Congress is entitled to condition its disbursement of highway construction funds on each state's willingness to adopt twenty-one as its minimum drinking age.[17] Congress can deny a portion of the anticipated funds to any state that retains a lower legal drinking age.

In *Garcia v. San Antonio Metropolitan Transit Authority* (1985), the High Court determined that Congress is also entitled to require a local community to pay its bus drivers in accordance with the minimum wage and overtime provisions of federal law, even though they work for a local government agency.[18] However, there is evidence that the current Court, under Chief Justice Rehnquist, may take a less generous view toward federal power than any Court since World War II.

In *United States v. Lopez (1995)*, the majority invalidated the Gun-Free School Zones Act of 1990 that made it a federal offense to possess a firearm in or near a school.[19] It concluded that this statute exceeded Congress's power to regulate interstate commerce because the *possession* of guns on school grounds (unlike their sale or importation) is completely unrelated to commerce. *Lopez* may have been the opening salvo in a battle by the Rehnquist Court to reduce federal power over states and communities. If so, more than fifty years of precedents could be in jeopardy.[20]

[16]*Id.*

[17]483 U.S. 203.

[18]469 U.S. 528.

[19]18 U.S.C. section 922(q)(2)(A).

[20]In 1996, the Rehnquist Court fired a second salvo at federal power when it decided *Seminole Tribe of Florida v. Florida,* 116 S. Ct. 1114, wherein the Court held unconstitutional a provision of a federal statute that permitted Indian tribes to sue states in federal court for failing to negotiate in good faith about conducting gambling operations on reservations. The majority concluded that the provision of the Indian Gaming Regulation Act, 25 U.S.C. §2710(d), which permitted such suits violated the Eleventh Amendment, which prohibits suits in federal courts against a state by citizens of

CIVIL LIBERTIES

Civil liberties cases concern the relationship between government power and individual rights. They attempt to reconcile government's interests in public safety, order, and health with the individual's interests in personal and political freedom.

Civil liberties cases typically feature claims that a federal or state government agency violated one or more of the individual rights contained in the First, Fourth, Fifth, Sixth, or Eighth Amendments to the Constitution. These are the most litigated provisions in the **Bill of Rights,** which includes the first ten amendments to the Constitution.

On April 30, 1789, when the Constitution went into effect, it did not contain a Bill of Rights because the Constitutional Convention had unanimously rejected a proposal to draft one.[21] However, at the ratifying conventions in several states, public opinion forced supporters of the Constitution to promise a Bill of Rights as the price of ratification. In Virginia, James Madison, seeking to win election to the House of Representatives, promised his would-be constituents that if elected, he would propose a Bill of Rights as soon as the first Congress met.[22] Madison proposed twelve amendments to the Congress, ten of which the Congress approved and three-fourths of the states ratified, thus adding the Bill of Rights to the Constitution.

The Bill of Rights played a limited role in American law during the eighteenth and nineteenth centuries. Constitutional cases during those years concerned mostly separation of powers and federalism issues. However, civil liberties cases gradually became more numerous, especially after World War II. Today, they are the most numerous category of constitutional case on the Supreme Court docket. After

---

another state. The majority reached that conclusion even though Article I, section 10, clause 3 of the Constitution gives Congress the preeminent power to regulate commercial relations between the United States and Indian tribes, and even though the Seminoles are residents of the state that they sued, which appears to make the Eleventh Amendment inapplicable. Chief Justice Rehnquist, who wrote the majority opinion, read the Eleventh Amendment broadly, concluding that in most instances it prevents Congress from authorizing lawsuits by private parties against states that do not consent to be sued. *Seminole Tribe,* therefore, suggests that the pro-state stance the Court assumed in *Lopez* was not an aberration, but rather, a sign of an apparent shift in the Court's views on federalism issues.

[21] Jensen, *The Making of the American Constitution,* p. 95.

[22] *Id.,* p. 148.

World War II, the Court also shifted its civil liberties focus from protecting property rights by invalidating legislation that regulated business, to protecting "cultural freedoms"—such as speech, press, worship, and association—and the rights of persons accused of crimes. The postwar Court assumed that economic legislation was constitutional as long as it had a rational relationship to a legitimate governmental purpose. For example, in *Williamson v. Lee Optical (1955)*, the Court upheld an Oklahoma law that prohibited opticians from duplicating or replacing eyeglass lenses without a written prescription from an ophthalmologist or optometrist.[23] Conceding that the law imposed a requirement that was frequently wasteful, the Court nevertheless held that the Oklahoma legislature may have concluded that eye examinations were sufficiently important that they should accompany all changes in frames and duplications of lenses.

However, the Court viewed with suspicion governmental actions that appeared to restrict cultural freedoms.[24] This **double standard,**[25] predicated on the notion that the cultural freedoms are **preferred freedoms,** still shapes Supreme Court jurisprudence today.[26]

In another important twentieth-century development, the Court gradually applied most of the rights contained in Amendments One through Eight of the Constitution to the states. The Bill of Rights originally protected Americans only against the federal government

[23] 348 U.S. 483.

[24] Henry J. Abraham and Barbara A. Perry, *Freedom and the Court: Civil Rights and Liberties in the United States,* sixth edition (New York: Oxford University Press, 1994), p. 11.

[25] *Id.,* p. 9.

[26] The double standard and the concept of preferred freedoms upon which it rests originated in a footnote that Justice Harlan Stone appended to the opinion of the Court in *United States v. Carolene Products Company,* 304 U.S. 144 (1938). Stone suggested in the first paragraph of the famous "Footnote Four" that the Court should examine legislation that appears to restrict the First Amendment freedoms of religion, speech, press, assembly, and petition with a greater degree of scrutiny than it accords to legislation that restricts property rights in pursuit of national economic goals. Abraham and Perry, *Freedom and the Court,* p. 19. In paragraph two, Stone advocated special judicial scrutiny of legislation that restricts political processes—notably voting— because those processes preserve all other rights in a democracy. Finally, in paragraph three, Stone called for that same degree of scrutiny of legislation that appears designed to restrict the rights of "discrete and insular minorities," that is, unpopular racial, religious, and political minorities. *Id.*

because its framers feared tyranny by the federal government, not by state governments. The vehicle for **incorporating,** or applying to the states, these rights is the **due-process clause** of the Fourteenth Amendment. This clause declares that no state shall "deprive any person of life, liberty, or property, without due process of law." In the Court's view, due process of law includes most of the rights contained in Amendments One through Eight.[27] As a result, states cannot subject their citizens to **unreasonable searches and seizures** or **cruel and unusual punishments** today any more than the federal government can.

The following cases reflect the double standard and the application of the Bill of Rights to federal and state authorities. In *Texas v. Johnson,* the Supreme Court invalidated a Texas law that prohibited the desecration of a venerated object in a way likely to offend others.[28] The Court concluded that the statute violated the freedom of speech that the First Amendment guarantees. In *United States v. Eichman,* cited earlier, the Court invalidated for the same reason the Flag Protection Act of 1989, a Congressional statute that prohibited desecration of the American flag.[29]

In *Miranda v. Arizona (1966)*, the justices held that the Constitution requires state and local police officers to inform an arrestee of the Sixth Amendment right to counsel and the Fifth Amendment rights to remain silent and to revoke at any time during questioning prior consent to interrogation.[30] *Johnson, Eichman,* and *Miranda* reflect the Supreme Court's desire to protect personal autonomy against the intrusive and coercive power of government.[31]

[27] A few less "preferred" freedoms—including the Fifth Amendment right to indictment by a grand jury, the Seventh Amendment right to a jury trial in civil cases, the Eighth Amendment freedoms from excessive bail and fines, the Second Amendment right to bear arms, and the Third Amendment protection against involuntary quartering of troops in private homes—remain applicable only to the federal government.

[28] 491 U.S. 397 (1989). The statutory provision that Mr. Johnson violated was Tex. Penal Code Ann. section 42.09 (a)(3) (1989).

[29] 496 U.S. 310 (1990).

[30] 384 U.S. 436.

[31] Federalism permits state courts to interpret the rights contained in state constitutions differently from federal constitutional rights, so long as the result is greater protection for individual rights under state law than under federal law. That was precisely the result in *Claremont School District v. Governor,* 138 N.H. 183 (1993) and *State v. Kirchoff,* 156 Vt. 1, 587 A.2d 988

INTERPRETING CONSTITUTIONAL LANGUAGE

Introduction

Constitutional scholars no longer debate whether courts should ever exercise judicial review, but they vigorously debate in which cases and by what methods courts should do so. There is no consensus about how to decide what the Constitution means; hence, every method that courts use to resolve constitutional cases is controversial.

Methods of Constitutional Interpretation

The methods of **constitutional interpretation** are the: **historical, textual, structural, doctrinal, prudential,** and **ethical.**[32]

Historical

The historical method is also known as the method of "original intent" and as "interpretivism." Its proponents are known as "originalists." In recent years, this method has been the subject of a national debate in the legal community that began when former Attorney General of the United States Edwin Meese III publicly endorsed it and urged courts to use it.[33]

The historical method interprets the Constitution according to the intent of the "framers," those persons who drafted and ratified the Constitution and its amendments. This method resolves constitutional cases by relying on express provisions of the Constitution, or on values that those provisions clearly imply, and by interpreting

---

(1991). In *Claremont School District*, the New Hampshire Supreme Court held that the New Hampshire Constitution requires that state to adequately fund its public schools. In *Kirchoff*, the Vermont Supreme Court held that the Vermont Constitution prohibits warrantless searches of "open fields" (permissible under the federal Constitution) where the owner has taken steps to exclude the public. Neither decision is reviewable by the United States Supreme Court because it rests entirely on state constitutional law.

[32] Philip Bobbitt, *Constitutional Interpretation* (Cambridge, MA: Basil Blackwell, 1991), pp. 12–13.

[33] Edwin Meese III, "Toward a Jurisprudence of Original Intention," v. 45 *Public Administration Review* 701 (1985).

constitutional language according to its commonly held meaning at the time the framers wrote it.

An originalist judge such as Robert Bork, formerly of the United States Court of Appeals, or current Supreme Court Justice Clarence Thomas, whom President Bush appointed in 1991, views the judicial task in constitutional cases as translating the framers' intent into a rule of law that can govern modern circumstances that the framers could not have foreseen.[34] The judge extracts from the text, structure, and history of the Constitution a value that the framers wanted to protect and preserve. If the judge determines that the statute or executive action at issue in the present case threatens that value, then she must invalidate the offending statute or executive action.[35]

The judge must not create new constitutional rights or destroy old ones. According to Judge Bork, the Supreme Court violated this principle in *Roe v. Wade* when it predicated the right to receive an abortion upon a larger constitutional **right of privacy**.[36] The Court created a new constitutional right because abortion, like privacy, is not rooted in the text, structure, or history of the Constitution.[37]

Nevertheless, Judge Bork argues that the historical method need not be a straitjacket. For example, although the framers of the Fourth Amendment were unfamiliar with **wiretapping,** it is nevertheless a "search" under the Fourth Amendment and ordinarily requires a warrant because the framers intended to prohibit warrantless searches of the person and personal property.[38]

The historical method is faithful to the democratic principle of majority rule. The Constitution creates a political system in which

---

[34] Robert H. Bork, "Tradition and Morality in Constitutional Law," in Cannon and O'Brien, eds. *Views from the Bench* (Chatham, NJ: Chatham House, 1980), pp. 171–172. For an excellent summary of Justice Thomas's originalist views, see Christopher E. Smith, "Bent on Original Intent: Justice Thomas Is Asserting a Distinct and Cohesive Vision," *American Bar Association Journal* (October 1996): pp. 48–52.

[35] Robert H. Bork, *The Tempting of America: The Political Seduction of the Law* (New York: Simon & Schuster, 1990), p. 162.

[36] 410 U.S. 113 (1973).

[37] See "Nomination of Robert H. Bork to be Associate Justice of the Supreme Court of the United States: Hearings before the Senate Subcommittee on the Judiciary." 100th Cong., 1st Sess. (1987): p. 185.

[38] Philip Bobbitt, *Constitutional Interpretation*, p. 92.

legislation, not litigation, is to be the primary instrument of social change.[39] Legislatures, not courts, have the major responsibility for solving social problems because legislatures contain popularly elected representatives who discuss policy options in open public debates and who build coalitions among themselves to achieve legislative majorities.[40] The legislation they pass reflects the view of the voters who elected them. Therefore, courts should uphold legislation unless it violates the intent of the "supermajority" that ratified the Constitution (thirteen states) or of the supermajority that ratified its amendments (two-thirds of Congress and three-fourths of the state legislatures).

Critics of the historical method respond that the "framers" include not only those who drafted and signed the Constitution, but also those who ratified it in state conventions in 1787 and 1788, the Members of Congress who voted for its twenty-seven amendments, and the state legislators who ratified those amendments. Every constitutional provision therefore has a large number of "framers" who undoubtedly voted for it for a wide range of reasons and had different ideas about its meaning and purpose. Under such circumstances, it is virtually impossible to identify a collective "intent" regarding any particular provision.

Critics of the historical method also charge that it does not end the influence of personal values in judicial decisions. Former Supreme Court Justice William Brennan maintained that reliance on the historical method is "arrogance cloaked as humility."[41] In Brennan's view, originalists profess a desire to eliminate the influence of personal policy preferences from judicial decisions, but arrogantly presume that they can discern the framers' intent and apply it to contemporary issues of which the framers were completely unaware.

Furthermore, critics of the historical method note that the Constitution contains important words and phrases that are either vague

---

[39] J. Clifford Wallace, "Interpretivism and the Fourteenth Amendment: An Inquiry into Judicial Limitation," in National Legal Center for the Public Interest and the American Studies Center, *Politics and the Constitution,* (Washington, DC: 1990), p.68.

[40] *Id.*

[41] William J. Brennan Jr., "The Constitution of the United States: Contemporary Ratification," in Rakove, ed., *Interpreting the Constitution* (Boston: Northeastern University Press: 1990), p. 25.

(due process, equal protection) or evaluative (unreasonable searches and seizures, cruel and unusual punishment), thereby requiring interpretation. The necessity of interpretation makes it inevitable that value judgments will enter into judicial opinions. Professor Judith Baer contends that the best evidence that originalism does not eliminate value judgments from court decisions is that Justice Black believed that all the rights contained in Amendments One through Eight apply to the states as well as to the federal government, whereas fellow originalist Edwin Meese disagrees. Professor Baer concludes that "[w]hen the same approach [to constitutional interpretation] permits contradictory conclusions, it is hard to see how it restrains judges or provides consistency."[42]

The critics' most frequent charge against the historical method is that it permits the views of framers who died long ago to control human lives late in the twentieth century. The renowned constitutional scholar Edward Corwin observed that, as a document, the Constitution came from its framers; but as law it "comes from and derives all its force from the people of the United States of this day and hour."[43] Therefore, the Constitution is contemporary law, and courts are justified in rejecting the original understanding of a constitutional provision when it clearly fails to address contemporary values and needs.

Brown v. Board of Education (alluded to in Chapter One) illustrates this point. Congress did not intend the equal-protection clause of the Fourteenth Amendment to prohibit racial segregation in public schools. Indeed, in 1864, two years before enacting the amendment, Congress authorized racial segregation in the District of Columbia's public schools.[44] However, Congress did intend the equal-protection clause to give blacks legal equality with whites, including the same rights to own property, sue, enforce contracts, and testify in court.[45]

---

[42] Judith A. Baer, "Reading the Fourteenth Amendment: The Inevitability of Noninterpretivism," in National Legal Center for the Public Interest and the American Studies Center, *Politics and the Constitution* (Washington, DC: 1990), p.75.

[43] Quoted in Gregory Bassham, *Original Intent and the Constitution* (Lanham, MD: Rowman & Littlefield Publishers, 1992), p. 101.

[44] *Id.*, p. 106.

[45] Raoul Berger, *Government by Judiciary: The Transformation of the Fourteenth Amendment* (Cambridge, MA: Harvard University Press, 1977), p. 133.

In *Brown*, the Court concluded that the real purpose of the equal-protection clause was to prevent the legal subjugation of blacks and that, by the moral standards of 1954, racial segregation in public schools amounted to the legal subjugation of blacks; therefore, segregation laws were unconstitutional. Critics of the historical method contend that *Brown* shows that constitutional interpretation must flow from the aspirations of contemporary Americans, not from the political interests of long-dead legislators.

Finally, the critics claim that the historical method too often permits the majority to limit the rights of a numerical minority, which is inconsistent with the purpose of the Bill of Rights.[46] The words of former Supreme Court Justice Robert Jackson in *West Virginia State Board of Education v. Barnette* (1943) eloquently express this argument.[47] In *Barnette*, the Court invalidated a West Virginia law that required public schoolchildren to salute the American flag and recite the "Pledge of Allegiance" each school day. Justice Jackson wrote:

> *The very purpose of a Bill of Rights was to withdraw certain subjects from the vicissitudes of political controversy, to place them beyond the reach of majorities and officials and to establish them as legal principles to be applied by the courts. One's right to life, liberty, and property, to free speech, a free press, freedom of worship and assembly, and other fundamental rights may not be submitted to vote; they depend on the outcome of no elections.*[48]

The critics contend that the historical method permits majorities to tyrannize unpopular minorities, like the Jehovah's Witnesses in *Barnette*, precisely the sorts of people the Bill of Rights exists to protect.

A famous example of the historical method is Justice Black's concurring opinion in *New York Times Co. v. United States* (1971).[49] In that case, the Supreme Court rejected the Nixon administration's request for a permanent injunction to prevent the *New York Times* and the *Washington Post* from publishing a classified Defense Department study popularly known as the "Pentagon Papers." Justice Black's opinion shows that the historical method does not necessarily produce politically conservative decisions, even though conservatives such as Edwin Meese and Robert Bork most often endorse it.

[46] Bassham, *Original Intent and the Constitution*, p. 41.
[47] 319 U.S. 624.
[48] *Id.* at 638.
[49] 403 U.S. 713.

Justice Black stated that the framers of the First Amendment knew precisely what they intended when they wrote the words: "Congress shall make no law . . . abridging the freedom . . . of the press. . . ." He wrote, "[b]oth the history and language of the First Amendment support the view that the press must be left free to publish news, whatever the source, without censorship, injunctions, or prior restraints."[50]

Therefore, he concluded that "in revealing the workings of government that led to the Vietnam war, the newspapers did precisely that which the Founders hoped and trusted they would do," notwithstanding President Nixon's claim that publication would compromise the national security.[51] Liberals cheered this decision while many conservatives, especially those who worked in the Nixon administration, criticized it.[52]

Textual

The textual method of constitutional interpretation, also known as the "meaning of the words" method, is closely related to the historical method. It resolves constitutional cases by discovering the meaning of the word or clause in question at the time of its drafting and ratification, that is, what its framers intended it to mean. Justice Black's dissent in *Tinker* uses the historical and textual methods in tandem to conclude that the First Amendment protects oral and written communication, but not **symbolic expression.**

Nevertheless, the textual and historical methods are not identical. In determining the meaning of constitutional language, the textual method relies on a close analysis of the constitutional text instead of the broad examination of historical evidence that originalists favor. Supporters claim that the textual method reduces judicial policy making by forcing judges to be faithful to the literal meaning of constitutional language. Indeed, it restricts such policy making even more than the historical method does because the textualist judge

---

[50] *Id.* at 717.

[51] *Id.*

[52] However, Black's dissent in *Tinker v. Des Moines Independent Community School District,* reprinted at the end of Chapter One, indicates that he did not believe that the framers intended the First Amendment to protect symbolic expression as it protects spoken and written words. In *Tinker,* unlike in the Pentagon Papers Case, Justice Black's opinion pleased more conservatives than liberals.

need not attempt to discover the "intent of the framers" on the basis of meager or contradictory evidence; instead, he merely applies to the case at hand the words that the ratifiers approved.[53]

However, textual constitutional analysis is difficult. Most constitutional language is more than two hundred years old, and evidence of its meaning at the time the framers drafted it is often unavailable or inconclusive. Textual analysis is also likely to be unnecessary in cases in which the constitutional text speaks clearly—such as in Article II, section 1, clause 4, which requires the President to be at least thirty-five years old—and inadequate in cases in which the text is vague or ambiguous. In the latter, courts must use other interpretive methods to illuminate the meaning of the Constitution.

The reason for this use of other methods is that context is extremely important in determining the meaning of constitutional language. Context is as crucial to interpreting the Constitution as it is to construing statutes (see Chapter Two). The context of a constitutional provision includes not only related provisions and case law, but the information, values, and assumptions that the provision's drafters and audience shared.

It is necessary to consult such sources because most constitutional language, when read apart from its context, fails to express one clear meaning. Article II, section 1, clause 4, which requires the president to be a "natural born citizen," provides a simple example. This provision could impose a requirement upon either the place or the manner of the president's birth. Only when read in the context of its history does it clearly restrict the place, not the manner, of birth.[54]

Moreover, evaluative constitutional phrases such as *due process of law, cruel and unusual punishment,* and *unreasonable searches and seizures* are virtually meaningless when read apart from the history that produced them, the values that underlie them, and the prior case law that interprets them. As a result of the ambiguities of constitutional language and the importance of context, courts seldom use the textual method alone to interpret the Constitution.

Konigsburg v. State Bar (1960) illustrates the textual method.[55] California rejected Mr. Konigsburg's application for admission to the practice of law in that state because he had refused to answer a question

[53] Bassham, *Original Intent and the Constitution,* p. 47.
[54] *Id.,* p. 27.
[55] 366 U.S. 36.

about his present or past membership in the Communist Party. Konigsburg argued that California's action violated his First Amendment freedoms of speech and association.

Justice John Marshall Harlan II, writing for the majority, disagreed, reasoning that the First Amendment does not protect speech and association absolutely, and that courts should not read it literally.[56] Regulatory statutes may limit speech and association when such limitations are necessary to the exercise of a valid governmental function; in such instances, courts "balance" the governmental interest against the individual's First Amendment interests.[57] California's interest in inquiring about bar applicants' possible membership in the Communist Party outweighed Konigsburg's First Amendment interests.

Justice Black's dissent countered that the "First Amendment's unequivocal command that there shall be no abridgment of the rights of free speech and assembly shows that the men who drafted our Bill of Rights did all the 'balancing' that was to be done in this field."[58] He further argued that the purpose of the First Amendment was to prevent government from restricting the freedoms of speech and association by "balancing" them against the claimed interests of government.[59] Therefore, California violated Konigsburg's First Amendment rights by denying him admission to the bar for refusing to indicate whether he was ever a member of the Communist Party. The difference of opinion in *Konigsburg* illustrates that the textual method does not end the influence of personal policy preferences in judicial decisions, even when the language in question is as apparently clear as: "Congress shall make no law abridging the freedom of speech."

Structural

The structural method of constitutional interpretation derives the rules that resolve cases from the various structures within the Constitution—especially federalism and the separation of powers—and from the relationships that such structures require. First, the court will make an uncontroversial statement in its written opinion about the structure of the Constitution. For example, the **supremacy**

---

[56] *Id.* at 49.
[57] *Id.* at 50–51.
[58] *Id.* at 61.
[59] *Id.*

clause contained in Article VI makes the Constitution and all federal laws that conform to constitutional requirements the supreme law of the land; it also obligates states to obey that supreme law. Next, the court will deduce from the structure noted in statement one an important power relationship that will influence the outcome of the case. A hypothetical example might read: "Congress, pursuant to its commerce power under Article I, section 8, clause 3, has complete authority to legally 'recognize' and manage relations with Indian tribes, and states cannot apply their laws to Indian reservations unless Congress specifically permits them to do so." Such deductions are not the inevitable results of indisputable logic that court opinions sometimes make them appear to be. Judges' values and public policy preferences influence those deductions, just as they influence other aspects of legal reasoning.

The court will next make a factual assertion that highlights the constitutional conflict in the case. An example might read: "The state of Arizona ignores the fact that the Navajo Nation is a federally recognized Indian tribe, and seeks to enforce state hunting and fishing laws on the Navajo Reservation." Finally, the court will draw a conclusion that provides the rule that resolves the case: "Congress possesses the exclusive power to 'recognize' Indian tribes, and federal recognition includes tribal control over hunting and fishing on reservations unless Congress decides otherwise. Arizona's enforcement of state law on the Navajo Reservation is unconstitutional because state law must comply with Congressional policy." Notice how the deduction that Congress possesses complete authority to "recognize" Indian tribes and manage relations with them leads to the conclusion that Arizona's enforcement of its hunting and fishing laws on the Navajo Reservation is unconstitutional.

An actual example of the structural method is Chief Justice John Marshall's opinion for the Supreme Court in *McCulloch v. Maryland* (1819).[60] The Court held that Congress possessed the power to incorporate the Bank of the United States in 1816, and that Maryland could not tax the Baltimore branch of the bank without violating the Constitution. Marshall reasoned that, pursuant to the supremacy clause, the federal government, "though limited in its powers, is supreme" within its sphere of action.[61] Article I, section 8, clause 18

[60] 17 U.S. (4 Wheaton) 315.
[61] *Id.* at 406.

empowers Congress to "make all laws necessary and proper" to carry out its express powers. Banks are necessary to conduct interstate commerce; hence, Congress's power to charter a bank is implicit in its express power over interstate commerce. Thus he reasoned that the law that created the Bank was constitutional.

The supremacy clause also made Maryland's tax on the Bank of the United States unconstitutional. That clause makes the federal government supreme over the states. Maryland's tax meant the regulation and potential destruction of a federal institution by a state institution. To uphold the Maryland tax, then, would be to turn the Constitution on its head; if a state could tax a federal bank, it could also tax and potentially destroy the mail, the mint, and other federal institutions. Thus, the Maryland law was unconstitutional.[62]

Doctrinal
The doctrinal, or precedent-based, method of constitutional interpretation resolves cases by applying rules derived from decisions reached in prior cases. In other words, it features the **reasoning by analogy** component of legal reasoning. Courts do not often use the doctrinal method in constitutional cases. Precedent is less important in constitutional than in statutory cases because Congress can overturn a statutory decision of the Court by passing a new statute, but only judicial action or a constitutional amendment can overturn a constitutional precedent. A constitutional amendment has overturned a Supreme Court decision only four times since 1789; hence,

[62] Two scholars have constructed fascinating theories of constitutional interpretation based on structural arguments. Robert Lowery Clinton argues that the framers intended federal courts to exercise judicial review only in cases of "a judicial nature," that is, cases that arise when the legislative or executive branch of the federal government usurps judicial power. In all other cases, the elected branches of the federal government should ultimately determine the constitutionality of their respective actions. See Robert Lowery Clinton, *Marbury v Madison And Judicial Review* (Lawrence, KS: University Press of Kansas, 1989). John Hart Ely argues that the principal purpose of the Constitution is to ensure an open political process and, therefore, that courts should exercise judicial review only where the political process fails to function properly, such as in cases of legislative malapportionment, racial discrimination in voting, or denials of the freedom of speech. John Hart Ely, *Democracy and Distrust* (Cambridge, MA: Harvard University Press, 1980). Each author argues that the structure of the Constitution restricts the exercise of judicial review to a limited category of cases in which vigorous judicial scrutiny is warranted.

judicial action is the most likely means of correcting an unjust constitutional precedent.[63]

One way a court can use the doctrinal method is to analogize the case at hand to a prior case, then apply the rule of the earlier case to the present one. For example, in *Mapp v. Ohio* (1961),[64] the Supreme Court applied to the states the famous **exclusionary rule** of *Weeks v. United States* (1914), which prohibits prosecutors from introducing in federal court evidence obtained in violation of the Fourth Amendment prohibition of unreasonable searches and seizures.[65] Justice Tom Clark, writing for the majority in *Mapp*, noted the following:

> *Presently, a federal prosecutor may make no use of evidence illegally seized, but a State's attorney across the street may, although he supposedly is operating under the enforceable prohibitions of the same Amendment. Thus, the State, by admitting evidence unlawfully seized, serves to encourage disobedience to the Federal Constitution which it is bound to uphold.*[66]

The Court remedied that inequity by applying the rule of *Weeks* to the states in *Mapp*.

Another way in which a court may use the doctrinal method is to examine a group of precedents, identify general legal principles that underlie the group, and then apply those principles to the present case. For example, in *Lemon v. Kurtzman* (1971) the Supreme Court invalidated two laws, ruling that each was an **establishment of religion** in violation of the First Amendment.[67] One was a Pennsylvania law that reimbursed church-related elementary and secondary

---

[63] The Eleventh Amendment overturned *Chisholm v. Georgia,* 2 U.S. 419 (1793), which held that a resident of one state could sue another state in federal court. The Thirteenth Amendment reversed *Dred Scott v. Sandford,* 60 U.S. 393 (1856), which held in effect that Blacks were not American citizens whom the Constitution protects. The Sixteenth Amendment invalidated *Pollock v. Farmers' Loan & Trust Company,* 158 U.S. 601 (1895), which held the federal income tax unconstitutional. The Twenty-sixth Amendment overturned *Oregon v. Mitchell,* 400 U.S. 112 (1970), which held unconstitutional a federal statute that lowered the minimum voting age in state elections to eighteen.

[64] 367 U.S. 643.

[65] 232 U.S. 383.

[66] 367 U.S. at 657.

[67] 403 U.S. 602; the First Amendment states that "Congress shall make no law respecting an establishment of religion. . . ."

schools for the cost of teachers' salaries, textbooks, and instructional materials; the other was a Rhode Island law that provided a state subsidy to teachers in church-related elementary schools amounting to 15 percent of their annual salaries. The Court applied principles derived from two prior decisions—*Board of Education v. Allen* (1968) [68] and *Walz v. Tax Commission* (1970) [69]—to articulate the three-part *"Lemon* test," which states that any statute must:

1. possess a **secular** (i.e., nonreligious) purpose;
2. possess a principal or primary effect that *neither helps nor harms* religion; and
3. not create an **excessive entanglement** between church and state.

A statute that fails any one of the three prongs of this test is unconstitutional.

The Court declared the Rhode Island and Pennsylvania laws unconstitutional because they created excessive entanglements between church and state. Chief Justice Burger, writing for the majority, observed that:

> *[a] comprehensive, discriminating, and continuing state surveillance will inevitably be required to ensure that [the teachers who benefit from state assistance teach only secular subjects, and the books and other materials that state funds purchase address only such subjects] and the First Amendment [is] otherwise respected. These prophylactic contacts will involve excessive and enduring entanglement between state and church.* [70]

The doctrinal method limits but does not eliminate judicial discretion. Judges are free to choose the constitutional precedents that they believe are most relevant to the present case, and to apply the former to the latter (see Chapter One). Judges' moral and political values are likely to influence their choices of precedents. Consequently, members of an appellate court may disagree about whether a certain prior case should control the decision at hand.

In *Wallace v. Jaffree* (1985), for example, the majority, using the *"Lemon* test," concluded that an Alabama law that authorized a

[68] 392 U.S. 236.
[69] 397 U.S. 664.
[70] 403 U.S. at 619.

moment of silence "for meditation or voluntary prayer" in all public schools was an unconstitutional establishment of religion because it had a **religious purpose,** namely, returning prayer to public schools.[71] Justice John Paul Stevens, writing for the majority, reasoned that inclusion of the words "or voluntary prayer" in the statute "indicates that the State intended to characterize prayer as a favored practice."[72] He then concluded that "[s]uch an endorsement is not consistent with the established principle that the government must pursue a course of complete neutrality toward religion."[73]

Chief Justice Burger, in dissent, supported the *"Lemon* test," but concluded that the majority had misapplied it in this case. He argued that the Alabama law did not have an unconstitutional religious purpose merely because it offered students a moment of silence, during which they could pray if they chose. The Chief Justice wrote that "[t]o suggest that a moment-of-silence statute that includes the word 'prayer' unconstitutionally endorses religion, while one that simply provides for a moment of silence does not, manifests not neutrality but hostility toward religion."[74]

Justice Rehnquist, also in dissent, rejected the *"Lemon* test" altogether on the ground that it is not rooted in the history of the First Amendment. He argued further that the purpose of the establishment clause is to prohibit a national religion and, perhaps, to prevent government from favoring one religion over another. The framers did not intend that clause to require the government to be neutral toward religion, as the *"Lemon* test" demands. Therefore, he concluded, Alabama should be able to enact a moment-of-silence statute, even if doing so endorses religion, because "nothing in the Establishment Clause, properly understood, prohibits any such generalized 'endorsement' of prayer."[75]

Prudential
The prudential method of constitutional interpretation, also known as "balancing," decides cases by identifying the competing interests

[71] 472 U.S. 38.
[72] 472 U.S. at 60.
[73] *Id.*
[74] *Id.* at 85.
[75] *Id.* at 113–114.

involved and then fashioning rules that reasonably accommodate those interests. In *United States v. Leon* (1984), the Supreme Court used the prudential method to determine the constitutionality of a **good-faith exception** to the exclusionary rule.[76] The exclusionary rule, as noted earlier, prohibits the use in a criminal court of illegally obtained evidence.

The issue in *Leon* was whether that rule applies when police officers, acting in the good-faith belief that their search is legal, obtain evidence in a manner that a court later concludes violates the Fourth Amendment. Justice Byron White, writing for the majority, observed that the purpose of the rule is to punish police misconduct; hence, there is no benefit to society in applying it when the police have acted responsibly. However, there is a significant social cost in applying it to such cases because exclusion of the challenged evidence may result in the release of a guilty defendant. Consequently, the Court announced a good-faith exception to the exclusionary rule that permits the use in court of illegally seized evidence obtained in what the police believed was a lawful search.

Critics of the prudential method charge that it requires courts to compare the burdens and benefits of a particular rule absent any common unit of measure. For example, in *United States v. Leon* the Court could not possibly have compared, by a common unit of measure, the cost to society of freeing guilty defendants who were subject to good-faith, but illegal, searches, and the benefit to society of prohibiting the police from enforcing the law by breaking it. It might be possible to measure quantitatively the cost of freeing guilty defendants, but it is not possible to similarly measure the benefit of constitutional restraints on police behavior.

A second criticism of this method is that it diminishes the importance of constitutional interpretation by reaching conclusions via a balancing of interests more appropriate to the legislative process. Courts should use constitutional cases to affirm fundamental principles (e.g., the freedom of speech), and to ratify changes in those principles (e.g., speech includes symbolic speech) that reflect the evolving consensus of society. The methods used should be textual analysis, examination of precedent, and, occasionally, reference to

[76] 468 U.S. 897.

America's ethical traditions; the mere balancing of conflicting interests is inappropriate in constitutional cases.[77]

Justice Brennan, for example, dissenting in *Leon*, argued that the
exclusionary rule is an integral part of the Fourth Amendment;
therefore courts cannot balance it against the public's desire to curb
crime any more than they can balance the Fourth Amendment itself
against that desire. A search that is unconstitutional remains so even
though the police officers who conducted it thought it was legal,
and the fruits of that search are inadmissible in court, regardless of
the urgency of crime control.

A final criticism is that this method is so flexible and adaptable
that judges can use it to justify any conclusion to which their personal policy preferences lead them. Justice Brennan expressed this
view in *Leon:*

> When the Court's analysis is examined carefully ... it is clear that we have
> not been treated to an honest assessment of the merits of the exclusionary
> rule, but have instead been drawn into a curious world where the "costs"
> of excluding illegally obtained evidence loom to exaggerated heights and
> where the "benefits" of such exclusion are made to disappear with a mere
> wave of the hand.[78]

Nevertheless, the prudential method is useful for resolving unprecedented cases because it does not rely on analogy to prior cases
or on prior interpretations of constitutional language. *United States v.
Nixon*, cited earlier, illustrates this point.[79] In *Nixon*, the Supreme
Court considered the novel question of whether a prosecutor could
force President Nixon to release tape recordings of conversations between the president and members of his staff. The Court acknowledged President Nixon's interest in confidential communications
and weighed it against the interest of the criminal justice system in
obtaining evidence for trial. The Court concluded that the president's
interest, which in this case was general and unrelated to national

---

[77] For thoughtful critiques of "balancing," see John H. Garvey and T. Alexander Aleinikoff, *Modern Constitutional Theory: A Reader*, second edition
(St. Paul, MN: West Publishing, 1991); and T. R. Van Geel, *Understanding Supreme Court Opinions* (White Plains, NY: Longman, 1991).

[78] 468 U.S. at 929.

[79] Van Geel, *Understanding Supreme Court Opinions*, p. 49.

security, must yield to the legal system's interest in obtaining all available evidence for a pending criminal trial. Chief Justice Burger, writing for a unanimous Court, stated that:

> *when the ground for asserting privilege as to subpoenaed materials sought for use in a criminal trial is based only on the generalized interest in confidentiality, it cannot prevail over the fundamental demands of due process of law in the fair administration of criminal justice. The generalized assertion of privilege must yield to the demonstrated, specific need for evidence in a pending criminal trial.*[80]

The justices therefore ordered the president to release the requested material; they might have reached a different conclusion, however, had the president demonstrated a national security reason to withhold the tapes.

Ethical

The ethical method of constitutional interpretation, also known as "noninterpretivism," resolves constitutional cases on the basis of moral or political values that the majority concludes are fundamental to American culture and consistent with the Constitution, even though the text does not mention them. Conclusions about what is good policy and how society ought to function underlie court decisions based on the ethical method. Former Justices Brennan and William Douglas were noninterpretivists who believed that the Supreme Court should expound in its decisions national ideals of fairness and individual freedom, even when the words in the Constitution do not express those particular ideals. Brennan believed that the fundamental guiding principle of constitutional jurisprudence is "human dignity."[81]

A court is most likely to use this method when the others fail to produce an argument that satisfactorily resolves the case. If, for example, the consideration of precedents and the balancing of interests yield opposing arguments that are equally or almost equally plausible, a court will probably favor the argument that is closest to its view of justice or sound public policy. This scenario occurs most

---

[80] 418 U.S. at 713.
[81] Brennan, "The Constitution of the United States," p. 31.

frequently in civil-liberties cases that require interpretation of the Fourteenth Amendment's due-process and equal-protection clauses, the Fourth Amendment's prohibition of unreasonable searches and seizures, or the Eighth Amendment's prohibition of cruel and unusual punishments.

The ethical method is controversial. Originalists criticize it vehemently as "social engineering" by judges who appear to have forgotten that their job is to read the Constitution, not to write it. The originalists further argue that such judges, in effect, rewrite the Constitution by means of an illegitimate "amendment" process. Noninterpretivists counter that constitutional principles must be sufficiently elastic to address the needs of an ever-changing society and, therefore, that courts are justified in rejecting the framers' intent when it is unresponsive to the contemporary world. The Supreme Court, for example, is justified in using the equal-protection clause to protect women against discrimination, even though its framers intended it to protect only blacks, because it promises, and contemporary Americans aspire to, equal treatment for all.

The ethical method is not new, nor does it necessarily produce politically liberal decisions. Indeed, the most famous early example of this method is *Lochner v. New York* (1905), wherein the Court declared unconstitutional a New York law that prohibited employers from requiring bakers to work more than sixty hours per week.[82] The majority concluded that the law violated **liberty of contract,** namely, the freedom of employer and employee to negotiate the employee's wages. Today, professors of constitutional law routinely pummel the *Lochner* majority for basing its decision on a principle that existed in the judges' minds, but not in the Constitution, as well as on an antiquated and unrealistic view (even in 1905) of the freedom of employees to negotiate wages with their employers. Indeed, some professors refer to the act of basing a constitutional decision entirely on one's policy preferences as "Lochnerizing."

Currently, critics most often accuse the Supreme Court of "Lochnerizing" in cases that concern the right of privacy, which restricts governmental intervention in matters concerning marriage, family life, and procreation. The critics charge that in *Griswold* and *Roe,* as in *Lochner,* the Court invalidated a law because of a "fundamental right"

---

[82] 198 U.S. 45.

that is neither explicit nor implicit in the Constitution. According to this view, if one rejects *Lochner* as a back-door constitutional amendment, one must also reject *Griswold* and *Roe* as the same thing.[83]

Supporters of the right of privacy disagree. They argue that the First Amendment's freedoms of thought, conscience, and association; the Third Amendment's protection against having to quarter soldiers in one's home during peacetime; and the Fourth Amendment's prohibition of unreasonable searches and seizures all suggest that the Constitution values and protects personal privacy. They also cite the Ninth Amendment, which states, "The enumeration in the Constitution of certain rights shall not be construed to deny or disparage others retained by the people."

Professors Lawrence Tribe and Michael Dorf contend that the Ninth Amendment requires the Court to recognize and protect "unenumerated rights" that are consistent with the rights specified in Amendments One through Eight.[84] The right of privacy in intimate matters meets that standard because it coincides with the protections that the First, Third, and Fourth Amendments provide for personal autonomy and the sanctity of the home. Thus, privacy, unlike liberty of contract, is rooted in constitutional principles.

There has been disagreement within the Supreme Court about the right of privacy ever since *Griswold*. Today, that disagreement is as likely to be about how far the right extends as it is about whether the right exists. For example, in *Bowers v. Hardwick* (1986), the Court considered the constitutionality of a Georgia law that prohibited consensual sodomy.[85] Justice White, writing for the majority, concluded that the Constitution does not protect a right to homosexual

[83] One thing about which supporters and critics of the privacy decisions will surely agree is that those decisions are substantive due-process decisions. In substantive due-process cases, the Court determines whether the substance or content of a statute violates due process because the statute is "arbitrary," "capricious," or "irrational." The other form of due process, procedural, concerns the manner in which government officials carry out a law. *Miranda v. Arizona, Mapp v. Ohio,* and *United States v. Leon,* cited earlier in this chapter, are examples of procedural due process cases because they concern constitutional issues of law enforcement procedure. Due-process cases are much more numerous than substantive due-process cases.

[84] Lawrence H. Tribe and Michael C. Dorf, *On Reading the Constitution* (Cambridge, MA: Harvard University Press, 1991), p.110.

[85] 478 U.S. 186.

sodomy because the Court's precedents indicate that the right of privacy only encompasses child rearing, education, marriage, procreation, contraception, and abortion, a presumptively heterosexual sphere. He wrote, "we think it evident that none of the rights announced in [prior right of privacy] cases bears any resemblance to the claimed constitutional right of homosexuals to engage in acts of sodomy, that is asserted in this case."[86]

The majority further reasoned that even if the precedents did not contain an exhaustive list of the practices that the right of privacy protects, that right did not protect homosexual sodomy because—unlike child rearing, education, marriage, procreation, contraception, and abortion—homosexual sodomy did not meet two important tests that the Court set. These tests were that it is neither "implicit in the concept of ordered liberty," that is, necessary to the preservation of liberty and justice in this country, nor "deeply rooted in this Nation's history and tradition," which "rights not readily identifiable in the Constitution's text" must be in order to warrant judicial protection.[87]

Justice Harry Blackmun countered, in dissent, that the issue here was not a right to homosexual sodomy, but a much broader "right to be let alone."[88] He wrote that "what the Court really has refused to recognize [in this case] is the fundamental interest all individuals have in controlling the nature of their intimate associations with others."[89] In Blackmun's view, that is what the right of privacy protects. Therefore, it guarantees the freedom of adults, heterosexual and homosexual, to make choices about the intimate aspects of their lives, including the conduct of personal relationships. Moreover, the right of privacy assuredly protects conduct, like Hardwick's in this case, that occurs in one's own home. Justice Blackmun observed that "the right of an individual to conduct intimate relationships in the intimacy of his or her own home seems to me to be the heart of the Constitutional protection of privacy."[90] Thus, Justice Blackmun concluded that the right of privacy encompasses homosexual sodomy between consenting adults.

[86] 478 U.S. at 190–191.
[87] *Id.* at 191–192.
[88] See Justice Louis Brandeis's dissenting opinion in *Olmstead v. United States,* 277 U.S. 438 (1928).
[89] *Id.* at 206.
[90] *Id.* at 208.

Evaluating Constitutional Opinions

There is no one *right* way to interpret the Constitution, just as there is no one *right* way to interpret the Bible. That is why there are originalists and noninterpretivists, just as there are Southern Baptists and Unitarians. However, some constitutional opinions are better than others, and a well-reasoned opinion can win the votes of both originalists and noninterpretivists on an appellate court.

The well-reasoned opinion often features several methods of constitutional interpretation. The harder the case is to decide, the more methods the opinion is likely to use. The legendary Justice Benjamin Cardozo wrote that in a difficult case, a judge must "balance all his ingredients, his philosophy, his logic, his analogies, his history, his customs, his sense of right, and all the rest, and adding a little here and taking out a little there, must determine, as wisely as he can, which weight shall tip the scales."[91]

Even when the judge decides the case on the basis of a compelling moral or political value, if he also considers history, text, and precedent in analyzing the case, his opinion is more likely to command a majority. That is because he has read the Constitution, not written it.

The well-reasoned constitutional opinion integrates the following four elements:

1. the rules of constitutional law, as reflected in statutes and prior court decisions;
2. the facts of the case that emerged at trial;
3. "social background" or "legislative" facts, which are social conditions that have created or affected the case; and
4. moral values held in the community in which the case occurs.[92]

It reaches a result that does not depend upon

1. an incorrect factual determination reached at trial;
2. a false assumption about relevant social conditions;
3. a mistaken reading of a rule of constitutional law, or
4. a value judgment that the community will surely reject.

[91] Benjamin N. Cardozo, *The Nature of the Judicial Process* (New Haven: Yale University Press, 1921), p. 162.

[92] Carter, *Reason In Law,* p. 221.

Lochner v. New York is not a well-reasoned opinion for two reasons. First, it "rewrote" the Constitution to enshrine therein the Court majority's economic philosophy, which fiercely opposed governmental regulation of business. Second, it ignored two important social background facts, namely, workers' lack of bargaining power and the adverse health effects of working more than sixty hours per week in a bakery.

You should examine constitutional opinions for evidence of faulty foundations. Remember, though, that in some cases the facts, rules of law, and values involved are all controversial. Such cases often produce well-reasoned majority and dissenting opinions. The authors have read rather than written the Constitution, but disagree about the *right* way to read it.

CONCLUSION

Constitutional interpretation, like statutory construction, is the exercise of discretion, subject to constraints. Prior decisions, societal values, and the language and history of the Constitution limit, but do not eliminate, judicial discretion. Courts exercise discretion in constitutional cases because the document is often vague and/or ambiguous; prior decisions exert a reduced influence in constitutional matters; and dominant societal values may conflict with cherished individual rights. To identify the fundamental values of the American political system and apply them to contemporary controversies is to choose among competing values and alternative outcomes. That is why debates occur among appellate judges and in constitutional law classes.

EPILOGUE: THE CONSTITUTIONALITY OF A VETERANS' PREFERENCE LAW

The following case tests the constitutionality of a state law that requires the state to hire veterans before nonveterans for its civil-service jobs. A female nonveteran challenged the law, claiming that it discriminates against women in violation of the equal-protection clause of the Fourteenth Amendment. The case shows that the majority and the dissenters can use the same method of constitutional interpretation yet arrive at opposite conclusions. When reading the case, try to identify the interpretive method used and the reason(s) why it led to conflicting conclusions. After reading the case, ask yourself whether the law in question intentionally treats men and women differently and, if so, whether that is necessary to achieve an important public policy goal.

Personnel Administrator of Massachusetts v. Feeney *442 U.S. 256 (1979)*

MR. JUSTICE STEWART delivered the opinion of the Court.

This case presents a challenge to the constitutionality of the Massachusetts veterans' preference statute on the ground that it discriminates against women in violation of the Equal Protection Clause of the Fourteenth Amendment.

I.

A.

The Federal Government and virtually all of the States grant some sort of hiring preference to veterans. The Massachusetts preference, which is loosely termed an "absolute lifetime" preference, is among the most generous. It is available to "any person, male or female, including a nurse," who was honorably discharged from the United States Armed Forces after at least ninety days of active service, at least one day of which was during "wartime." Persons who are deemed veterans and who are otherwise qualified for a particular civil service job may exercise the preference at any time and as many times as they wish.

All applicants for [state] employment [in Massachusetts] must take competitive examinations. Candidates who pass are then ranked in the order of their respective scores on an "eligible list." [State law] requires, however, that disabled veterans, veterans, and surviving spouses and surviving parents of veterans be ranked—in the order of their respective scores—above all other candidates. Although the veterans' preference thus does not guarantee that a veteran will be appointed, it is obvious that the preference gives to veterans who achieve passing scores a well-nigh absolute advantage.

B.

[Editor's note: In 1971, Helen Feeney received the second highest score on a Massachusetts civil-service examination and in 1973 the third highest score on another such examination. Ms. Feeney, a nonveteran, was in both instances ranked below several male veterans who had achieved lower scores. In neither case, therefore, did she make the list of three candidates from which the agency filled its vacancy. Similar results followed subsequent examinations that Ms. Feeney took.]

C.

The veterans' hiring preference in Massachusetts, as in other jurisdictions, has traditionally been justified as a measure designed to reward veterans for the sacrifice of military service, to ease the transition from military to civilian life, to encourage patriotic service, and to attract loyal and well-disciplined people to civil service occupations. . . .

D.

Notwithstanding the apparent attempts by Massachusetts to include as many military women as possible within the scope of the preference, the statute today benefits an overwhelmingly male class. This is attributable in some measure to the variety of federal statutes, regulations, and policies that have restricted the number of women who could enlist in the United States Armed Forces, and largely to the simple fact that women have never been subjected to a military draft. . . .

II.

The sole question for decision on this appeal is whether Massachusetts, in granting an absolute lifetime preference to veterans, has discriminated against women in violation of the Equal Protection Clause of the Fourteenth Amendment.

A.

The equal protection guarantee of the Fourteenth Amendment does not take from the States all power of classification. When the basic classification is rationally based, uneven effects upon particular groups within a class are ordinarily of no constitutional concern. . . .

Certain classifications, however, in themselves supply a reason to infer antipathy. Race is the paradigm. A racial classification, regardless of purported motivation, is presumptively invalid and can be upheld only upon an extraordinary justification. *Brown v. Board of Education*, 347 U.S. 483; *McLaughlin v. Florida*, 379 U.S. 184.

III.

A.

The question whether [Massachusetts] establishes a classification that is overtly or covertly based upon gender must first be considered.

. . . Veteran status is not uniquely male. Although few women benefit from the preference, the nonveteran class is not substantially all female. To the contrary, significant numbers of nonveterans are men, and all nonveterans—male as well as female—are placed at a disadvantage. Too many men are affected by [this statute] to permit the inference that the statute is but a pretext for preferring men over women.

Moreover, as the District Court implicitly found, the purposes of the statute provide the surest explanation for its impact. The distinction made [by the Massachusetts veterans' preference statute] is between veterans and nonveterans, not between men and women.

B.

The dispositive question, then, is whether [Ms. Feeney] has shown that a gender-based discriminatory purpose has, at least in some measure, shaped the Massachusetts veterans' preference legislation.

1.

The contention that this veterans' preference is "inherently nonneutral" or "gender-biased" presumes that the State, by favoring veterans, intentionally incorporated into its public employment policies the panoply of sex-based and assertedly discriminatory federal laws that have prevented all but a handful of women from becoming veterans. There are two serious difficulties with this argument. First, it is wholly at odds with the District Court's central finding that Massachusetts has not offered a preference to veterans for the purpose of discriminating against women. Second, it cannot be reconciled with the assumption made by both [Ms Feeney] and the District Court that a more limited hiring preference for veterans could be sustained. Taken together, these difficulties are fatal.

2.

The decision to grant a preference to veterans was of course "intentional." It would thus be disingenuous to say that the adverse consequences of this legislation for women were unintended, in the sense that they were not volitional or in the sense that they were not foreseeable.

"Discriminatory purpose," however, implies more than intent as volition or intent as awareness of consequences. It implies that the decisionmaker, in this case a state legislature, selected or reaffirmed a particular course of action at least in part "because of," not merely "in spite of," its adverse effects upon an identifiable group. Yet nothing in the record demonstrates that this preference for veterans was originally devised or subsequently re-enacted because it would accomplish the collateral goal of keeping women in a stereotypic and predefined place in the Massachusetts Civil Service.

IV.

Veterans' hiring preferences represent an awkward—and, many argue, unfair—exception to the widely shared view that merit and merit alone should prevail in the employment policies of government. The substantial edge granted to veterans by [Massachusetts law] may reflect unwise policy. [Ms. Feeney], however, has failed to demonstrate that the law in any way reflects a purpose to discriminate on the basis of sex.

Reversed and remanded.

MR. JUSTICE MARSHALL, with whom MR. JUSTICE BRENNAN joins, dissenting.

In my judgment, Massachusetts' choice of an absolute veterans' preference system evinces purposeful gender-based discrimination. And because the statutory scheme bears no substantial relationship to a legitimate governmental objective, it cannot withstand scrutiny under the Equal Protection Clause.

I.

The District Court found that the "prime objective" of the Massachusetts veterans' preference statute . . . was to benefit individuals with prior military service. . . .

That a legislature seeks to advantage one group does not, as a matter of logic or of common sense, exclude the possibility that it also intends to disadvantage another. Individuals in general and lawmakers in particular frequently act for a variety of reasons. . . . Thus, the critical constitutional inquiry is not whether an illicit consideration was the primary or but-for cause of a decision, but rather whether it had an appreciable role in shaping a given legislative enactment. . . .

To discern the purposes underlying facially neutral policies, this Court has . . . considered the degree, inevitability, and foreseeability of any disproportionate impact as well as the alternatives reasonably available. . . .

Although neutral in form, the [Massachusetts] statute is anything but neutral in application. It inescapably reserves a major sector of public employment to an already established class which, as a matter of historical fact, is 98 percent male.

Particularly when viewed against the range of less discriminatory alternatives available to assist veterans, Massachusetts' choice of a formula that so severely restricts public employment opportunities for women cannot reasonably be thought gender-neutral. . . .

II.

To survive challenge under the Equal Protection Clause, statutes reflecting gender-based discrimination must be substantially related to the achievement of important governmental objectives. See *Califano v. Webster,* 430 U.S. 313, 316–317 (1977); *Craig v. Boren,* 429 U.S. 190, 197 (1976); *Reed v. Reed,* 404 U.S. 71, 76 (1971). [Massachusetts] here advance[s] three interests in support of the absolute-preference system. . . .

With respect to the first interest, facilitating veterans' transition to civilian status, the statute is plainly overinclusive. By conferring a permanent preference, the legislation allows veterans to invoke their advantage repeatedly, without regard to their date of discharge.

Nor is the Commonwealth's second asserted interest, encouraging military service, a plausible justification for this legislative scheme. . . . I am unwilling to assume what [Massachusetts] made no effort to prove, that the possibility of obtaining an *ex post facto* civil service preference significantly influenced the enlistment decisions of Massachusetts residents. Moreover, even if such influence could be presumed, the statute is still grossly overinclusive in that it bestows benefits on men drafted as well as those who volunteered.

Finally, the Commonwealth's third interest, rewarding veterans, does not "adequately justify the salient features" of this preference system. *Craig v. Boren, supra,* at 202–203. Here, there are a wide variety of less discriminatory means by which Massachusetts could effect its compensatory purposes. For example, a point preference system, such as that maintained by many States and the Federal Government . . . or an absolute preference for a limited duration would reward veterans without excluding all qualified women from upper level civil service positions.

I would affirm the judgment of the court below.

 ## QUESTIONS FOR DISCUSSION

1. How does the Massachusetts veterans' preference law classify applicants who qualify for civil-service appointments in that state?

2. How does the Massachusetts law differ from the federal veterans' preference law?

3. Why does Ms. Feeney contend that the Massachusetts law discriminates against women in violation of the equal-protection clause of the Fourteenth Amendment?

4. What social background facts contribute to the result that the Massachusetts law overwhelmingly benefits males?

5. What must Ms. Feeney show in order to meet her burden of proof that the Massachusetts law violates the equal-protection clause?

6. Why is she unable to meet that burden of proof?

7. Why does Justice Marshall, dissenting, conclude that Ms. Feeney has demonstrated that the Massachusetts veterans' preference law intentionally discriminates against women?

8. Under what circumstances can a law intentionally discriminate against women yet still be constitutional?

9. Why does Justice Marshall conclude that the Massachusetts law is not substantially related to easing veterans' adjustments to civilian life?

10. Why does Justice Marshall conclude that the Massachusetts law is not substantially related to encouraging military service?

11. Why does Justice Marshall conclude that the purpose of rewarding veterans for their military service does not justify the absolute lifetime preference contained in the Massachusetts law?

12. Is the Massachusetts veterans' preference law a rational classification or unconstitutional gender-based discrimination?

CHAPTER 4

Common-Law Decision Making

Introduction

The Common-Law Tradition

The Common Law in Action

Conclusion

Epilogue: The Psychotherapist's Duty of Care

Questions for Discussion

INTRODUCTION

American judges resolve disputes even when no statute or constitutional provision governs the issues raised in those disputes. Such cases occupy what Justice Cardozo called "the land of mystery,"[1] where a judge must rely for guidance on the lessons learned from prior cases, "whether stored in his mind or hidden in the books."[2] When judges resolve disputes by comparing the case at hand to prior cases, and by applying to the case at hand principles derived from those prior cases, they engage in **common-law decision making.**

Common-law decision making produces judge-made law. Judge-made law includes principles and rules that are as much a part of "the law" as any statute or constitutional provision. Indeed, most of the principles and rules contained in the law of **contracts** and **torts** (personal injuries) are judge-made law. Statutes are superior in authority to common-law decisions because, as Chapter Two explained, the doctrine of legislative supremacy states that legislative lawmaking power is greater than judicial lawmaking power. Legislative lawmaking power is greater because it derives from the will of the majority of the electorate.[3] That means, in principle, that a statute can change the common law, but a common-law decision cannot change a statute.[4]

In practice, though, courts' authority to construe statutes enables courts to expand and contract the scope and power of those statutes. Indeed, the vagueness, ambiguity, and limited scope of statutory language often require courts to use common-law principles to determine whether the statute or the common law should control the outcome of a case.[5] Recall, for example, that in *Riggs v. Palmer,* a grandson due to inherit money from his grandfather murdered the grandfather yet maintained that he was still entitled to receive his

[1] Benjamin N. Cardozo, *The Nature of the Judicial Process* (New Haven: Yale University Press, 1921), p. 18.

[2] *Id.*, p. 19.

[3] F. Reed Dickerson, *The Interpretation and Application of Statutes* (Boston: Little, Brown, 1975), p. 18.

[4] E. Allan Farnsworth, *An Introduction to the Legal System of the United States,* third edition (New York: Oceana Publications, 1996), p. 75.

[5] *Id.*, p. 79. See also Norman J. Singer, *Sutherland Statutory Construction,* fifth edition, v. 2B (New York: Clark Boardman Callaghan, 1992), p. 90.

inheritance.[6] The governing statute was silent on this subject, so the New York Court of Appeals voided the inheritance by reasoning from the common-law principle that the law should not permit one to profit from one's own wrongdoing. The statute's silence and the court's authority to construe the statute created plenty of room for common-law decision making.

Riggs v. Palmer was a state court decision. Only state courts engage in common-law decision making. There is no federal substantive common law, so federal courts reason from federal statutes and, when those statutes are vague and/or ambiguous, federal courts apply the common law of the respective states in which they are located.[7] Either a federal or a state statute can supersede the common law. In tort and contract law, though, federal and state statutes have supplemented, not supplanted, the common law; hence, common-law decision making remains significant.

Common-law decision making begins with judicial scrutiny of the relevant precedents, and a comparison of those precedents to the case at hand. It then derives from the precedents an underlying principle, and applies that principle to the case at hand, thereby creating the rule that resolves the case.

Ploof v. Putnam (1908) illustrates this process.[8] Sylvester Ploof, his wife, and their two children sustained injuries when a storm destroyed their boat, casting them into a lake. Earlier, the Ploofs had attempted to moor their boat to Putnam's dock, but Putnam's servant unmoored it, leaving the Ploofs at the mercy of the storm. The Vermont Supreme Court extracted from the precedents the principle of **necessity,** which justifies entries on another person's land that would otherwise constitute trespassing.

According to the court, this principle "applies with special force to the preservation of human life."[9] It permits one to damage the personal property of another in order to save one's own life or the life of another. After analogizing the precedents to the facts in *Ploof,*

[6] 115 N.Y. 506 (1889).

[7] In *Erie Railroad Company v. Tompkins,* 304 U.S. 64 (1938), the Supreme Court stated that there is no federal substantive common law and that federal courts should apply the common law of the respective states in which they sit.

[8] 81 Vt. 471, 71 A. 188.

[9] 81 Vt. at 475.

the court used deductive reasoning to apply the principle of necessity to those facts. The result was the rule that when a storm threatens boaters' personal safety, they may moor their boats at another person's dock without trespassing. Thus, the *Ploof* decision extended the reach of an established principle to circumstances that principle had not previously addressed.

Thoughtful judges extract and apply the controlling principle in such a way that the resulting rule not only resolves the present dispute but also guides the resolution of comparable disputes in the future. They recognize that principles derived from prior cases are not final answers, but rather, in Justice Cardozo's words, "working hypotheses to be continually retested."[10] Common-law principles are working hypotheses because modern society is an ongoing "experiment" wherein continually changing conditions produce new legal issues that necessitate the creation of new legal rules. Justice Cardozo captured this reality when he said: "Nothing is stable. Nothing absolute. All is fluid and changeable."[11] In this environment, legal principles and rules that fail to govern human affairs fairly and effectively will soon die, or judges will reinterpret and alter them.

Nevertheless, both lawyers and clients want the law to be stable and predictable as much as they want it to be flexible and adaptable. This is especially true in business and in personal financial matters, in which clients rely on current law in conducting their affairs. They want the contract or will their lawyer drafts today to be valid a year from now, not void because a court rejects the precedents on which the drafter relied. In litigation, clients want courts to treat similar cases similarly; it is frustrating to lose a case that the precedents indicated you would win.

Judges attempt to reconcile the tension between the public's competing desires for predictability and adaptability by following precedents in cases in which predictability is most important, yet distinguishing those precedents from the current case and creating a new rule when the law must adapt to new social conditions. When predictability is most important, as in the requirements of a valid will or deed, judges are usually content to let change occur by

[10] Cardozo, *The Nature of the Judicial Process*, p. 23.
[11] *Id.*, p. 28.

means of legislation rather than litigation.[12] When adaptability is most important and there is less reason to rely on current law—as when a new product causes a new illness—judges are more likely to create change themselves by common-law decision making.[13]

Chapter One observed that judges can create change without appearing to do so. Judges can change the law while honoring **stare decisis** (precedent) by (1) relying on different precedents in the current case than their predecessors relied on in prior similar cases, and (2) applying the precedents they prefer to the facts they think are most important in the current case. "Fact freedom" and "precedent freedom," as noted in Chapter One, enable judges to create "controlled" change that balances the public's competing interests in predictability and adaptability. Judges cannot ignore precedent in pursuit of personal visions of truth, goodness, and justice; neither are they chained to the past when circumstances demand change. Thus, they reconcile the two by "pouring new wine into old bottles."[14] The old bottles are long-standing rules, and the new wine consists of exceptions to those rules. The old rules remain in force, which ensures predictability, but the exceptions deprive them of their former power, which ensures that the law adapts to new circumstances.

Section III will describe changes in the law of dangerous products and the law of employer-employee relations that illustrate this process. First, though, Section II will discuss the historical roots of common-law decision making.

THE COMMON-LAW TRADITION

When modern American judges engage in common-law decision making, they practice a tradition that dates back to the conquest of England in 1066 by the Norman King William the Conqueror. King William strictly enforced his royal rights as the undisputed lord of all land in the country. The **common law** of England, which the

---

[12] Lief H. Carter, *Reason in Law*, third edition (New York: HarperCollins, 1988), p. 150.

[13] *Id.*, pp. 155–56.

[14] Arthur R. Hogue, *Origins of the Common Law* (Hamden, CT: Archon Books, 1974), p. 11.

colonists brought to America in the seventeenth and eighteenth centuries, developed from the king's enforcement of his royal rights.[15]

The common law began as a series of **writs,** which were written orders the king issued that commanded the recipient to remedy an injury the recipient had caused, or to appear before the king or one of the king's officers to explain why the injury had occurred. The king issued writs in response to requests from injured parties. Gradually, writs evolved from personal requests for royal intervention into standardized forms that injured parties used to bring various complaints to court. By the thirteenth and fourteenth centuries, when formal courts replaced royal intervention, writs were the "keys" to the courthouse for injured parties. A landowner who sought to evict a squatter requested a **writ of trespass,** one who sought repayment of money loaned requested a **writ of debt,** and one who wished to recover stolen goods requested a **writ of replevin.**[16]

Three core principles of the common-law tradition took root during the thirteenth and fourteenth centuries. The most fundamental principle is the **supremacy of law.** All acts of government agencies are subject to examination in the courts, and no individual is beyond the courts' jurisdiction.[17] Courts must resolve disputes by using established procedures (i.e., "due process") that apply to all litigants in all cases, not just to those in the present case.[18] They must decide by reasoning from principles that society generally accepts, not by arbitrarily imposing their will.[19]

The second principle is that courts should judge like cases alike.[20] Courts can achieve this goal through reasoning by analogy from prior cases. When courts judge like cases alike, litigants are more likely to obey the law because they trust courts to resolve their disputes according to the law rather than personal bias.

The third principle is that judges bear the major responsibility for interpreting the law.[21] They interpret the law by deciding cases. They should decide unprecedented cases with particular care because the

[15] Theodore F. T. Plucknett, *A Concise History of the Common Law,* fifth edition (Boston: Little, Brown, 1956), p. 13.
[16] Hogue, *Origins of the Common Law,* p. 12.
[17] *Id.,* p. 179.
[18] *Id.*
[19] *Id.*
[20] *Id.,* p. 190.
[21] *Id.*

power to interpret the law is the power to make the law, especially when there are no precedents to guide the interpreter.

Those three principles remained preeminent even during the seventeenth and eighteenth centuries, when Parliament began to enact legislation with increased frequency, and to rival the monarchy as the supreme political authority in England. The colonists brought those principles to America and built colonial law and, later, American law, upon them. Indeed, English common law influenced the development of American law so profoundly, both before and after the Revolutionary War, that modern scholars speak and write about an "Anglo-American common-law" system.[22]

Countries outside the English-speaking world did not adopt legal systems based on the common law. Instead, the countries of continental Europe, Central America, and South America adopted legal systems based on the **civil law,** which drew its inspiration from ancient Roman law.[23]

Civil-law systems differ from common-law systems in two overarching ways. First, civil-law systems are rooted in comprehensive codes of written laws, originally Emperor Justinian's **Corpus Juris Civilis** (Body of Civil Law), and later the **Napoleonic Codes.**[24] The codes are unified bodies of statutory law designed to articulate, systematically and completely, the law concerning a particular subject (e.g., crimes, commercial transactions, etc.).[25] Second, in civil-law systems, professors are more important interpreters of the law than judges are.[26] Judges in civil-law systems tend to follow the prevailing opinion of the professors, expressed in books and articles, rather than relying primarily on prior decisions as judges in common-law

[22] *Id.,* pp. 236–37.

[23] It is important to distinguish between the two meanings of the term civil law. One meaning refers to the legal systems that exist on the European continent and in Central and South America. The other meaning refers to the body of noncriminal (e.g., contracts, property, personal injuries, etc.) law that exists in the United States. One who understands this distinction avoids considerable confusion.

[24] George A. Zaphiriou, "Introduction to Civil Law Systems," in Richard A. Danner and Marie-Louise H. Bernal, *Introduction to Foreign Legal Systems* (New York: Oceana, 1994), pp. 47–48.

[25] Harold J. Berman and William R. Greiner, *The Nature and Functions of Law,* fourth edition (Mineola, NY: The Foundation Press, 1980), p. 572.

[26] Martin Shapiro, *Courts: A Comparative and Political Analysis* (Chicago, IL: University of Chicago Press, 1981), p. 147.

systems do.[27] Professors in civil-law systems also write interpretive notes at the conclusion of published court opinions in which they discuss those opinions in relationship to particular code provisions and legal principles.[28] The notes are usually more important to the development of the law than are the court decisions on which they comment.

Therefore, the French or Italian lawyer who faces a legal problem first consults the relevant provision in the code, then the professors' interpretations of it, to find an answer. Court decisions can be helpful because the codes are not always as clear or complete as they could be. Nevertheless, court decisions are not the most important tool for answering a legal question.[29]

In contrast, the common law derives from principles and rules that judges create while answering questions that particular cases present. Consequently, the British or American lawyer who faces a legal problem first consults prior court decisions in order to find an answer. Court decisions are more important than professors' writings because the common law, in contrast to the civil law, is based on experience, not logic.[30]

The common law took root in America because it was the only system of law with which the colonists were familiar. However, it survived and even thrived because, by and large, it satisfied Americans' desire for both certainty and flexibility in the law. Analogical reasoning from prior decisions fostered certainty because it honored the past, and it resolved cases by extracting controlling principles through a well-established and respected method. The same reasoning process promoted flexibility because no single case fixed the limits of a controlling principle for all time. As new cases arose that reflected new conditions, lawyers and judges either expanded that principle to fit the new conditions or replaced it with a new principle that did.[31]

[27] Alan Watson, *The Making of the Civil Law* (Cambridge, MA: Harvard University Press 1981), p. 174.

[28] *Id.*, p. 177.

[29] Phillippe Bruno, "The Common Law from a Civil Lawyer's Perspective," in Danner and Bernal, *Introduction to Foreign Legal Systems*, p. 9.

[30] Zaphiriou, "Introduction to Civil Law Systems," p. 52.

[31] Roscoe Pound, *The Spirit of the Common Law* (Boston: Beacon Press, 1963), p. 182.

The common law's flexibility permitted Americans in the eighteenth and nineteenth centuries to adapt their legal arrangements to the unique circumstances of the frontier. They did so by abandoning legal principles that did not suit the conditions of life there. Most of the discarded principles concerned land ownership, which was the major subject of the common law in preindustrial England. The nature of land ownership was different in America than it had been in England, and new circumstances necessitated new legal arrangements.

Americans, for example, abandoned the common-law presumption that when two or more persons hold interests in the same land, they are **joint tenants** who share the same undivided legal interest in their land. Neither joint tenant can sell the land without the other's approval, and when one dies, the other joint tenant inherits the entire piece of land.[32] Americans favored a presumption that persons who own land together are **tenants in common,** each of whom owns a separate legal interest in the land. A tenant in common can sell her interest in the land without the approval of the other tenant(s). At one tenant's death, her legal interest in the land passes to her heir(s), not to the other tenant(s). Therefore, her heir(s) will own whatever portion of the land she owned, and the other tenant(s) will own the rest.

The presumption of joint tenancy worked well in England, where family members often owned land jointly and wanted to keep it in the family from one generation to the next. However, it did not fit conditions in early America, where unrelated individuals often owned land together and wished to sell it quickly for profit. American courts therefore rejected it early in the nineteenth century in favor of the presumption of tenancy in common.[33] The change enabled speculator A to sell to farmer C A's interest in land jointly owned with speculator B without having to obtain speculator B's consent.

That change of presumptions in land law reflected the view of early Americans that the principal purpose of the common law was to protect individual freedom. The right to buy and sell land with

---

[32] Lawrence M. Friedman, *A History of American Law,* second edition (New York: Simon & Schuster, 1985), pp. 234–235.
[33] *Id,* p. 235.

minimal legal restrictions was essential to that freedom. In other words, law existed primarily to protect individual freedom, and it did so by protecting property. The individualism of the early Americans reflected their Puritan roots. The Puritans believed that individuals should be free to make choices about how to live their lives and that government should not coerce them in those matters. However, they also believed that individuals must live with the consequences of their choices; they should not expect government to rescue them from their mistakes.[34] In other words, early Americans believed that government existed to protect individuals' freedom to make choices, not to protect individuals from the adverse consequences of their choices.[35]

Nineteenth-century tort law illustrates the influence of Puritan individualism in American law. Tort law compensates persons who have suffered physical or psychological injuries, property damage or loss, or damage to their reputations and/or careers as a result of the wrongful conduct of another person. It also compensates the heirs of persons whose injuries result in death. The wrongful conduct usually does not violate the criminal law, but instead violates a **duty of care** that the **defendant** owes to the injured party (**plaintiff**). The defendant **breaches** (violates) the duty of care, and the injuries of which the plaintiff complains are foreseeable results of that breach of duty. The law characterizes the defendant's conduct in such circumstances as negligence, for which the plaintiff is entitled to recover damages (financial compensation).[36]

[34] Pound, *The Spirit of the Common Law*, p. 42.

[35] This Puritan ethic underlay the United States Supreme Court's decision in *Lochner v. New York*, discussed in Chapter Three. *Lochner* turned on the constitutional principle of liberty of contract, which stated that employers and employees negotiate wages and working hours and that government deprives both parties of freedom when it regulates wages and working hours. Liberty of contract was a classic Puritan notion because it presumed that individuals were free to make choices about how to manage their property (employer) or earn a living (employee). It therefore opposed laws that restricted that freedom in order to protect workers whose choices of employment harmed their health or family lives.

[36] The plaintiff who alleges that the defendant was negligent must prove that: (1) the defendant owed the plaintiff (or the plaintiff's deceased relative) a duty of care; (2) the defendant breached that duty; (3) that breach was the proximate cause of the plaintiff's injury, which means that the injury was a foreseeable result of the breach; and (4) the plaintiff has incurred damages (e.g. medical bills, hospital bills, lost wages, etc.) as a result of the

For example, a lifeguard at a beach has a duty of care to persons who swim there while the lifeguard is on duty. If the lifeguard leaves her chair to play volleyball while she should be working, she will be **liable** to the heirs of the swimmer who drowns because she was inattentive to her duties. The heirs are likely to sue the lifeguard and her employer in an effort to recover damages for the loss of their relative caused by the defendants' negligence. This type of tort case is a **wrongful-death** case.[37]

---

injury. The plaintiff who proves all of the above meets the burden of proving that the defendant was negligent. The defendant will then be liable to the plaintiff unless the defendant can prove either that: (1) he did not owe the plaintiff a duty of care; (2) he satisfied his duty of care; (3) he breached his duty but the plaintiff's injuries were not the foreseeable result of his breach of duty; or (4) he breached his duty and the plaintiff's injuries were a foreseeable result of that breach, but the plaintiff's own negligence was partially responsible for the injuries, which reduces his liability.

Not all torts, though, result from negligence. Sometimes the defendant's conduct is not merely negligent, but "willful, wanton, or reckless," which amounts to an **intentional tort.** Negligent conduct is unintentional. In cases of intentional torts, the defendant's conduct may not only be **tortious,** but it may also violate the criminal law. Therefore, one incident can result in both a criminal prosecution and a tort action for damages, as did the highly publicized murders of Nicole Brown Simpson and Ronald Goldman in Los Angeles on June 12, 1994. The plaintiff in an intentional tort action must prove that the defendant: (1) knew that the circumstances required him to exercise ordinary care and diligence in order to prevent injury to another person; (2) was able to prevent the injury that the plaintiff (or **decedent**) suffered by using ordinary care and diligence; and (3) failed to use such care and diligence, even though the average person would have recognized that injury would probably result from that failure. Ronald Goldman's parents met that burden of proof, and in February, 1997, a jury awarded them damages for defendant O. J. Simpson's intentional tort against Ronald. In an earlier criminal prosecution, using essentially the same evidence introduced in the civil trial, a jury found Mr. Simpson not guilty of murder. For thorough discussions of negligence and intentional torts, see Stuart M. Speiser, Charles F. Krause, and Alfred W. Gans, *The American Law of Torts* (Rochester, NY: Lawyers Cooperative Publishing, 1983), v.1.

[37] The civil suit that Ronald Goldman's parents, who are divorced, filed against O. J. Simpson, was a wrongful-death suit. A California jury found Mr. Simpson liable for Mr. Goldman's death, and awarded Mr. Goldman's parents $8.5 million in **compensatory** damages, to compensate them for the loss of their son, and $12.5 million in **punitive** damages, to punish Mr. Simpson for his conduct. Nicole Brown Simpson's parents filed a companion suit, known as a **survival action,** on behalf of Ms. Simpson's two children, seeking to compensate the children for the loss of their mother as

In nineteenth-century America, steamboats, trains, and work-place machinery were major causes of injury and death. Between 1812 and 1860, steamboats, railroads, and water-powered mills revolutionized the American economy, but at a high price in human suffering and death. Workplaces became increasingly dangerous as machines gradually replaced skilled artisans in the production of goods.[38] As a result, by 1860, tort suits, which were virtually unknown prior to the American Revolution, became a common feature of court dockets in the United States.[39]

By and large, injury victims did not fare well in nineteenth-century tort cases. That is because the Puritan ethic of free choice and minimal governmental assistance to the unfortunate underlay the rules that courts devised to govern tort law. Those rules limited the liability that companies could incur as a result of industrial accidents, thereby requiring injured individuals to bear the costs of their choices to ride a train or work with certain machinery. In assigning the costs of industrial accidents to the victims, early tort law rewarded entrepreneurs and punished their unfortunate employees and consumers. That is primarily because most judges shared the individualism of the commercial and professional classes, which caused them to welcome industrialism and to regard expanded corporate liability for injuries as a grave threat to economic progress.

Four tort principles were especially helpful to industry and harmful to accident victims. They were (1) **contributory negligence,** (2) **assumption of the risk,** (3) the **fellow-servant** rule, and (4) the prohibition on wrongful-death suits.[40]

Contributory negligence prevented a plaintiff from recovering damages for an injury that resulted from the defendant's negligence

---

a result of Mr. Simpson's tortious conduct. That suit was also successful, and the Simpson children will share $12.5 million, half of the $25 million in punitive damages that the jury awarded. See B. Drummond Ayres, "Jury Decides Simpson Must Pay $25 Million in Punitive Award," *New York Times,* February 11, 1997, p. A1; for thorough discussions of survival actions and wrongful-death suits, see Stuart M. Speiser, Charles F. Krause, and Juanita M. Madole, *Recovery for Wrongful Death and Injury,* third edition (New York: Clark Boardman Callaghan, 1992), v.1.

[38]Kermit L. Hall, William M. Wiecek, and Paul Finkelman, *American Legal History: Cases and Materials* (New York: Oxford University Press, 1991), p. 115.
[39]*Id.,* p. 140.
[40]*Id.,* pp. 179–180. See also Friedman, *A History of American Law,* p. 473.

if the defendant could prove that the plaintiff's own negligence contributed in even a small way to the accident. Assumption of the risk prevented a plaintiff from recovering damages for an injury that resulted from the defendant's negligence if the plaintiff willingly assumed a dangerous position, such as a railroad employee, miner, or factory worker.

The fellow-servant rule prohibited an injured employee from suing his employer for negligence if his injuries resulted from the negligence of one or more coworkers; he could sue only if the employer's misconduct caused the injuries. This severely restricted access to the courts for injured employees because industrial accidents were much more likely to result from negligence by a coworker than by the employer.

The prohibition on wrongful-death suits reflected the ancient rule of English common law that when individuals die, they carry with them to the grave any personal injury claims they had during their lifetimes. The deceased person's family members cannot file suit to recover damages from the person(s) whose negligence caused the death. Ironically, an employer whose negligence injured one of his employees might have to pay damages if the employee survived, but he would not have to pay damages if the employee died. It was more profitable for employers if employees died than if they merely suffered injuries.[41]

American tort law favored defendants, especially employers, for most of the nineteenth century. However, after 1890, social conditions became more conducive to change. Victims, often speaking through labor unions, became increasingly adamant in demanding changes in tort law. They had ample reason to make such demands, as industrial accidents increased after 1890 at a rate that the earlier generations of judges who had crafted tort law did not foresee. The railroad injury rate alone doubled between 1889 and 1906.[42] By 1900, industrial accidents were claiming approximately thirty-five thousand lives and inflicting nearly two million injuries, annually.[43]

Slowly, courts began to respond to victims' pleas and to relax the rigid rules that had dominated tort law for two generations. Courts were not sealed off from the changes that swirled around them after

[41] Friedman, *A History of American Law*, pp. 473–474.
[42] *Id.*, p. 482.
[43] *Id.*

1890. Indeed, their behavior in the tort field at the dawn of the new century illustrates Justice Cardozo's famous statement that "[t]he great tides and currents which engulf the rest of men do not turn aside in their course and pass the judges by."[44] That behavior also illustrates the relationship between the common-law tradition, the Puritan tradition, and Americans' litigiousness, or tendency to seek judicial resolutions to disputes. In the common-law tradition, courts bear the primary responsibility for deciding what the law is. In the Puritan tradition, law exists principally to protect individual freedom. Those traditions joined forces in America and created an environment in which judges are major public policy makers, and individuals who wish to change public policy routinely petition courts to do so.

Thousands of tort suits flooded into courts after 1890, and judges devised two new tort principles, *res ipsa loquitur* (the thing speaks for itself) and the **last clear chance** doctrine, that made it easier for a plaintiff to recover damages from a defendant.

Res ipsa loquitur enables the plaintiff to shift the burden of proof to the defendant when the plaintiff can show that the accident and resulting injury could not possibly have occurred without negligent conduct, for which the defendant should be held responsible. For example, a barrel does not fall out of a warehouse window absent negligence; therefore, the owner of the warehouse must demonstrate why she should not be held liable for the injury that the plaintiff suffered when the barrel struck him on the head.[45]

The last clear chance doctrine diminishes the power of contributory negligence by assigning liability for an accident to the party who had the last clear chance to prevent it. For example, the rancher who allows a cow to stray on to a railroad track will not have to absorb the loss when the train destroys the cow if the train engineer had the last clear chance to prevent a collision, but failed to do so.

Those changes reflected a growing judicial awareness that economic and technological change had radically altered the relationships between businesses and their consumers, and employers and their employees in America. Judges began to realize that new legal

[44] Cardozo, *The Nature of the Judicial Process*, p. 168.
[45] The case of the runaway barrel is *Byrne v. Boadle*, 2 H. & C. 722 (1863), an English court decision that torts textbooks used in American law schools frequently cite.

arrangements would be necessary in the new century because urbanization and industrialization would require individuals to depend on each other more, yet would also enable them to injure each other more severely than ever before. Section III discusses in detail two examples of twentieth-century common-law decision making that created new legal arrangements in response to new social conditions. Part A shows how the New York Court of Appeals, early in this century, made it easier for consumers who suffered injuries from defective products to recover damages from manufacturers. Part B shows how the Vermont Supreme Court, in the 1990s, has made it more difficult for employers to fire employees arbitrarily and unfairly. Both changes occurred gradually, but their effects were significant.

THE COMMON LAW IN ACTION

Dangerous Products

Between 1852 and 1916, the New York Court of Appeals, the highest court in New York State, significantly changed the law in that state concerning the liability of manufacturers for injuries that their products cause. In 1852, New York followed the English rule that a manufacturer, A, has a duty to furnish a safe product only to an **immediate purchaser,** B: that is, the person to whom the manufacturer sells the product directly. That is because the manufacturer and the immediate purchaser contract for the purchase and sale of the product. The law termed this legal relationship **privity of contract;** it said that the two parties had a contractual relationship.

Under the rule of privity of contract, the manufacturer had no duty to furnish a safe product to a third person, C, who purchased it from the immediate purchaser. The rule allowed only one exception under which the consumer, C, could recover damages for the negligence of A, the manufacturer. The exception was for products that were **inherently dangerous;** that is, products that, if made negligently, presented an imminent danger to human life.

The rule of privity of contract may have been appropriate to conditions in New York State in 1852. By and large, the state was rural, and consumers purchased products directly from manufacturers such as millers, blacksmiths, and wheelwrights. In other words, the consumer was usually the immediate purchaser. In the cities, industry was in its infancy, and it might not have matured had it faced liability from consumers who were injured by defective products they purchased from retailers.

In *Thomas v. Winchester* (1852) the New York Court of Appeals ruled for the injured plaintiff, Mrs. Thomas, based on the inherently dangerous exception.[46] Mrs. Thomas became seriously ill after ingesting belladonna, a deadly poison, which she thought was the extract of dandelion that her physician had prescribed for her. An employee of Winchester, the manufacturer, had mislabelled the jars of extracts that Winchester maintained.

Mr. Thomas purchased the mislabelled belladonna for his wife from a physician who had purchased it from a druggist who had, in turn, purchased it from Winchester, who manufactured and sold vegetable extracts for medicinal purposes. Winchester's lawyer moved to dismiss the case on the ground that, as a manufacturer, Winchester had a duty to furnish a safe product only to an immediate purchaser, which Mrs. Thomas was not. The Court of Appeals acknowledged that generally, a manufacturer's duty to furnish a safe product for sale extends only to the immediate purchaser. In so doing, the Court deferred to the rule of privity of contract, and to *Winterbottom v. Wright* (1842), the English case that established that rule.[47]

Nevertheless, the Court of Appeals opted to distinguish *Winterbottom* from *Thomas* because in *Winterbottom* the product that caused injury was a stagecoach, which was not inherently dangerous, whereas in *Thomas* the product was belladonna, an inherently dangerous poison. The inherent dangerousness of belladonna dictated the court's decision to reject *Winterbottom* as a precedent, and to follow instead another English case, *Longmeid v. Holliday*, an 1851 decision.[48] In *Longmeid*, the court held that a manufacturer is liable for injuries that a third party suffers when the manufacturer's negligence puts the third party's life in imminent danger. Thus, the inherently dangerous exception to the rule of privity of contract was born.

Having analogized *Thomas* to *Longmeid*, the court then reasoned deductively and applied the rule of *Longmeid* to *Thomas* because the evidence indicated that Mrs. Thomas's physicians initially believed

[46] 6 N.Y. 397.
[47] 10 Meeson & Welsby 109.
[48] 155 Eng. Rep. 752.

that her life was in great danger. Winchester's negligence put Mrs. Thomas's life in imminent danger; therefore, Winchester was liable to Mrs. Thomas on the basis of the inherently dangerous exception announced in *Longmeid*. Thus, the Court of Appeals affirmed the jury's verdict for Mrs. Thomas.

Despite its decision in *Thomas,* the New York Court of Appeals was not about to cast overboard the rule of privity of contract. Indeed, throughout the nineteenth century the inherently dangerous exception remained precisely that, an exception to the general rule under New York law. The exception was a narrow one because the Court of Appeals was reluctant to expand the category of inherently dangerous products beyond items like explosives and poisons.

For example, in *Loop v. Litchfield* (1870) the court held that Litchfield, the manufacturer of a defective flywheel that killed Loop, was not liable to Loop's estate for his death.[49] Litchfield sold the flywheel and attached it to the buyer's circular saw. The buyer informed Litchfield that the flywheel was defective, but the buyer continued to use it nevertheless. Five years later, the buyer loaned the flywheel to Loop; when Loop used the flywheel, it burst, causing his death.

Reasoning by analogy, the court determined that a flywheel, like a stagecoach, is not an inherently dangerous product. A flywheel does not present an imminent threat to human life. Indeed, despite the flywheel's defect, the buyer in the present case had used it safely for five years. Therefore, the rule of privity of contract controlled, the inherently dangerous exception did not apply, and Litchfield was not liable to Loop's estate because Loop was not the immediate purchaser of the flywheel.

Similarly, in *Losee v. Clute* (1873), the court concluded that Clute was not liable for the destruction of two buildings that Losee owned.[50] The damage occurred when a boiler that Clute constructed improperly and sold to Losee's neighbor exploded. The force of the explosion hurled the boiler onto Losee's property and through his buildings. Drawing an analogy between *Losee* and *Loop,* the court observed that a boiler, like a flywheel, is not inherently dangerous. Therefore, the inherently dangerous exception did not apply and Clute was not liable to Losee for property damage because Losee did not purchase the boiler from Clute.

[49] 42 N.Y. 351.
[50] 51 N.Y. 494.

However, New York law began to change in favor of injured consumers in *Devlin v. Smith*, an 1882 decision in which the Court of Appeals expanded the category of inherently dangerous products.[51] Devlin fell to his death when the scaffold on which he was sitting while painting the inside of a courthouse dome broke. Devlin's estate sued Smith, a painting contractor who was Devlin's employer, and Stevenson, who manufactured the scaffold.

The Court of Appeals absolved Smith of liability, but found Stevenson liable for Devlin's death. The judges reasoned that a ninety-foot scaffold, like the jar of belladonna in *Thomas*, is inherently dangerous because, if made negligently, it puts human life in imminent danger. Reasoning deductively, they then applied the rule of *Thomas* that a manufacturer who negligently produces an inherently dangerous product is liable for the injuries that a third party suffers when using the product. Thus, the inherently dangerous exception controlled the outcome in *Devlin*, negating the rule of privity of contract.

At the time of the *Devlin* decision, in 1882, urbanization and industrialization were well under way in New York State. By 1900, social and economic conditions there had changed dramatically. Industry had matured and was considerably more able than it had been fifty years earlier to absorb liability for defective products. The beginning of nationwide distribution of name-brand merchandise meant that consumers increasingly purchased products from retailers instead of from manufacturers. The consumer was no longer the immediate purchaser; in the new commercial environment, the retailer was typically the immediate purchaser. Consumers relied on the manufacturer's brand name as evidence of quality, but the rule of privity of contract prevented them from holding a manufacturer liable for injuries that resulted from defects unless the product was inherently dangerous. That rule seemed increasingly inappropriate; therefore, conditions were ripe for change through common-law decision making.[52]

Change came, albeit gradually. In *Torgesen v. Schultz*, decided in 1908, the New York Court of Appeals reversed a lower court decision for Schultz, whose corporation filled and marketed bottles of

[51] 89 N.Y. 470.
[52] Melvin Aron Eisenberg, *The Nature of the Common Law* (Cambridge, MA: Harvard University Press, 1988), pp. 73–74.

aerated water.[53] One of those bottles, placed in ice on a hot day, exploded, causing Torgesen to suffer the loss of an eye.

The evidence indicated that Schultz had put on the market, without appropriate warnings to consumers, a bottle that he knew was prone to explode if subjected to a dramatic change in temperature, thereby causing potentially severe injury to anyone using it. That evidence pointed to liability, even though Torgesen had not purchased the bottle directly from Schultz, because the bottle was an inherently dangerous product subject to the rule of *Thomas v. Winchester.* Thus, bottles of aerated water joined poisons and scaffolds in the category of products whose manufacturers were liable to consumers for negligence under the inherently dangerous exception.

Torgesen began an expansion of the category of inherently dangerous products that continued in *Statler v. Ray Manufacturing Company,* a 1909 decision.[54] A large coffee urn manufactured by the Ray Company exploded, severely scalding Statler. Statler's company purchased the urn from a wholesaler who had purchased it from the Ray Company. The court reasoned by analogy that the Ray Company, like the manufacturer of aerated bottles in *Torgesen,* had marketed a defective, inherently dangerous product with the foreseeable result that the product could injure one who used it. Under those circumstances, the inherently dangerous exception controlled the case, and the Ray Company was liable to Statler even though Statler did not enjoy privity of contract with the Ray Company. Thus, the court added coffee urns to the category of products to which the inherently dangerous exception applied.

The expansion of the inherently dangerous exception by the New York Court of Appeals culminated in *MacPherson v. Buick Motor Company,* decided in 1916.[55] MacPherson sustained injuries while driving his car when the wooden spokes on one of the wheels crumbled into fragments, causing the car to collapse. Buick, the manufacturer of the car, bought the wheel from another manufacturer, who made the wheel with defective wood. Buick sold the car to a retail dealer who, in turn, sold it to MacPherson. Therefore, MacPherson, as a consumer, was not an immediate purchaser of the car.

[53] 192 N.Y. 157.
[54] 195 N.Y. 478.
[55] 217 N.Y. 382, 111 N.E. 1050.

Nevertheless, the court found Buick liable for MacPherson's injury. Buick failed to inspect the wheels that the wheel manufacturer supplied, and a reasonable inspection could have revealed the defect in the wheel that caused MacPherson's injury. Buick owed MacPherson a duty to inspect the wheel for two reasons. One reason is that a car is within the category of products to which the inherently dangerous exception applies. That category, observed Judge (later Supreme Court Justice) Benjamin Cardozo, writing for the majority, "is not limited to poisons, explosives, and things of like nature, to things which in their normal operation are implements of destruction." [56] Instead, it includes any product that is "reasonably certain to place life and limb in peril when negligently made." [57] It certainly includes a car intended to travel at a speed of fifty miles per hour.

The second reason why Buick owed MacPherson a duty to inspect the wheel is that Buick knew that someone other than the immediate purchaser would use the car without benefit of inspection by the retailer. That knowledge was evident because Buick sold the car to a retailer, who Buick knew or should have known would not inspect the car before selling it, and equipped it with three seats, reflecting Buick's expectation that persons other than the retailer would ride in the car. Buick knew that the car would be dangerous if defective and that persons other than the retailer would use it; therefore, Buick was liable to MacPherson under the inherently dangerous exception.

MacPherson dramatically changed the law in New York State in the field that modern lawyers call **products liability.** The law of products liability, which developed partly from tort law, holds a seller (e.g., manufacturer, wholesaler, or retailer) liable for injury to the person or property of a buyer that results from a defect in the product that the seller sold to the buyer. Indeed, it is fair to say that *MacPherson* created the modern law of products liability in New York State because it adopted the rule under which courts there (and in the other forty-nine states) today hold manufacturers liable for injuries that their defective products cause. As a result of *MacPherson,* courts hold manufacturers liable for producing defective products that injure persons whose use of those products the manufacturer

[56] 217 N.Y. at 389.
[57] *Id.*

could reasonably have anticipated, whether those persons purchased the products from the manufacturer or from a retailer. The key issue is no longer whether there was privity of contract between manufacturer and injured party, but instead whether the manufacturer is responsible for the defect(s) that caused injury.[58]

MacPherson destroyed the old rule of privity of contract without overruling a single case. It did so by expanding the inherently dangerous exception to cover any product that, if produced negligently, could cause injury to an anticipated user. Appearing to follow *Thomas v. Winchester,* the court in *MacPherson* in fact greatly broadened the ruling in *Thomas* by labelling products as inherently dangerous that the court in *Thomas* did not view that way. In this fashion, the New York Court of Appeals changed the law dramatically without appearing to have changed it at all. Judge Cardozo's majority opinion effectively reconciled competing societal needs for predictability and adaptability.

As a result of *MacPherson,* a New York jury or trial judge could find a manufacturer liable for injuries that a consumer incurred while using any product if the consumer could demonstrate that the manufacturer was responsible for the defect(s) that caused those injuries.

[58] Products liability is the offspring of torts and contracts. In the past, the plaintiff who sustained injuries from using defective products sued the seller on the ground that the seller had been negligent or had breached a **warranty** (legally enforceable promise), either express or implied, that the product was safe for its intended use. Today, products liability is distinct from torts and contracts because of the principle of **strict liability,** which is the law in more than forty states. In those states, the defendant can be liable for damages because of a defect in the product or its design, or for failure to warn of the dangers associated with using the product, whether or not the defendant was negligent or breached a warranty. The purpose of strict liability is to ensure that manufacturers, not injured consumers, bear the costs of defective products. Manufacturers are financially better able than consumers are to absorb those costs. The plaintiff in a products liability case, even in states in which strict liability is not the law, must prove that: (1) she suffered personal injury or property damage because the defendant manufactured and/or sold her a defective product; (2) the product was defective when it left the defendant's control; and (3) the defect was the proximate (foreseeable) cause of the plaintiff's injury or property damage. For a thorough discussion of products liability, see Timothy E. Travers, ed., *American Law of Products Liability,* third edition (Rochester, NY: Lawyers Cooperative Publishing, 1987).

Privity of contract remained the rule, but the inherently dangerous exception now covered so many products that it swallowed the rule, and privity faded away. The modern law of products liability was born.

Employer-Employee Relations

The law of employer-employee relations provides a modern example of common-law decision making. Employment law is contract law, and contract law, like tort law, has developed largely as a result of common-law decision making by state courts. Between 1985 and 1993, the Vermont Supreme Court made an important change in employment law in that state. The court created the **implied-contract exception** to the common-law principle of **employment-at-will.** A by-product of Puritan individualism, employment-at-will dominated employment law in Vermont and most other states beginning in the late nineteenth century. Employment-at-will gives both the employer and the employee the right to end their relationship at any time. The underlying premise is that both parties have an equal right to end the employment relationship.[59]

However, employers typically possess far more economic power than employees do; therefore, the equality of rights that employment-at-will envisions rarely exists in the workplace. The employer can usually absorb the loss of an employee much more easily than an employee can absorb the loss of a job.[60] Thus, the major implication of employment-at-will is that, unless a contract or statute creates an exception that protects an employee, an employer can fire that employee for a good reason, a bad reason, or no reason at all.

In Vermont, employment-at-will became the law as a result of the Vermont Supreme Court's decision in *Mullaney v. Goss Company*

---

[59] Stephen F. Befort, "Employee Handbooks and the Legal Effect of Disclaimers," *Industrial Relations Law Journal,* vol. 13 (1992), p. 329.

[60] The assumption that employers and employees have equal power to end an employment relationship, which underlies employment-at-will, is reminiscent of the assumption that employers and employees have equal power to set wages and work hours, which underlay liberty of contract and the *Lochner* decision. The United States Supreme Court abandoned liberty of contract and *Lochner* in 1937, but state courts clung to employment-at-will tenaciously until the early 1980s, when they created the implied-contract exception.

in 1923.[61] The court held in *Mullaney* that when an employment contract is for an indefinite period of time, the legal relationship between employer and employee is an employment-at-will relationship, and either party may end it at any time.

Employment-at-will remains the law in Vermont today; however, it is now subject to numerous exceptions that have dramatically reduced its influence. One of those is the **public-policy exception.** In *Jones v. Keough* (1979)[62] and in *Payne v. Rozendaal* (1986)[63] the Vermont Supreme Court said that exception applies when there is a clear and compelling public policy against the reason for which an employer has fired an employee.[64] For example, employment-at-will does not permit an employer to fire an employee in retaliation for serving on a jury, filing a workers' compensation claim, or refusing to give perjured testimony. In *Brower v. Holmes Transportation, Inc.* (1981) the court added that employment-at-will does not govern when an employer fires an employee as a result of the employer's bad faith, malice, or desire to retaliate.[65]

The public-policy exception to employment-at-will is important, but the implied-contract exception is more helpful to employees because it applies even when the employer does not act in an outrageous manner. The implied-contract exception is especially helpful

[61] 97 Vt. 82.
[62] 137 Vt. 562, 409 A.2d 581.
[63] 147 Vt. 488, 520 A.2d 586.
[64] The text of this chapter discusses the public-policy and implied-contract exceptions to employment-at-will, but several other exceptions exist too. One applies when an employer and an employee negotiate a contract that states a definite term of service, such as one year. A second exception applies when a labor union negotiates a contract with an employer that prohibits the employer from firing employees without a reason permitted by that contract. A third exception applies when a statute prohibits employers from firing employees for certain reasons. For example, a federal statute, Title VII of the Civil Rights Act of 1964, 42 U.S.C. section 2000e-2, prohibits employers from firing employees because of their race, color, religion, sex, or national origin. Another federal statute, the Age Discrimination In Employment Act of 1967, 29 U.S.C. section 623, prohibits employers from firing employees over age forty because of their age. In Vermont, the Vermont Fair Employment Practices Act, 21 V.S.A. section 495(a)(1), prohibits employers from firing employees because of their race, color, religion, ancestry, national origin, sex, sexual orientation, place of birth, age, or handicapping condition.
[65] 140 Vt. 114, 435 A.2d 952.

to employees today because of the sharp decline in labor union membership in recent years. The proportion of non–farm workers in the United States that belongs to labor unions declined from over 30 percent during the mid-1960s to 15.5 percent in 1994; in Vermont, only 9.4 percent of all non–farm workers were labor-union members in 1994.[66] Therefore, few workers now benefit from the **collective bargaining agreements,** or contracts, that unions negotiate with employers for whom their members work. Those agreements usually prohibit employers from firing employees without a good reason and without following procedures specified in the agreements.[67]

The Vermont Supreme Court first stated that an implied contract between employer and employee can negate an employment-at-will relationship in *Sherman v. Rutland Hospital, Inc.,* a 1985 decision.[68] The hospital fired Sherman because of dissatisfaction with his management of its housekeeping staff. Sherman won a $30,000 jury verdict at trial, and the hospital appealed.

On appeal, the hospital argued that Sherman's employment was for an indefinite period of time, which created an employment-at-will relationship. Sherman countered that employment-at-will did not apply here because he and the hospital had agreed, by implied contract, that the hospital could only fire him after following the disciplinary procedures specified in its personnel policy manual.

The Vermont Supreme Court agreed with Sherman. The court, citing *Mullaney,* acknowledged that employment for an indefinite time period is usually employment-at-will. Nevertheless, an exception exists when employer and employee agree to other terms. In other words, the court reasoned, the law presumes that an employment-at-will relationship exists, but an employer and employee can defeat that presumption and cancel the employment-at-will relationship by agreeing to alternative termination procedures. Sherman and the hospital did precisely that. When Sherman expressed

[66] Befort, "Employee Handbooks and the Legal Effect of Disclaimers," p.331; See also U.S. Department of Commerce, *Statistical Abstract of the United States 1995* (Washington, DC: U.S. Government Printing Office, 1995), pp. 443–444.

[67] Befort, "Employee Handbooks and the Legal Effect of Disclaimers," p. 331.

[68] 146 Vt. 204, 500 A.2d 230.

concern about job security during a job interview at the hospital, the interviewer gave him a copy of the hospital's personnel policy manual and referred him to the disciplinary procedures stipulated in the manual. When Sherman commenced employment at the hospital, he signed and returned to the personnel office there a card that indicated that he had read the manual and understood it.

The court concluded that those actions created an implied contract exception to employment-at-will that prohibited the hospital from firing Sherman without following the procedures stipulated in the manual. The hospital violated the implied contract; therefore, the court affirmed the jury verdict in Sherman's favor. After *Sherman, Mullaney v. Goss Company* was still good law, and Vermont courts continued to presume an employment-at-will relationship absent an express contract to the contrary. An employee could rebut that presumption, though, by showing that she and her employer had impliedly contracted for an alternative termination procedure.

Sherman did not hold, however, that the mere existence of a personnel policy manual creates an implied contract exception to employment-at-will. The result in *LaRose v. Agway*, decided in 1986, demonstrates that.[69] LaRose alleged that Agway fired him without notice or warning after he completed a probationary period. He added that in so doing, Agway violated its own personnel manual, which promised a warning in response to an employee's first instance of unsatisfactory performance. Agway responded that LaRose was an employee-at-will; therefore, Agway could fire him at any time, for any reason. The court agreed with Agway despite the apparent similarities between this case and *Sherman*. The justices distinguished *Sherman* from *LaRose* because in *Sherman*, employer and employee bargained concerning job security and agreed that the employer could only fire the employee according to the procedures contained in the employer's personnel policy manual. In *LaRose*, however, employer and employee neither bargained nor reached an agreement concerning job security. The employer, Agway, adopted, implemented, enforced, and amended the policies in its personnel policy manual without negotiating with or soliciting opinions from its employees. Thus, in *LaRose*, the court rejected *Sherman* as a

[69] 147 Vt. 1, 508 A.2d 1364.

precedent and concluded that *Mullaney* controlled the outcome. There was no implied contract between LaRose and Agway to modify their employment-at-will relationship; hence, LaRose's claim failed.

Despite its decision in *LaRose,* the court found an implied-contract exception to an employment-at-will relationship just four months after *LaRose* in *Benoir v. Ethan Allen, Inc.,* another 1986 decision.[70] Ethan Allen fired Benoir for engaging in dangerous "horseplay" in violation of its personnel policy manual. A jury found that the firing was wrongful. Ethan Allen appealed and argued that Benoir was an employee-at-will.

The court disagreed because Ethan Allen's personnel policy manual established a three-step disciplinary procedure for rules violations that management consulted whenever it considered firing an employee. Under those circumstances, the manual became part of a binding and enforceable contract between Benoir and Ethan Allen. That contract prohibited Ethan Allen from firing Benoir without a good reason and without following the procedures contained in the personnel policy manual. The manual, by specifying disciplinary procedures, created an implied contract between Benoir and Ethan Allen that rebutted the presumption of at-will employment and bound Ethan Allen to follow its stated procedures in disciplining Benoir.

Benoir was an important victory for employees in Vermont because it was the first case in which the Vermont Supreme Court stated that an employee can enjoy job security without having to bargain for it individually. A personnel policy manual, at least when management customarily relies on it, can substitute for individual bargaining and create an implied-contract exception to employment-at-will. After *Benoir,* the presumption of employment-at-will announced in *Mullaney* remained in force, but it was subject to a broadened implied-contract exception.

The court also found that a personnel policy manual negated an at-will relationship in *Foote v. Simmonds Precision Products,* a 1992 decision.[71] Foote contended that Simmonds fired him in retaliation for having used the grievance procedure published in Simmonds's personnel policy manual. Simmonds countered that Foote was an at-will employee. The evidence supported Foote's contention that

[70] 147 Vt. 268, 514 A.2d 716.
[71] 158 Vt. 566, 613 A.2d 1277.

Simmonds had retaliated against him for using the grievance procedure. The court therefore affirmed a jury verdict in favor of Foote. Citing its decision in *Sherman,* the court observed that the common law presumes that an at-will relationship exists when employment is for an indefinite term. The court noted, however, that evidence to the contrary, such as a promise of nonretaliation in a personnel policy manual, can rebut that presumption. Simmonds's personnel policy manual stated that employees would not be "criticized or penalized in any way" for using Simmonds's grievance procedure.[72] That language, according to the court, defeated the presumption of an employment-at-will relationship because it promised nonretaliation for use of Simmonds's employee-grievance procedure, and Foote understandably relied on that promise when he questioned a hiring decision and changes in pay and benefits practices at Simmonds. Foote's reasonable reliance on that promise created an implied contract that modified his at-will employee status and prohibited Simmonds from firing him in retaliation for using its employee-grievance procedure.[73]

After *Sherman, Benoir,* and *Foote,* it was clear that the provisions contained in a personnel policy manual could modify an employment-at-will relationship in Vermont when an employee bargained for, agreed to, and/or relied on those provisions. It was

[72] 158 Vt. at 568, 613 A.2d at 1281.

[73] In *Foote,* the court based its conclusion that the personnel policy manual created an implied contract between Foote and Simmonds on the principle of **promissory estoppel.** Promissory estoppel governs when A makes a promise to B that A should reasonably expect will cause B to either take or refrain from taking a particular action, at some cost or disadvantage to B. When B behaves as A should have expected, the law **estops,** or prohibits, A from breaching the promise to B; in other words, promissory estoppel enforces A's promise to B. In *Foote,* promissory estoppel enforced Simmonds's promise to Foote that Simmonds would not retaliate against him for using the company grievance procedure. Foote's reliance on that promise, at the price of his job, prohibited Simmonds from arguing that it had made no such promise to Foote. Promissory estoppel varies slightly from the principle of implied contract because promissory estoppel required Foote to rely to his detriment on Simmonds's promise, whereas implied contract, as later cases will show, can protect an employee merely by making a promise in a personnel policy manual, whether or not the employee relies on that promise. Nevertheless, the two principles are similar because they can bind a promisor to a promise, under certain circumstances, absent a formal written agreement.

not clear, because of *LaRose*, whether the mere existence of such a manual containing a prescribed disciplinary procedure or a prohibition on retaliation could create an implied-contract exception to an employment-at-will relationship. The Vermont Supreme Court clarified that ambiguity in 1993 in *Taylor v. National Life Insurance Co.*[74]

The court in *Taylor* overruled *LaRose* and held that a personnel policy manual that contains provisions inconsistent with employment-at-will can create an implied contract exception to an employment-at-will relationship by its mere existence. The manual prohibits the employer from firing an employee without a good reason and without following the disciplinary procedures it prescribes, whether or not the employee knows about those procedures or agrees with them and regardless of whether the employer can change the procedures without the approval of its employees. There was no Vermont precedent for that proposition, so the court followed the lead of *Toussaint v. Blue Cross and Blue Shield of Michigan* (1980), in which the Michigan Supreme Court held that the mere existence of language in a personnel policy manual that contradicts employment-at-will can create an implied contract exception to an employment-at-will relationship.[75] Quoting *Toussaint*, the Vermont Supreme Court reasoned that the employer who publishes a manual that includes such language obtains an "orderly, cooperative and loyal work force."[76] In return for that benefit, the employer enters into an implied contract with its employees that prohibits the employer from firing any employee at-will. Thus, in *Taylor*, the Vermont Supreme Court did what it had been unwilling to do in *Sherman, Benoir,* and *Foote*; namely, craft an implied-contract exception to employment-at-will based on the contents of a personnel

---

[74] 161 Vt. 457, 652 A.2d 466.

[75] 408 Mich. 579, 292 N.W.2d 880. Ordinarily, state supreme courts follow only their own prior decisions. In major policy-making decisions like *Taylor*, though, state supreme courts often announce new rules that apply decisions that the supreme court of another state first announced. In the past, the California Supreme Court was often the first state supreme court to announce a new legal rule, and supreme courts in other states gradually adopted it. *Tarasoff v. Regents of the University of California*, which is printed in the epilogue to this chapter, is an example of that phenomenon.

[76] 292 N.W.2d at 892.

policy manual, rather than on whether an employee bargained for, agreed to, or used the manual.[77]

CONCLUSION

Common-law decision making occurs in cases in which no statute or constitutional provision controls the outcome. In such instances, judges compare the case at hand to prior, similar cases, and apply to the case at hand a governing principle that they derive from those cases. The result is judge-made law that is just as much "the law" as any statute or constitutional provision is. Much of the law of torts and contracts is judge-made.

The American public expects judges to adapt the law to new social and economic realities. The public also expects predictability, especially in the law of business and personal financial matters. Judges attempt to reconcile those competing goals by following precedent when predictability is essential and by effecting legal change, when it is necessary, without appearing to have done so. They often effect legal change by creating exceptions to an established rule that destroy much of the rule's power without obliterating the rule itself.

Common-law decision making flows from the common-law tradition that English colonists brought to America. That tradition, which makes judges the most important actors in the legal system, joins with the tradition of Puritan individualism to produce the litigiousness for which the United States is well known.

The power of judges in America helps to make many of their decisions controversial, especially in cases that have broad policy consequences. The case that appears in Section V is a good example. It shows that judges make important public-policy decisions even when no statute or constitutional provision controls and the case appears to be a purely private matter between the parties.

[77] Nevertheless, the court concluded that National Life was justified in firing Taylor because that firing was part of a company-wide reduction in force necessitated by adverse economic conditions. The implied contract exception can modify an employment-at-will relationship under ordinary circumstances, but that exception does not deprive an employer of the right to fire or lay off employees in order to reduce the costs of doing business when economic conditions are unfavorable.

EPILOGUE: THE PSYCHOTHERAPIST'S DUTY OF CARE

In the case printed below, the California Supreme Court held that a psychologist whose client expressed an intent to murder the plaintiffs' daughter had a legal duty to warn the intended victim of the danger she faced. While reading the case, try to determine whether (1) the psychologist had a legal duty to warn the victim, (2) the psychologist violated that duty, and (3) the victim's death was a foreseeable result of that violation. After reading the case, ask yourself whether the benefit to society from requiring the psychologist to warn the potential victim justifies a corresponding loss of confidentiality that may deter troubled people from seeking psychotherapy.

Tarasoff v. Regents of University of California
551 P.2d 334 (1976)

TOBRINER, J. On October 27, 1969, Prosenjit Poddar killed Tatiana Tarasoff. Plaintiffs, Tatiana's parents, allege that two months earlier Poddar confided his intention to kill Tatiana to Dr. Lawrence Moore, a psychologist employed by the Cowell Memorial Hospital at the University of California at Berkeley. They allege that on Moore's request, the campus police briefly detained Poddar, but released him when he appeared rational. They further claim that Dr. Harvey Powelson, Moore's superior, then directed that no further action be taken to detain Poddar. No one warned plaintiffs of Tatiana's peril.

[The Plaintiffs] allege that Tatiana's death proximately resulted from defendants' negligent failure to warn Tatiana or others likely to apprise her of her danger. Defendants, however, contend that in the circumstances of the present case they owed no duty of care to Tatiana or her parents and that, in the absence of such duty, they were free to act in careless disregard of Tatiana's life and safety.

In analyzing this issue, we bear in mind that legal duties are not discoverable facts of nature, but merely conclusory expressions that, in cases of a particular type, liability should be imposed for damage done.

In the landmark case of *Rowland v. Christian*, [443 P.2d 561 (1968)], Justice Peters recognized that liability should be imposed "for an injury occasioned to another by his want of ordinary care or skill" as expressed in section 1714 of the [California] Civil Code.

As a general principle, a defendant owes a duty of care to all persons who are foreseeably endangered by his conduct, with respect to all risks which make the conduct unreasonably dangerous.

Although, . . . under the common law, as a general rule, one person owed no duty to control the conduct of another, the courts have carved out an exception to this rule in cases in which the defendant stands in some special relationship to either the person whose conduct needs to be controlled or . . . the foreseeable victim of that conduct. Applying this exception to the present case, we note that a relationship of defendant therapists to either Tatiana or Poddar will suffice to establish a duty of care. . . .

Although plaintiffs' pleadings assert no special relation between Tatiana and defendant therapists, they establish as between Poddar and defendant therapists the special relation that arises between a patient and his doctor or psychotherapist. Such a relationship may support affirmative duties for the benefit of third persons. Thus, for example, a hospital must exercise reasonable care to control the behavior of a patient which may endanger other persons. A doctor must also warn a patient if the patient's condition or medication renders certain conduct, such as driving a car, dangerous to others.

Although the California decisions that recognize this duty have involved cases in which the defendant stood in a special relationship *both* to the victim and to the person whose conduct created the danger, we do not think that the duty should logically be constricted to such situations. Decisions of other jurisdictions hold that the single relationship of a doctor to his patient is sufficient to support the duty to exercise reasonable care to protect others against dangers emanating from the patient's illness. The courts hold that a doctor is liable to persons infected by his patient if he negligently fails to diagnose a contagious disease (*Hofmann v. Blackmon* (Fla. App. 1970) 241 So. 2d 752), or, having diagnosed the illness, fails to warn members of the patient's family.

Defendants contend, however, that imposition of a duty to exercise reasonable care to protect third persons is unworkable because therapists cannot accurately predict whether or not a patient will resort to violence.

We recognize the difficulty that a therapist encounters in attempting to forecast whether a patient presents a serious danger of violence. Obviously, we do not require that the therapist, in making that determination, render a perfect performance; the therapist need only exercise that reasonable degree of skill, knowledge, and care ordinarily possessed and exercised by members of that professional specialty under similar circumstances.

In the instant case, however, the pleadings do not raise any question as to failure of defendant therapists to predict that Poddar presented a serious danger of violence. On the contrary, the present complaints allege that defendant therapists did in fact predict that Poddar would kill, but were negligent in failing to warn. . . .

We realize that the open and confidential character of psychotherapeutic dialogue encourages patients to express threats of violence, few of which are ever executed. Certainly a therapist should not be encouraged routinely to reveal such threats; such disclosures could seriously disrupt the patient's relationship with his therapist and with the persons threatened. To the contrary, the therapist's obligations to his patient require that he not disclose a confidence unless such disclosure is necessary to avert danger to others, and even then that he do so discreetly, and in a fashion that would preserve the privacy of his patient to the fullest extent compatible with the prevention of the threatened danger.

We conclude that the public policy favoring protection of the confidential character of patient-psychotherapist communications must yield to the extent to which disclosure is essential to avert danger to others. The protective privilege ends where the public peril begins.

Our current crowded and computerized society compels the interdependence of its members. In this risk-infested society we can hardly tolerate the further exposure to danger that would result from a concealed knowledge of the therapist that his patient was lethal. If the exercise of reasonable care to protect the threatened victim requires the therapist to warn the endangered party or those who can reasonably be expected to notify him, we see no sufficient societal interest that would protect and justify concealment. The containment of such risks lies in the public interest.

[Editor's Note: The Court thus held that Tatiana's parents stated a legally sufficient claim of negligence against the defendant psychologists and their employer, the regents, and that the defendants must present a defense to it in the trial court or face liability for Tatiana's death.]

CLARK, J., dissenting. Until today's majority opinion, both legal and medical authorities have agreed that confidentiality is essential to effectively treat the mentally ill, and that imposing a duty on doctors to disclose patient threats to potential victims would greatly impair treatment. Further recognizing that effective treatment and society's safety are necessarily intertwined, the legislature has already decided effective and confidential treatment is preferred over a duty to warn.

The issue whether effective treatment for the mentally ill should be sacrificed to a system of warnings is, in my opinion, properly one for the legislature, and we are bound by its judgment. Moreover, even in the absence of clear legislative direction, we must reach the same conclusion because imposing the majority's new duty is certain to result in a net increase in violence.

McCOMB, J. concurred.

QUESTIONS FOR DISCUSSION

1. Who are the plaintiffs in this wrongful death case, and why have they sued the regents of the University of California? Who, besides the regents, are the defendants in this case?

2. What duty do the plaintiffs allege that Dr. Moore and Dr. Powelson had to Tatiana? In what way, according to the plaintiffs, did Dr. Moore and Dr. Powelson breach that duty?

3. Was Tatiana's death a foreseeable result of a breach of duty by Dr. Moore and Dr. Powelson?

4. What defense do the defendants offer to the plaintiffs' claim that a breach of duty by Dr. Moore and Dr. Powelson caused Tatiana's death?

5. Under what circumstances does the law impose a duty on *A* to control the conduct of *B* toward *C*?

6. According to the court, do the circumstances of this case impose upon the defendants a duty of care to Tatiana? If so, what is the nature of that duty?

7. Should the law impose that duty only if Dr. Moore had a special relationship to both Tatiana and Poddar, or do you think that

Dr. Moore's relationship to Poddar was sufficient to create a duty to Tatiana too?

8. Do you agree with the court that Dr. Moore's duty to Tatiana is analogous to a doctor's duty to warn the family of a patient who suffers from a contagious disease?

9. According to the court, when must a psychotherapist disclose a patient confidence to a potential victim or to those who can protect the potential victim?

10. What values does Justice Clark think that the court has sacrificed in its pursuit of public safety?

11. Is there a compelling reason why a legislature, instead of a court, should decide whether psychotherapists have a duty to warn the potential victims of their patients?

12. Who do you think reached the correct result in this case, the majority or Justice Clark?

CHAPTER 5

Administrative Regulation

Introduction

Agency Activities

Judicial Review of Agency Action

Conclusion

Epilogue: Passive Restraints Revisited

Questions for Discussion

INTRODUCTION

A much-publicized news story during the summer of 1996 reported President Clinton's announcement of new Food and Drug Administration (FDA) rules that will restrict advertising and sales of tobacco products to minors. The FDA contends that the Food, Drug and Cosmetic Act authorizes it to regulate tobacco products because they are delivery systems for the drug nicotine.[1] The new rules would eliminate vending machines except in facilities that prohibit children, would ban colorful billboards and name-brand advertising of cigarettes at sporting events, and would not allow glossy cigarette advertisements in magazines that significant numbers of teenagers read. They will also require six companies that the FDA charges have attracted the largest percentages of underage smokers to run an advertising campaign that warns children and teenagers about the dangers of using tobacco products. President Clinton's announcement provoked an angry reaction from the tobacco industry. That was not surprising, as the cigarette makers filed suit in a federal court in North Carolina to block the rules soon after the FDA proposed them, more than six months before the president announced them.[2] The cigarette makers contend that the Food, Drug and Cosmetic Act does not give the FDA authority to regulate nicotine as a drug, and that restrictions on tobacco advertising violate the freedom of speech.

The new rules on cigarette advertising and sales to minors illustrate the two major themes to be addressed in this chapter: first, that administrative agencies that Americans barely notice, like the FDA, regularly make decisions that profoundly affect our daily lives, and second, that regulated parties frequently challenge agency decisions

---

[1] The Food, Drug and Cosmetic Act begins at 21 U.S.C.A. section 301.

[2] Stephen Barr and Martha M. Hamilton, "Tobacco Ad Restrictions Announced," The *Valley News* (West Lebanon, NH, August 24, 1996): p.A1. On April 25, 1997, the federal court in Greensboro, North Carolina, concluded that the Food, Drug and Cosmetic Act authorizes the FDA to regulate sales of tobacco products, such as by eliminating vending machines in certain facilities, but that the Act does not authorize the FDA to regulate tobacco advertising. The court therefore invalidated the agency's proposed restrictions on tobacco advertising on billboards, at sporting events, and in magazines. The case is on appeal, so the future of the advertising rules is uncertain at this writing. John Schwartz, "FDA Can Regulate Tobacco," The *Valley News*, April 26, 1997, p. A1.

in court on the grounds that those decisions are unconstitutional, unauthorized by statute, unsupported by evidence, or all of the above. As a result of both phenomena, much legal reasoning occurs nowadays in the context of administrative regulation.[3]

The tobacco example illustrates that the legislative, executive, and judicial branches of the federal government all participate in administrative regulation.[4] The remainder of this chapter will show how Congress, the presidency, the administrative agencies, and the courts interact in the administrative process. The principal focus will be the courts' role, but one cannot understand that role without first understanding the origins of the rules that courts review. The origin of rules is the principal subject of section II.

AGENCY ACTIVITIES

Rule Making

Statutes delegate to administrative agencies authority to perform **rule-making** (legislative), **rule-enforcement** (executive), and

[3] Several noteworthy books address in detail subjects that this chapter, because of space limitations, can only introduce. Those books include: Alfred C. Aman Jr., *Administrative Law in a Global Era* (Ithaca, NY: Cornell University Press, 1992); Alfred C. Aman Jr. and William T. Mayton, *Administrative Law* (St. Paul, MN: West Publishing, 1993); Lief H. Carter and Christine B. Harrington, *Administrative Law and Politics: Cases and Comments,* second edition (New York: HarperCollins, 1991); Kenneth Culp Davis and Richard J. Pierce Jr., *Administrative Law Treatise,* third edition (Boston: Little, Brown, 1994); Daniel Hall, *Administrative Law* (Albany, NY: Delmar Publishers and Lawyers Cooperative Publishing, 1994); Richard J. Pierce Jr., Sidney A. Shapiro, and Paul R. Verkuil, *Administrative Law and Process,* second edition (Mineola, NY: The Foundation Press, 1992); Bernard Schwartz, *Administrative Law,* third edition (Boston: Little, Brown, 1991); and Peter H. Schuck, *Foundations of Administrative Law* (New York: Oxford University Press, 1994).

[4] The legislative, executive, and judicial branches of state governments also participate in administrative regulation. State legislatures delegate legislative power to state administrative agencies, and state courts review the actions of those agencies. However, this book has a national focus and space limitations; therefore, it will concentrate on federal administrative regulation. Students who are interested in state administrative regulation should read James R. Bowers, *Regulating the Regulators: An Introduction to the Legislative Oversight of Administrative Rulemaking* (New York: Praeger, 1990) and Arthur Earl Bonfield, *State Administrative Rulemaking* (Boston: Little, Brown, 1986).

rule-adjudication (quasi-judicial) functions. Because the Constitution, in Article I, assigns all legislative powers to the Congress, any exercise of legislative power by an administrative agency (i.e., rule making) can only occur pursuant to a **delegation** by Congress in a statute signed by the president. The Supreme Court interprets Article I to mean that Congress's legislative power is supreme, but not exclusive, and, therefore, that Congress can delegate a portion of its power to administrative agencies.[5]

That interpretation prohibits Congress from delegating all of its legislative power concerning a particular subject. Congress must retain the primary legislative power whenever it delegates by setting statutory standards that reflect its policy choices, and it must also direct the agency to which it delegates to implement those standards. Statutory language should not be so open-ended that it leaves policy choices to the agency because in a democratic society, elected legislators, not appointed administrators and career civil servants, must make those choices. Thus, the Supreme Court has held that Congress cannot delegate to an administrative agency power to impose workplace health standards without having to consider the seriousness of the health risks to be eliminated or the expense of eliminating them.[6] Only Congress can decide whether "the statistical possibility of future deaths should ever be disregarded in light of the economic costs of preventing those deaths."[7] Rule making establishes the mechanisms by which the federal government puts a legislative purpose into practice. It supplies the technical details that are often missing in statutes, and it informs regulated parties what their rights and responsibilities under a new statute will be. Thus, statutes and rules are interdependent. Statutes provide the legal bases for rules, and rules furnish the technical details that make statutes work.[8]

Rule making also performs political functions. It frees Congress to concentrate on broad policy designs instead of on the details of implementation that strain Congress's limited expertise and create discord that inhibits the passage of legislation. It also enables a legislator

---

[5] Aman Jr. and Mayton, *Administrative Law*, p. 9.

[6] *Industrial Union Dep't., A.F.L.-C.I.O. v. American Petroleum Institute*, 448 U.S. 607 (1980).

[7] *Id.*, p. 672.

[8] Cornelius M. Kerwin, *Rulemaking: How Government Agencies Write Law and Make Policy* (Washington, DC: Congressional Quarterly Press, 1994), p. 8.

to directly assist her constituents in their dealings with agencies, which typically improves her prospects for reelection.

Administrative agencies make rules by means of a multistep process in which each step affects the one that follows it. The steps do not always occur in chronological order. Several may occur simultaneously, or when the rule is simple and noncontroversial, the agency may omit one or more of them. The steps are as follows:

1. Legislation

Legislation establishes the purpose for agency rule making on a particular subject and determines the number of rules that will be necessary, the deadline by which the agency must write them, the amount of discretion the agency will exercise concerning their content, and the procedures that the agency must observe in writing and announcing them. No rule is valid unless it promotes a statutory purpose.

2. Assigning Responsibility for Rule Making

Agencies differ in the manner in which they assign staff members to write rules. Frequently, the office that enforces the particular statute that forms the basis for the proposed rule requests permission to begin rule making from the individual or committee charged with reviewing such requests. Upon approval of the request, the requesting office begins staffing the work group that will write the rule, but a higher ranking office or permanent committee may oversee the process. The importance of the rule, the range of issues that the rule writers must resolve during rule making, the variety of viewpoints within the agency on those issues, and the nature of the information that the agency must gather in order to resolve such issues will determine how many and which agency staffers will write the rule.

3. Developing a Draft Rule

The rule writers must be sensitive to statutory mandates, such as a requirement that they consult the scientific community or that they not produce a rule that inhibits the creation of small businesses. Typically, they will consult reliable sources of technical information. For example, EPA personnel writing an air-pollution rule would likely consult academic and government scientists and engineers, air-quality experts employed by industry, and their counterparts from environmental organizations in search of relevant data.

Rule writers usually also keep important constituencies informed about their progress, even though the law does not require public participation until after a draft of the proposed rule is complete. The EPA personnel writing the air-pollution rule would likely apprise industry and environmental groups of their progress in order to anticipate, and perhaps avoid, potential challenges to the rule.

After collecting and analyzing the relevant data, the rule writers will draft a proposed rule and its **preamble.** The preamble identifies for the nonexpert the basis and purpose for the rule.

4. Internal Review
The internal review of a draft rule occurs both **horizontally** and **vertically;** *horizontally* refers to agency offices other than the one that wrote the draft examining it to determine whether they can support it, and *vertically* refers to supervisors and senior officials evaluating it for compliance with the agency's policies and programs.

5. External Review
The external review is performed by an administrative agency other than the one whose employees wrote the draft. The drafting agency may request external review by an agency that possesses relevant expertise or that regulates parties that the rule is likely to affect. A statute may also require external review. The most significant external reviewer is the **Office of Management and Budget (OMB),** the budgetary arm of the president, which scrutinizes proposed rules for conformity to the president's policy goals.

6. Publication
The Administrative Procedure Act of 1946 (APA), which governs rule making generally, requires agencies to publish a **Notice of Proposed Rulemaking,** including the text of the draft rule or a description of its subject matter, in the *Federal Register,* in which agencies publish all their rules and related decisions.[9] The rules of the *Federal Register* itself require publication of a preamble. Most agencies publish both preamble and text as a matter of practice. The preamble, which is often longer and more informative than the draft rule, explains the data and analyses that convinced the agency to propose the rule.

[9] 5 U.S.C.A. section 553(b).

7. Public Participation

The APA requires that federal agencies permit interested parties to participate in rule making through "submission of written data, views, or arguments. . . ."[10] Interested parties must submit their written comments within thirty days of publication of the draft rule.[11] That is the minimum amount of participation to which the public is entitled in the rule-making process. Most rule making occurs subject to these **notice and comment** requirements; it is known as **informal rule making.**

However, many statutes require agencies to provide more and better opportunities for public participation than the APA mandates, such as legislative-type hearings wherein agency personnel solicit the views of witnesses who testify on behalf of interested parties (e.g., timber companies, the Sierra Club, etc.), and even quasi-judicial hearings in which interested parties may cross-examine agency personnel. The rule making that occurs under statutes that permit quasi-judicial hearings is known as **formal rule making.**

In both formal and informal rule making, the agency must collect, retain, and make available to the public all comments and materials that the interested parties submit. They are part of the **record** of a rule making, which is especially important when there is a court challenge to a rule. The court will hold the agency accountable to the public by requiring that the record reveal the process by which the agency produced the challenged rule.

8. Action on the Draft Rule

If, at the conclusion of the public comment period, the draft rule does not require any changes, it will become a **final rule.** The agency will publish a **Notice of Final Rulemaking** in the *Federal Register,* and the new rule will take effect on the designated date. The rule writers may make minor revisions without internal or external review. However, if public comments raise questions that the rule writers cannot answer without additional information, the agency may solicit more public comment. If major revisions are necessary, the agency may produce a new draft rule, start on a new rule from scratch, or decide not to write the rule after all. The agency must publish in the *Federal Register* notice of a decision not to write the rule.

[10] 5 U.S.C.A. section 553(c).
[11] 5 U.S.C.A. section 553(d).

Rule making is an open-ended process; it lacks a clearly-defined conclusion. Shortly after publication of a final rule in the *Federal Register,* a lawsuit may challenge it as unconstitutional, irrational, or beyond the authority of the agency that wrote it. More often, the agency revises the rule as a result of reinterpretations by agency staff, petitions by affected parties for change or clarification, or technical corrections of minor errors. A rule is subject to challenge and change, in whole or in part, at any time.

Congressional and Presidential Oversight

Congressional Oversight

Congress oversees rule making in order to correct agency violations of statutory aims, and it wields several tools in pursuit of that end. One is the power of the purse contained in Article I of the Constitution. Congress can punish agencies that violate its statutory goals by forbidding them to spend appropriated funds for certain purposes (e.g., abortions), or by imposing restrictive conditions on such expenditures (e.g., agencies must spend the funds within a specified time period). A second oversight tool is **program evaluation,** whereby the **General Accounting Office,** Congress's investigatory arm, reviews the results of programs that statutes authorize and agency rules implement.

A third oversight tool is direct statutory control of agency authority. One statutory control is the **hammer,** which requires an agency to take certain action within a specified time period and imposes a congressionally determined result if the agency misses the statutory deadline. Other statutory controls require agencies to report regularly to Congress via testimony or in writing, or to notify Congress about new rules and wait for it to approve them before implementing them; still another **sunsets,** or terminates, programs unless Congress reauthorizes them by a specified date. The most controversial statutory control is the **legislative veto,** which authorizes an agency to make pertinent rules but reserves the right of one house or both to veto those rules within sixty days after notification by the agency. Congress need not pass a new statute to veto a proposed rule.

In *Immigration and Naturalization Service v. Chadha,* a 1983 decision, the Supreme Court declared the legislative veto unconstitutional because it sidesteps the legislative process that the Constitution requires; namely, passage by both houses of Congress, and **presentment** to the president for signature or veto.[12] Nevertheless, the legislative veto survives in a modified form, which requires agencies to obtain approval for certain actions from the House and Senate Appropriations Committees, because it is more efficient than the regular legislative process.[13]

Presidential Oversight

Presidents oversee rule making to ensure that rules reflect presidential policy goals. The president is America's only nationally elected leader; therefore, the president's goals, not those of locally elected legislators or unelected agency personnel or lobbyists, are most likely to reflect the views of a majority of Americans. Presidents oversee rule making by means of the **executive order (E.O.)**, a directive to an agency to implement a statute, treaty, or constitutional provision in a specified way. Executive orders derive from Article II, section 3 of the Constitution, which requires the president to "take Care that the Laws be faithfully executed." The responsibility to ensure faithful execution of the laws carries with it power to instruct agency officials how to execute those laws.

President Reagan's E.O. 12,291, issued in 1981, reflected his belief that many of the rules that federal agencies write are needless and burdensome. It required agencies to justify proposed rules likely to result in at least a $100 million annual impact on the economy by means of a **Regulatory Impact Analysis (R.I.A.).** E.O. 12,291 prohibited an agency from writing a new rule unless the agency concluded in its R.I.A., and convinced the budgetary "watchdogs" at the OMB, that the rule's potential benefits outweighed its potential costs, and that it would cost less than any available alternative. That "cost-benefit analysis" enabled the OMB to induce agencies to change and even withdraw proposed rules that the OMB opposed. The OMB's aim was not to conform rules to legislative intent, but

---

[12] 462 U.S. 919.

[13] Louis Fisher, "Micromanagement by Congress: Reality and Mythology," in Peter H. Schuck, ed., *Foundations of Administrative Law* (New York: Oxford University Press 1994), pp. 248–257.

instead, to frustrate the policy goals of congressional Democrats in order to advance the president's rather different policy goals.[14] Another Reagan order, E.O. 12,498, issued in 1985, required agencies to notify the OMB almost as soon as an idea for a new rule arose and to obtain OMB approval to develop a draft rule.

Both orders resulted from President Reagan's conviction that only he possessed the political will and broad-based popular support necessary to reduce the size and budget of the federal government. He was convinced that members of Congress would not do so because creating programs and spending money enables them to benefit constituents and improve their chances for reelection. Agencies would not do so either because new federal programs increase their budgets and their power. Both orders helped President Reagan, a Republican, to achieve some of his budgetary goals at a time (1980–1988) when Democrats, most of whom did not share those goals, controlled at least one house of Congress.[15]

Such presidential actions influence rule making. For example, during the Reagan presidency, the OMB pressured the EPA to withdraw two proposed rules that would have imposed strict controls on the production and use of asbestos, a mineral used in insulation, which can cause a lung disease known as "asbestosis."[16] Thus, it is not surprising that President Clinton repealed the two Reagan orders and substituted E.O. 12,866, which reduced the OMB's veto power over proposed rules, and increased its accountability to the public.[17] Like President Reagan, President Clinton understood the need and the potential for presidential influence in rule making.

[14] Joseph Cooper and William F. West, "Presidential Power and Republican Government: The Theory and Practice of OMB Review of Agency Rules," *Journal Of Politics* 50 (1988): pp. 864–895.

[15] Democrats were the majority party in the House of Representatives throughout President Reagan's tenure in office, from 1980 through 1988. In the Senate, Republicans were the majority party from 1981 through 1986. Democrats regained majority status in the Senate in the 1986 elections; therefore, they controlled the Senate during the final two years of Mr. Reagan's presidency.

[16] Kerwin, *Rulemaking*, p. 239.

[17] For a thorough discussion of President Clinton's E.O. 12,866, see Richard H. Pildes and Cass R. Sunstein, "Reinventing the Regulatory State," *University of Chicago Law Review* 62 (Winter 1995), pp. 1–129.

Rule Enforcement and Adjudication

Federal agencies also enforce and adjudicate rules. Whenever possible, they seek enforcement without adjudication because adjudication is time-consuming and expensive. One enforcement technique is the **consent settlement,** in which an agency and a regulated party negotiate a resolution to their dispute. Agencies attempt to prevent disputes by issuing **advisory opinions** in response to requests from regulated parties for interpretations of unclear rules or rule provisions. Some agencies, such as the **Nuclear Regulatory Commission (NRC),** publish **industry guides** that instruct regulated parties how to comply with new rules.

Agencies frequently punish rules violations by means of financial sanctions. For example, a public-school district that receives federal financial assistance can lose it by discriminating against students or employees on the basis of race, religion, gender, or national origin.[18] An agency may levy an **administrative fine** instead, or revoke a violator's tax-exempt status, as the IRS did to Bob Jones University because of the University's prohibitions on interracial dating and marriage by its students.[19]

Agencies can also revoke a license, such as the license to operate a nuclear power facility. Finally, when a governing statute imposes criminal sanctions (fine, imprisonment, or both) for certain rules violations, an agency may seek such penalties, as the IRS does for tax fraud. However, agencies cannot impose and enforce criminal penalties; only courts can do so.[20]

When agencies and regulated parties cannot settle their disputes, they proceed to **adjudication,** which usually is **informal;** that is, it does not feature trial-like procedures. Instead of holding a hearing, the **Administrative Law Judge (A.L.J.)** who decides the matter acts strictly on the basis of written materials that the participants

[18] Title VII of the Civil Rights Act of 1964 (beginning at 42 U.S.C.A. section 2000) prohibits discrimination in employment on account of race, religion, sex, or national origin. Title IX of the Education Amendments of 1972 (20 U.S.C.A. sections 1681–1688) prohibits discrimination on account of sex in any educational program that receives federal funds.

[19] See *Bob Jones University v. United States,* 461 U.S. 574 (1983), and the discussion of it in Chapter Two.

[20] Carter and Harrington, *Administrative Law and Politics,* p. 316.

submit.[21] Such adjudication often concerns requests for exceptions or waivers to agency rules; a factory seeking to postpone installation of air-pollution control equipment that a new EPA rule requires might make that sort of request.[22]

Formal adjudication occurs when a statute or a court's interpretation of a statute requires it. In such instances, the APA requires the agency to notify the regulated party of (1) the time, place, and nature of the adjudication hearing; (2) the statutory provision or court decision that is the legal basis for the hearing; and (3) the factual and legal issues that are the subjects of the hearing.[23]

The A.L.J. has considerable discretion to determine the formality of the hearing. He may permit oral presentation of evidence, but he may insist on written evidence instead. He may prohibit cross-examination. He determines whether to exclude certain evidence. His decision in the dispute must rest upon a **preponderance of the evidence** presented at the hearing.

At the conclusion of the hearing, both sides submit legal briefs that present their arguments and lists of factual findings and legal conclusions that they believe resolve the dispute appropriately. After reviewing those materials and the hearing record, the A.L.J. prepares either an **initial** or a **recommended** decision. An initial decision becomes the agency's final decision unless an agency appeal panel or the head of the agency reverses it. A recommended decision, on

[21] A.L.J.s are employees of the various federal agencies, but the APA attempts to ensure their impartiality by placing decisions about their job security and compensation in the hands of the independent Office of Personnel Management instead of the agencies for which the A.L.J.'s work. Agencies can only fire A.L.J.'s for cause (e.g., incompetence, dishonesty, violation of the law), and only after a hearing before the independent Merit Systems Protection Board. The APA also prohibits agency personnel who perform investigative or prosecutory functions in adjudicated cases from discussing a case with the A.L.J. assigned to it.

[22] Increasingly, agencies and affected parties try to resolve disputes informally by means of mediation or arbitration. Both procedures feature an impartial referee chosen by the participants in the dispute. The **mediator** assists the two sides in negotiating a settlement, but cannot impose a decision on them. Labor disputes often involve mediation. An **arbitrator** can impose a decision if a statute or an agreement between the participants provides for **binding** and **mandatory arbitration.** Arbitration is common in labor and contract disputes.

[23] Aman and Mayton, *Administrative Law,* p. 222.

the other hand, cannot take effect until the head of the agency, or someone whom that person designates, reviews and approves it. When the A.L.J. issues an initial decision, it must include **findings of fact,** which **substantial evidence in the record** supports, and **conclusions of law.**

JUDICIAL REVIEW OF AGENCY ACTION

A dissatisfied party that exhausts the agency adjudication process may seek judicial review of a final agency decision in the United States Court of Appeals. Judicial review aims to ensure that agencies do not exceed their statutory or constitutional authority in performing their duties. Unlike congressional and presidential oversight, judicial review does not hold agencies accountable to the electorate, but rather, to the constitutional principles of separated powers and due process.

In so doing, courts consider *what* action(s) the agency is authorized to take, *why* the agency decided to act (or not to act), and *how* the agency acted. The APA empowers courts to (1) compel an agency to take actions that it unlawfully withholds or unreasonably delays; and (2) void agency actions that are (a) arbitrary or capricious; (b) unconstitutional; (c) in excess of statutory authority; (d) contrary to procedures required by law; (e) unsupported by substantial evidence; or (f) unwarranted by the facts of the case.[24]

The *what* question requires a determination whether Congress properly delegated legislative power to the agency, and, if so, whether the agency exceeded its delegated power. Judicial review, therefore, checks Congress's power as much as it checks agency power, for courts must often decide whether a particular delegation is constitutional. The Supreme Court faced that question in 1989 in *Mistretta v. United States.*[25]

The issue in *Mistretta* was the constitutionality of a delegation by the **Sentencing Reform Act** of 1984 to the **United States Sentencing Commission** of authority to establish sentencing guidelines

[24] 5 U.S.C.A. section 706.
[25] 488 U.S. 361.

for federal crimes.[26] The sentencing guidelines ended judicial control over sentencing and replaced it with a grid composed of offense (e.g., bank robbery, committed with gun, $2500 stolen) and offender (e.g., one prior conviction not resulting in imprisonment) categories and prison terms of varying lengths. The guidelines require a judge to sentence an offender to the prison term that the grid specifies for the categories of offender and offense present in the case. The judge can depart from the guidelines if she finds aggravating or mitigating factors that the guidelines do not consider, but she must state in writing the specific reason for imposing a sentence different from the one that the guidelines contain.

Mistretta, who was serving a federal sentence for trafficking in cocaine, argued that the sentencing guidelines were the product of an unconstitutional delegation of legislative power to the Sentencing Guidelines Commission. The Supreme Court disagreed. Justice Blackmun analogized this case to prior cases in which the Court held that delegations of legislative power to administrative agencies are constitutional as long as they contain an **intelligible principle** to guide the agency.[27] The Court approved broad delegations to agencies to (1) prevent an inequitable distribution of voting power among stockholders;[28] (2) set fair commodity prices;[29] (3) determine reasonable rates for electric power;[30] and (4) regulate broadcast licensing.[31] It did this because each delegation contained an intelligible principle to guide agency action. Justice Blackmun then applied the "intelligible principle" standard to the Sentencing Guidelines Commission and concluded that the Sentencing Reform Act guided the commission's actions sufficiently to satisfy constitutional requirements.[32]

Congress established three goals for the commission, namely to (1) meet the purposes of sentencing as set forth in the Sentencing Reform Act, (2) provide certainty and fairness in sentencing by

[26] One portion of the Sentencing Reform Act begins at 18 U.S.C.A. section 3551, and the other portion is located at 28 U.S.C.A. sections 991–998.

[27] See *J. W. Hampton Jr. & Company v. United States,* 276 U.S. 394 (1928).

[28] *American Power & Light Company v. Securities and Exchange Commission,* 329 U.S. 90 (1946).

[29] *Yakus v. United States,* 321 U.S. 414 (1944).

[30] *Federal Power Commission v. Hope Natural Gas Company,* 320 U.S. 591 (1944).

[31] *National Broadcasting Company v. United States,* 319 U.S. 190 (1943).

[32] 488 U.S. at 374.

avoiding unwarranted disparities in the sentences that offenders with similar records receive for the same offense, and (3) reflect advancement in knowledge about human behavior as it relates to criminal justice. Congress also specified four purposes for the commission to pursue in constructing sentencing guidelines, namely, to (1) provide just punishment for each offense, (2) deter criminal conduct, (3) protect the public from the defendant, and (4) provide the defendant with correctional treatment.

In order to achieve those statutory aims, Congress directed the commission to develop a system of **sentencing ranges** for each category of offense involving each category of defendant. Congress also directed the commission to construct offense categories and offender categories, and specified the factors that the commission should consider in constructing both. Justice Blackmun concluded that this delegation fit within constitutional bounds. He wrote "Developing proportionate penalties for hundreds of different crimes by a virtually limitless array of offenders is precisely the sort of intricate, labor intensive task for which delegation to an expert body is especially appropriate." [33]

Justice Blackmun acknowledged that Congress had delegated to the commission discretion to determine the relative severity of federal crimes and the relative weight of offender characteristics in constructing offense and offender categories. Congress also gave the commission the power to decide which federal crimes courts had punished too severely or too leniently in the past. Justice Blackmun further noted, however, that precedents made it clear that "Congress is not confined to that method of executing its policy which involves the least possible delegation of discretion to administrative officers." [34] Moreover, the Sentencing Reform Act limits the commission's discretion by identifying the policy goals that prompted its creation and by explaining what the commission should do and how it should do it, its sentencing guidelines represent a constitutionally permissible delegation of legislative power to an administrative agency. Thus, the Supreme Court upheld the Sentencing Reform Act of 1984 because its sentencing guidelines represent a constitutionally permissable delegation of legislative power to an administrative agency.

[33] 488 U.S. at 379.
[34] See *Yakus v. United States*, 321 U.S. at 425-426.

A court may uphold a delegation of legislative power to an agency but can void the agency's action because that action exceeds statutory authority. The Supreme Court did that in *Industrial Union Department, A.F.L.-C.I.O. v. American Petroleum Institute* (1980), better known as the **benzene case.**[35] In that case, the Court reviewed a rule that the secretary of labor issued that required industry to limit the presence of benzene in the workplace to no more than one part per one million parts of air. The secretary issued the rule pursuant to section 6(b)(5) of the **Occupational Safety and Health Act (OSHA)** of 1970, which authorized him to set exposure standards for toxic materials that will assure that "no employee will suffer material impairment of health or functional capacity" as a result of workplace hazards.

The secretary believed that it was impossible to determine a safe exposure level for cancer-causing chemicals like benzene. He therefore concluded that section 6(b)(5) required him to set an exposure standard for benzene at the lowest level that current technology could achieve that would not destroy the economic health of the industries affected. Thus, he substituted the one p.p.m. benzene standard for the existing ten p.p.m. standard.

The Court acknowledged the secretary's statutory authority to set workplace exposure standards for toxic chemicals but concluded that he had exceeded that authority in this case. That conclusion followed a painstaking construction of the Occupational Safety and Health Act. Justice Stevens, writing for the majority, reviewed the text and history of the act and construed it not to require employers to provide risk-free workplaces. Instead, it requires them to eliminate *significant* health risks, whenever feasible. Justice Stevens noted, in discussing the history of the act, that Congress amended section 6(b)(5), which originally directed the secretary to assure that no worker suffers *any* impairment of health as a result of exposure to toxic chemicals, to direct instead that no worker should suffer *material* impairment of health as a result of such exposure. Moreover, the legislative history indicated that the industrial hazards to which witnesses referred in hearings and to which legislators referred in debates, all posed "unquestionably significant" risks, which suggests that Congress intended to eliminate from the workplace major, but not all, risks to health and safety.

[35] 448 U.S. 607.

Therefore, Justice Stevens wrote, Congress did not intend to give the secretary the unprecedented regulatory power that he exercised in establishing the benzene rule. Accordingly, the secretary exceeded his statutory power, and the benzene rule is void. However, Congress did give the secretary authority to establish standards "reasonably necessary or appropriate to provide safe or healthful employment." [36] That means that before the secretary can announce a new health or safety standard, he must find that there is a significant risk present in the workplace that the new standard can reduce or eliminate. In this case, the statute requires him to find that exposure to ten p.p.m. of benzene poses a significant health risk to workers before he can substitute a different standard. The secretary failed to make that threshold finding regarding benzene; therefore, he exceeded his statutory authority in announcing the benzene rule.

If a delegation of legislative power and agency actions pursuant to it are proper, a court then considers the why and the how of agency action. The why question necessitates a review of the fact-finding that preceded the action. A court will usually accept an agency's findings of fact because the agency's expertise exceeds the court's. A court will not void a rule that informal rule making produces unless the fact-finding that preceded it was arbitrary or capricious; that is, not the product of rational thought. A court will not void a rule that formal rule-making produces unless the record lacks **substantial evidence** that supports the fact-finding that produced the rule. The "substantial evidence" standard used to be stricter than the "arbitrary or capricious" standard by requiring the agency to identify evidence in a written record that supported its findings of fact. Today, that distinction is unclear because statutes and court decisions require agencies to compile a written record and base their findings of fact on it in both informal and formal rule-making.

In practice, then, courts accept agency fact-finding that results from **reasoned analysis.** An agency demonstrates reasoned analysis in rule making by explaining in its statement of basis and purpose why it rejected alternatives and why it departed from prior policies in writing the rule. Administrative policy change should result from the careful consideration of data, not solely from the replacement of a Democratic administration by a Republican administration or vice

[36] 29 U.S.C.A. section 652(8).

versa. Courts do not try to guarantee that agencies make the best decisions possible, but instead, that agencies make well-reasoned decisions. Thus, a legal challenge to an agency rule is most likely to succeed by demonstrating that there is no evidence for the facts that the agency claims support the rule. If there is evidence, but the experts disagree about it, the prospects for a successful challenge dim considerably.

Motor Vehicle Manufacturers' Association v. State Farm Mutual Insurance Company, a 1983 Supreme Court decision, illustrates a lack of reasoned analysis in fact-finding.[37] The question before the Court was whether the National Highway Traffic Safety Administration, an office within the Department of Transportation, acted arbitrarily or capriciously in 1981, when it reversed a rule that it wrote in 1977. The rule, Motor Vehicle Safety Standard 208, required that car manufacturers equip new cars produced after September 1982 with "passive restraints;" that is, airbags or automatic seatbelts. The Court concluded that the reversal was indeed arbitrary, and ordered the agency to "either consider the matter further or adhere to or amend Standard 208 along lines which [the agency's own] analysis supports."[38]

The **National Traffic and Motor Vehicle Safety Act** of 1966 directs the Secretary of Transportation, or the Secretary's designee, to issue motor vehicle safety standards. Pursuant to that authority, in 1977, Brock Adams, President Carter's secretary of transportation, issued Standard 208, which required the phasing in of passive restraints beginning in model year 1982. It left to the manufacturers the choice of installing airbags or automatic seatbelts. In 1981, Drew Lewis, President Reagan's secretary of transportation, reopened rule making in this matter, and after receiving written comments and holding public hearings, the National Highway Traffic Safety Administration (the agency) rescinded the passive-restraint rule. The agency reasoned that because manufacturers planned to install automatic seatbelts, instead of airbags, in 99 percent of their new cars, and because car owners could easily detach the belts and leave them detached, Standard 208 would not significantly improve traffic safety.

The Court reviewed that decision according to the "arbitrary or capricious" test, which applies to informal rule making, because informal rule making sets automobile safety standards. That test also

[37] 463 U.S. 29.
[38] 463 U.S. at 34.

applies when, as here, an agency rescinds a motor vehicle safety standard. Justice White, writing for the majority, noted that agency action is "arbitrary or capricious" when an agency fails to "examine the relevant data and articulate a satisfactory explanation for its action including a 'rational connection between the facts found and the choice made.'"[39]

Justice White concluded that the reversal of Standard 208 was arbitrary for several reasons. First, when the agency learned that manufacturers planned to equip new cars with automatic seatbelts instead of airbags, it abandoned Standard 208 altogether instead of requiring airbags in all new vehicles. The likelihood that vehicle owners would detach the automatic seatbelts did not justify abandoning airbags too, particularly because the agency found in 1977 that airbags produce significant safety benefits.

Secondly, Justice White noted that the agency was "too quick to dismiss the safety benefits of automatic seatbelts."[40] He observed that there is general agreement that wearing seatbelts reduces traffic injuries and prevents fatalities, and that if vehicle owners use automatic seatbelts, the benefits realized will easily justify the cost of implementing Standard 208. There was no evidence in the record to support the agency's finding that the standard would not produce a substantial benefit because vehicle owners would detach their automatic seatbelts. Citing the agency's own data, Justice White wrote that the "empirical evidence on the record, consisting of surveys of drivers of automobiles equipped with passive belts, reveals more than a doubling of the usage rate experienced with manual belts."[41]

Thirdly, the agency's decision ignored Congress's intent that safety should be the preeminent concern in the setting of motor vehicle standards. Reviewing legislative history, Justice White quoted the report of the Committee in the House of Representatives that considered the National Traffic and Motor Vehicle Safety Act. The report states that "[t]he Committee intends that safety shall be the overriding consideration in the issuance of standards under this bill."[42]

[39] 463 U.S. at 43, quoting *Burlington Truck Lines, Inc. v. United States*, 371 U.S. 156 (1962).

[40] 463 U.S. at 51.

[41] 463 U.S. at 53.

[42] 463 U.S. at 55, quoting H.R. Rep. No. 1776, 89th Cong., 2d Sess., 16 (1966).

Therefore, he reasoned that if the agency chose to reconsider Standard 208, it would have to reevaluate the likely cost of requiring installation of automatic belts in light of Congress's expressed desire to improve highway safety.

Finally, the agency failed to explain why it did not require nondetachable seatbelts in all new vehicles. That failure violated the "arbitrary or capricious" test because it did not show a "rational connection between the facts found and the choice made" in abandoning Standard 208.[43] The agency could change its view on the acceptability of nondetachable seatbelts, but it would have to explain its reasons for doing so.

Thus, the agency's decision to rescind Motor Vehicle Safety Standard 208 violated its statutory authority. The decision was arbitrary because the primary basis for it was not new evidence about the cost or effectiveness of passive restraints, but apparently, the Reagan administration's dislike for regulation.

The question of *how* an agency acted requires a review of its procedures for gathering and analyzing data, and for notifying interested parties of its conclusions. For example, an agency must disclose the data and methodology it used to produce a proposed rule, and it must respond to significant comments. In responding to a lawsuit, an agency must show how it produced a rule from available data and explain how that rule relates to statutory goals. Failure to satisfy any of those criteria is likely to result in a successful legal challenge to the agency.

In *United States v. Nova Scotia Food Products Corp.*, a 1977 decision by the United States Court of Appeals for the Second Circuit, a regulated party successfully challenged an FDA rule on the grounds that in writing the rule, the agency failed to disclose the scientific data on which it relied and also failed to respond to significant public comments.[44] The rule required that fish processors heat smoked fish at a continuous temperature of 180 degrees for at least thirty minutes, or 150 degrees for at least thirty minutes, depending on the salt content of the fish. The goal was to minimize the growth of *Clostridium botulinum* Type E bacteria, which can cause botulism, a form of food poisoning. Nova Scotia Food Products Corporation (Nova Scotia),

[43] 463 U.S. at 56. See also *Burlington Truck Lines, Inc. v. United States,* 371 U.S. 156 (1962).
[44] 568 F.2d 240.

which processed smoked whitefish for commercial sale, challenged the rule on the grounds mentioned.

The court agreed with Nova Scotia on both claims. The FDA did not inform interested parties of the scientific data it used to write the challenged rule, which effectively limited public comment because the FDA itself, and not the interested parties, had collected the relevant data. The FDA's failure to inform prevented interested parties from commenting on the data, which, in turn, prevented FDA from taking into account all relevant factors in making its decision. It is "arbitrary or capricious" for an agency not to take into account all relevant factors in making a decision[45] because "[t]o suppress meaningful comment by failure to disclose the basic data relied upon is akin to rejecting comment altogether."[46] Thus, the court concluded that when a scientific decision is the basis for a proposed rule, the agency must make available to interested parties the data that produced the rule.

The FDA also did not produce an adequate statement of basis and purpose, as the Administrative Procedure Act requires.[47] The FDA's statement failed to respond to (1) Nova Scotia's comment that heating whitefish at high temperatures will destroy the product and ruin the whitefish industry, and (2) a comment by the Interior Department's Bureau of Commercial Fisheries that processors can prevent the growth of botulism-causing bacteria without damaging fish by adding nitrite and salt instead of by heating fish at high temperatures. By failing to respond to those comments, the FDA acted arbitrarily because "[i]t is not in keeping with the rational process to leave vital questions, raised by comments which are of cogent materiality, completely unanswered."[48]

The court acknowledged that the Food, Drug and Cosmetic Act requires the FDA to ban from interstate commerce "adulterated" food, including food prepared or packed under unsanitary conditions,[49] and that public health supersedes the commercial feasibility of a product or an industry. Nevertheless, the court noted that the

---

[45] 568 F.2d at 251, quoting *Hanly v. Mitchell*, 460 F.2d 640 (2d Cir.), *cert. denied*, 409 U.S. 990 (1972).

[46] 568 F.2d at 252.

[47] 5 U.S.C.A. section 553.

[48] 568 F.2d at 252.

[49] 21 U.S.C.A. section 342(a)(4).

APA requires that an agency that faces those issues must at least disclose whether it considers a proposed rule to be commercially feasible and, if not, whether other considerations take precedence over commercial feasibility in the rule-writing process. Because the FDA failed to disclose such information, its fish-processing rule was invalid.

Judicial review examines not only how an agency writes a rule, but also how it adjudicates a dispute. In adjudication, the agency can deprive an individual of a **liberty** or **property** interest that the federal Constitution's Fifth Amendment, which limits the powers of federal agencies, or its Fourteenth Amendment, which limits the powers of state agencies, protects only if the agency observes the requirements of **due process**.[50] Failure to do so will invalidate the result of the adjudication.

Goldberg v. Kelly, a 1970 Supreme Court decision, illustrates this point.[51] The question before the Supreme Court in *Goldberg* was whether a state agency that terminates welfare benefits without an opportunity for an evidentiary hearing prior to termination denies the recipient due process in violation of the Fourteenth Amendment. Welfare recipients challenged a rule of New York City's Department of Social Services, which permitted evidentiary hearings after, but not before, termination of benefits. The Court agreed with the plaintiffs that "when welfare is discontinued, only a pre-termination evidentiary hearing provides the recipient with procedural due process."[52]

Goldberg required the Court to interpret the due-process clause of the Fourteenth Amendment to the Constitution. Justice Brennan, writing for the majority, observed that the Fourteenth Amendment protects against the termination of welfare benefits without due process because those benefits are a statutory entitlement that gives the recipient a property right to continue receiving them so long as the recipient remains eligible.[53] He noted that precedents require

[50] The due-process clause of the Fourteenth Amendment protects against deprivations of life, as well as liberty and property, without due process of law. However, agency decisions rarely, if ever, threaten to deprive one of life, so plaintiffs who challenge agency adjudications on constitutional grounds typically allege deprivations of liberty and/or property without due process.

[51] 397 U.S. 254.

[52] 397 U.S. at 264.

[53] In August 1996, the Congress enacted and President Clinton signed legislation that ends the statutory entitlement to receive welfare benefits. In the future, Congress will provide **block grants,** containing fixed sums, to

due process in the loss of other statutory entitlements—namely, the disqualification for unemployment compensation, the denial of a tax exemption, and the discharge from public-sector employment—and reasoned by analogy that due process is also required when welfare benefits are at stake.[54] The question that remained was whether due process requires an evidentiary hearing prior to the termination of welfare benefits.

Justice Brennan surveyed the precedents and extracted the well-established principle that the amount of process due in a particular case depends on whether the individual's private interest in avoiding the loss of an entitlement outweighs the government's interest in cost-effective administration.[55] Applying that principle, he reasoned that the welfare recipient's interest in continuing to receive benefits is compelling because "termination of aid pending resolution of a controversy over eligibility may deprive an *eligible* recipient of the very means by which to live while he waits."[56] Therefore, more process is due the welfare recipient than one who seeks unemployment compensation or a tax exemption.

Justice Brennan concluded that the welfare recipient's interest in the uninterrupted receipt of benefits outweighs government's interest in cost-effective administration. He argued that government can realize its interests as well as provide due process "by developing procedures for prompt pre-termination hearings and by skillful use of personnel and facilities."[57] However, the welfare recipient is not entitled to a trial. Instead, due process requires that the state provide the recipient with "timely and adequate notice detailing the reasons for a proposed termination, and an effective opportunity to defend by confronting any adverse witnesses and by presenting his own arguments and evidence orally."[58] Due process does not require the state to provide an attorney for the recipient, but it does require

---

the states, from which the states will distribute welfare benefits. An individual may qualify for but not receive benefits if the funds available in the block grant are insufficient to serve the pool of eligible applicants. It remains to be seen how the end of this entitlement will affect the due process rights of welfare recipients.

[54] See *Sherbert v. Verner,* 374 U.S. 398 (1963); *Speiser v. Randall,* 357 U.S. 513 (1958); and *Slochower v. Board of Higher Education,* 350 U.S. 551 (1956).
[55] 397 U.S. at 263.
[56] 397 U.S. at 264.
[57] 397 U.S. at 266.
[58] 397 U.S. at 268.

that the recipient "be allowed to retain an attorney if he so desires."[59] Finally, due process requires that (1) the state's decision derive entirely from the legal rules and evidence presented at the hearing; (2) the official who makes that decision be impartial; and (3) he identify the reasons for his decision and the evidence on which he relies.

Despite *Goldberg* the Court concluded in *Mathews v. Eldridge* (1976) that due process does not require an evidentiary hearing prior to the termination of social security disability benefits.[60] Like welfare benefits, disability benefits are a statutory entitlement for those who qualify. The **Social Security Act** provides cash benefits to workers during periods in which they are completely disabled.[61] That entitlement creates a **property interest** that the Fifth Amendment's due process clause protects, although it does not prevent the Social Security Administration from terminating benefits when the worker returns to work or is no longer disabled.

In *Mathews,* the Court reiterated that due process is a flexible concept that calls for differing degrees of procedural protection in different situations. Echoing *Goldberg,* the Court added that in order to determine the process that is due in each case, it must consider (1) the private interest that the challenged government action affects; (2) the risk that the government's procedures will deprive that interest, and the value of additional or substitute procedures; and (3) the government's interest, including the function being performed and the costs of additional or substitute procedures.

Nevertheless, Justice Powell, writing for the majority, exercised fact freedom and concluded that the facts in *Goldberg* were sufficiently different from those in *Mathews* to justify rejecting *Goldberg* as a precedent in *Mathews*. The crucial fact that distinguished *Mathews* from *Goldberg* was that unlike eligibility for welfare benefits, eligibility for social security disability benefits is not based on financial need. One is eligible for disability benefits if completely disabled, regardless of the income one receives from other sources, such as veterans' benefits, a tort claim award, or private insurance. Therefore, the deprivation resulting from the loss of disability benefits is likely to be less than that resulting from the loss of welfare benefits. The loss of disability benefits, then, is not analogous to the loss of welfare

[59] 397 U.S. at 270.
[60] 424 U.S. 319.
[61] 42 U.S.C.A. section 423.

benefits, which warrants a pretermination hearing, but rather to the revocation of a driver's license[62] or the loss of a federal job,[63] in which a posttermination hearing provides due process. Therefore, a posttermination hearing will provide due process in social security disability cases too. The government's interest in cost-efficient administration outweighs the recipient's interest in the uninterrupted receipt of disability benefits.

Taken together, *Goldberg* and *Mathews* require state and federal agencies that adjudicate disputes to provide due process whenever a statutory entitlement gives an individual a liberty or property interest. The process that is due in each case will depend on the governmental and private interests to be balanced. Judicial review exists to ensure that agencies strike a balance that complies with constitutional requirements.

CONCLUSION

Federal agencies make and enforce rules and adjudicate disputes that profoundly affect individuals, businesses, and other institutions in the United States. Regulated parties challenge agency decisions in court often enough that much legal reasoning nowadays occurs in the context of administrative regulation. Courts hold agencies accountable to the constitutional principle of separated powers by requiring them to act within the scope of their statutory authority. Courts also hold agencies accountable to the constitutional principle of due process by requiring them to act fairly and reasonably in dealing with regulated parties. Thus, legal reasoning in the administrative context reconciles the need for regulation in an urban, technological society with two cherished American values, individual freedom and the rule of law.

There is general agreement that courts should reconcile those forces, but there is often disagreement in individual cases about whether an agency acted fairly, rationally, and within its statutory authority.

[62] See *Bell v. Burson,* 402 U.S. 535 (1971).
[63] See *Arnett v. Kennedy,* 416 U.S. 134 (1974).

EPILOGUE: PASSIVE RESTRAINTS REVISITED

The case printed below revisits the rule-making process that resulted in the requirement that automobile manufacturers equip all new cars with either airbags or automatic seatbelts. The discussion earlier in this chapter focused on the Reagan administration's rescission in 1981 of Motor Vehicle Safety Standard 208. The following case addresses the Carter administration's adoption of that rule in 1977 and challenges to it by the Pacific Legal Foundation; consumer activist Ralph Nader; and Public Citizen, an organization that Mr. Nader founded. As you read the case, try to determine whether it is about *what* action the agency took, *why* it acted, or *how* it acted. After reading the case, ask yourself whether the agency's action reflects "reasoned analysis."

Pacific Legal Foundation et. al. v. Department of Transportation
593 F.2d 1338 (D.C. Cir. 1979)

WRIGHT, Chief Judge:

[T]he petitioners in these two cases challenge from opposite sides Motor Vehicle Safety Standard 208, which requires "passive restraints," such as automatic seatbelts or airbags, in all passenger cars sold in this country after September 1, 1983. [The Pacific Legal Foundation et. al.] argue that there is insufficient empirical support for Standard 208, and that the Secretary of Transportation (Secretary) violated the Motor Vehicle Safety Act of 1966 (Safety Act) by failing to consider public reaction to passive restraints and by ignoring potential hazards posed by them. [Ralph Nader and Public Citizen], in contrast, insist that the Secretary improperly delayed implementation of the Standard and lacked good cause for permitting car manufacturers to introduce passive restraints gradually, rather than requiring full compliance by the effective date. We find that the Secretary acted within his statutory authority and validly issued the passive restraint order under his rulemaking powers.

[Editor's Note: Secretary Adams ordered a "phasing-in" of passive restraints pursuant to Standard 208. In model year 1982, all new cars with wheelbases above 114 inches would have to have full passive restraint systems for front seat occupants. In model year 1983, that standard would extend to all new cars with wheelbases between 100 and 114 inches, and in model year 1984, to all new cars.]

II.

The [Motor Vehicle Safety Act] requires that Motor Vehicle Safety Standards "shall be practicable, shall meet the need for motor vehicle safety, and shall be stated in objective terms." In addition, the Secretary must "consider relevant available motor vehicle safety data" and determine the appropriateness of the standard for the type of vehicle covered by it.

III.

A. *Effectiveness of Passive Restraints*

[Petitioners Pacific Legal Foundation et. al.] challenge . . . DOT's conclusion that laboratory tests and limited field experience establish the reliability of airbags which, given current technology and the rule before us, would probably have to be installed in 75 percent of American cars. After reviewing the record in this case, we find that the Secretary's decision was rational.

. . . DOT has conducted over two thousand crash tests of airbags, including 188 with human volunteers in the vehicles, 274 with dummies, and a handful with cadavers and baboons. Following these experiments, involving collisions at speeds of up to 50 miles per hour, the agency concluded that if airbags were installed in all cars over 9,000 fatalities and over 100,000 injuries would be averted.

Petitioners also insist that the Secretary's conclusion on airbag effectiveness is contradicted by experience with the twelve thousand airbag cars currently in operation in this country. Indeed, there have been more fatalities in frontal accidents involving airbag cars than the statistical projections from experimental data would have indicated. Nevertheless, in view of the relatively small sample involved, and the extraordinary nature of several of the accidents, this variation does not undermine the agency's conclusion that airbags are effective. Moreover, airbags have been very effective in reducing or preventing major injuries.

B. *Public Reaction*

Petitioners assert that the Secretary violated his statutory mandate by refusing to consider public reaction to his decision. The importance of popular response, they contend, can be seen in the Safety Act's requirements that a safety standard be "practicable." The Secretary stated in his order, however, that "public acceptance or rejection of passive restraints is not one of the statutory criteria which the Department is charged by law to apply in establishing standards." Although we agree with petitioners' view of the requirements of the Safety Act, we believe that the Secretary did take public reaction into account and satisfactorily explained his conclusion that widespread public resistance to passive restraints is unlikely.

[H]e adequately justified his action in terms of the anticipated public reaction. . . . Adams distinguished the ignition interlock affair [in which the public severely criticized a 1972 DOT rule requiring installation of devices that prevented a car from starting until lap and shoulder belts were connected, prompting Congress to ban the devices] from passive restraints on the basis of the nature of the intrusion on the individual. Passive restraints do not require independent action by passengers to activate them. In the 1976 decision [by the Ford administration not to require passive restraints because of anticipated public resistance], Secretary [of Transportation William T.] Coleman characterized his estimate of public resistance as "a matter of judgment." In our view Secretary Adams provided a sufficient explanation why his judgment differed from his predecessor's.

C. *Collateral Dangers*

Airbags may also present collateral dangers to the public, petitioners argue, which are not justified by the expected benefits from Standard 208. [T]he Safety Act charges the Secretary with authority to balance present injuries against possible risks posed by safety equipment.

The major danger associated with airbags is inadvertent deployment that might cause the driver to lose control of the car. There is evidence, however, that such deployments do not present a substantial hazard. In road experience three such incidents have occurred, and none caused a collision or injury, while tests with human volunteers have shown little loss of control by drivers. Moreover, the agency is optimistic that the causes of the three inadvertent deployments are understood and can be remedied, so there is some prospect of reducing their likelihood in the future. Even without such improvements, DOT gauges at one in 200 the chance that in a lifetime an individual would experience an inadvertent deployment as an occupant of a car.

Rapidly inflating airbags also may injure out-of-position passengers in the front seat, especially children. New methods of gas generation, however, permit an initially slower inflation, with the aim of more gently moving the occupant back from the dashboard and out of harm's way.

In view of these circumstances, we cannot conclude that the Secretary abused his discretion in assessing the tradeoffs between the expected benefits and the potential dangers of airbags.

IV.

Petitioners Nader et. al. [challenge] the delayed implementation of Standard 208.

Petitioners argue . . . that the Secretary did not satisfy the Safety Act's requirement that he demonstrate "good cause" for not implementing the new safety standard within one year of issuance. They contend that "mere" economic hardship cannot constitute such cause when the statute's central goal—greater vehicle safety—is at stake. In his decision the Secretary explained the delay until model year 1982 as an attempt to assure "orderly implementation" of the new standard. The four-year lead-in period, according to the Secretary, grants car and airbag manufacturers breathing room to gear up production. Moreover, by encouraging voluntary production of cars with passive restraints before the 1982 models the Secretary hopes to increase the public's familiarity with the systems and facilitate their eventual acceptance.

We cannot agree with petitioners on this point. Congress . . . provided the "good cause" exception along with the general requirement of practicability. When dealing with a "technology-forcing" rule like Standard 208, the agency must consider the abilities of producers to comply with the new requirement and of the public to grasp the need for the change. On this record, these concerns were good cause for the delay in implementation.

Petitioners also insist that the Secretary lacked statutory authority to schedule introduction of airbags according to the size of a car's wheelbase. We find no basis for this protest in the statute. [Editor's Note: The Safety Act requires the Secretary to consider whether a proposed standard "is reasonable, practicable and appropriate for the particular *type* of motor vehicle or motor vehicle equipment for which it is prescribed."] Petitioners . . . interpret "type" as referring to distinctions between vehicle functions, such as passenger cars and trucks, not vehicle size. We view the term as including both distinctions, in the effort to provide the Secretary with sufficient flexibility to tailor safety standards to engineering realities. The Secretary reasonably decided on a phase-in because of the difficulty of providing airbags in smaller cars and the likely usefulness to that endeavor of experience with larger cars.

Accordingly, the Secretary's order is
Affirmed.

QUESTIONS FOR DISCUSSION

1. Who are the plaintiffs in this combined case, and what allegations do they make?

2. Motor Vehicle Safety Standard 208 is the product of informal rule making; therefore, what standard of review, or "test" does the court apply to it?

3. Does the Pacific Legal Foundation (the Foundation) challenge the delegation of legislative power to the Department of Transportation (DOT) to set automobile safety standards? Does the Foundation challenge the fact-finding on which Motor Vehicle Safety Standard 208 is based?

4. Does the court agree with the Foundation that DOT's laboratory and field tests fail to establish airbag reliability? Explain.

5. Does the Foundation challenge the manner in which DOT gathered the data for Standard 208? What data did the Motor Vehicle Safety Act (the Safety Act) require Secretary Adams to consider?

6. Does the court agree with the Foundation that Secretary Adams refused to consider public reaction to his decision? Explain.

7. Suppose that the restraints mandated by Standard 208 required independent action by automobile occupants to activate them. How might that affect the rationality of Secretary Adams's decision and the result in this case?

8. What duty did the Safety Act impose on Secretary Adams concerning the potential dangers of airbags? Does the court agree with the Foundation that Secretary Adams breached his duty?

9. Do Ralph Nader and Public Citizen challenge the what, why, or how of Secretary Adams's decision? What statutory mandate do they allege that Secretary Adams violated in delaying and phasing-in implementation of Standard 208?

10. Does the court agree with them that Secretary Adams failed to demonstrate **good cause** for delaying implementation of Standard 208? Does the court agree that he lacked statutory authority to phase-in airbags according to the size of a car's wheelbase? Explain.

11. Do you agree with the court that Secretary Adams acted rationally in setting Motor Vehicle Safety Standard 208?

12. Did he act rationally in implementing Standard 208?

CHAPTER 6

Summary and Conclusion

Summary

Conclusion

SUMMARY

Undergraduate courses introduce students to a wide variety of methodologies for studying and attempting to resolve problems in disciplines ranging from forestry to linguistics. The purpose of this book has been to introduce students to legal reasoning, a methodology that instructors use in undergraduate courses but do not always adequately explain. The legal scholar, practicing lawyer, or judge uses legal reasoning for the same purposes that the biologist or the criminologist uses the scientific method, namely, to analyze, understand, and resolve a particular problem. Law, of course, presents its problems in the form of lawsuits, and legal reasoning resolves lawsuits.

Just as students who are interested in biology or criminology must understand the scientific method, students who are interested in law must understand legal reasoning. Indeed, legal reasoning addresses so many important controversies in American life today that undergraduate students of biology, criminology, and virtually every other discipline probably ought to study it alongside their classmates who plan to practice or teach law. At a time when the Supreme Court determines the constitutionality of state prohibitions on physician-assisted suicide, every thoughtful American should understand the fundamentals of legal reasoning.[1]

---

[1] During its 1996–1997 term, the Supreme Court heard oral arguments in *Vacco v. Quill* and *Washington v. Glucksberg*. *Vacco v. Quill* was an appeal of a decision by the United States Court of Appeals for the Second Circuit that declared unconstitutional a New York state law prohibiting physician-assisted suicide. *Washington v. Glucksberg* was an appeal of a decision by the United States Court of Appeals for the Ninth Circuit that declared unconstitutional a Washington state law against physician-assisted suicide. In late June, 1997, the Supreme Court announced its decisions in both cases. The Court reversed both lower court decisions. In *Washington*, the Court concluded that the state's ban on physician-assisted suicide did not violate the due process clause of the fourteenth amendment because: (1) the "liberty" that the amendment protects does not encompass a right to assistance in committing suicide; and (2) the ban was rationally related to a legitimate state interest in preserving life. *See* 65 L.W. 4669. In *Vacco*, the Court concluded that New York's ban on physician-assisted suicide did not violate the equal protection clause of the fourteenth amendment, even though New York permits patients to refuse life-saving treatment, because it was rational for the

Legal reasoning is the process by which lawyers argue and courts decide cases. There are three components to legal reasoning, one of which is reasoning by analogy. A court resolves today's case by reviewing prior cases for an analogous precedent that yields the principle that resolves the case. The court then reasons deductively and applies the governing principle to today's case. For example, in *Tinker v. Des Moines Independent Community School District*, the Supreme Court concluded that wearing a black armband as a political statement is "akin to pure speech," and therefore deserves the same First Amendment protection that an oral statement receives. When the case at hand is unprecedented, a court reasons inductively, creating a governing principle from the circumstances of that case. In *Griswold v. Connecticut*, for example, the Supreme Court fashioned a constitutional right for married couples to practice contraception and to receive information about and devices for contraception.

Reasoning by analogy does not ensure unanimous decisions, as the dissents in *Tinker* and *Griswold* illustrate, because fact freedom permits each member of an appellate court to choose the precedent(s) and the principle(s) that he or she believes control a case. The judges' choices reflect their values, aspirations, biases, and, in many high profile cases, their public-policy preferences. One result of fact freedom is that predicting court decisions is a risky business, as *McCollum v. Board of Education* and *Zorach v. Clausen* illustrate. A more important result is that American law is sufficiently flexible that it can change to meet new social, economic, and technological conditions.

A second component of legal reasoning is linguistic analysis, which courts use to resolve cases that require them to construe statutory or constitutional language. For example, in *United States v. Sheek*, the United States Court of Appeals for the Fourth Circuit used linguistic analysis to construe the word "parent" within the meaning of the Federal Kidnapping Act. In *Personnel Administrator of Massachusetts v. Feeney*, the Supreme Court used linguistic analysis to determine whether the Fourteenth Amendment's guarantee of "equal protection of the

New York legislature to draw a "line between killing and letting die." *See* 65 L.W. at 4699.

laws" prohibits a state from classifying job applicants according to whether or not they are veterans.

The third component of legal reasoning is judicial discretion, namely, judges' views about public-policy disputes and about the role that courts should play in those disputes. The law's capacity for change gives judges ample opportunity to exercise discretion. To judge is not to declare the law once and for all, but instead, to make difficult, even agonizing choices between competing values of equal or nearly equal worth.[2] In *Tinker*, the majority chose the freedom of expression over the rights of local school authorities to run their schools free from federal interference, but Justice Black chose the latter. A combination of subjective preferences and objective evidence influenced those choices, as Justice Black's disagreement with the majority about whether the "armband students" (Black's term) had disrupted classes indicates.

Thus, legal reasoning is a rich stew of analogies, linguistic analyses, and judicial discretion. In some cases, reasoning by analogy is the key ingredient in the mixture, while in other cases, linguistic analysis dominates. In still other cases, both ingredients are part of the court's opinion. The amount of discretion added varies from case to case, but it is always part of the stew. Judges stir the stew, and their stirring is *the craft of legal reasoning.*

Courts use legal reasoning in four distinct contexts: statutory construction, constitutional interpretation, common-law decision making, and administrative regulation. Those functions are distinct, but not mutually exclusive. Courts often perform two or more of them in a single case. Statutory construction requires courts to determine the meaning of the statutory language that governs a particular lawsuit. Courts begin by reading the statute but often find that it is unclear how, or even whether, the statute applies to the case at hand because legislative compromise has produced a vague and/or ambiguous text. As a result, courts must frequently examine sources other than the text of a statute to determine its applicability to the case at hand. Those sources include context, legislative history, statutory purpose, presumptions, and canons of statutory construction.

---

[2] Frank M. Coffin, *The Ways of a Judge: Reflections from the Federal Appellate Bench* (Boston: Houghton Mifflin, 1980), p. 246.

For example, in *United States v. Sheek*, the majority relied on a canon that favors reading criminal statutes narrowly to conclude that a biological mother who lost her parental rights was nevertheless a "parent" under the Federal Kidnapping Act. The dissent relied on a presumption against absurd results to conclude that one who has lost parental rights cannot be a "parent" under the act. That difference of opinion illustrates that statutory language and the techniques of construing it constrain judicial discretion only slightly; judges have ample opportunities in statutory construction to be creative and to choose between competing values.

Constitutional interpretation requires courts to determine the meaning of the constitutional language that governs a lawsuit. It gives dimensions and meaning to the principles of federalism and separated powers, as well as to the rights of individuals as contained in the Bill of Rights. Constitutional interpretation is the most controversial exercise of legal reasoning because it can nullify a state or federal statute that represents the will of the people, acting through their elected representatives. It is also controversial because there is no consensus about the method(s) that judges should use to interpret the Constitution; each method is the subject of debate among judges, practicing lawyers, and scholars. Originalists Robert Bork and Clarence Thomas argue that only the text, structure, and history of the Constitution should guide constitutional interpretation, whereas noninterpretivist William Brennan maintains that the goal of fostering human dignity should guide constitutional interpretation, even though the Constitution does not mention that goal or that term. Most judges adopt positions located somewhere between Bork's and Thomas's originalism and Brennan's noninterpretivism.

Like statutory construction, constitutional interpretation features judicial discretion, subject to limited constraints. The language and history of the Constitution, as well as societal values, constrain judges somewhat, but judges nevertheless exercise discretion regularly because constitutional language is often vague and/or ambiguous, precedents are less important in constitutional interpretation than in other fields of law, and societal values often conflict with important individual rights. In constitutional interpretation, as in statutory construction, judges must frequently choose between competing values and alternative public-policy outcomes.

In constitutional interpretation, though, the competing values are more likely than they are in statutory cases to be fundamental political goals. Therefore, the judges' choices in constitutional cases are more likely to be controversial than their choices in statutory cases. That is why a discussion of *Personnel Administrator of Massachusetts v. Feeney* sparked a lively debate in a constitutional law course that I taught several years ago. Like the Supreme Court majority, the future military officers in the class (mostly male) valued encouraging military service more than ensuring equal employment opportunities for women, whereas the remaining students (mostly female), like the dissenters in *Feeney,* made the opposite choice. Like the *Feeney* case itself, classroom discussion of it produced well-reasoned majority and dissenting opinions.

Common-law decision making requires courts to resolve disputes in which no statute or constitutional provision governs. In such cases, courts rely exclusively on precedents to guide them to the right results. They derive from precedents a governing principle and then apply that principle to the case at hand in order to produce the rule that resolves the case. The new rule will, in turn, guide the resolution of similar disputes in the future. Thus, common law is judge-made law. It grows out of principles and rules that judges create while answering the particular questions that lawsuits present. It therefore develops and changes as courts extend rules announced in earlier cases to new circumstances presented in later cases.

Tarasoff v. Regents of the University of California illustrates the mechanics of common-law decision making. In *Tarasoff,* the court extracted from the precedents—then applied to psychotherapists—the principle that one has a duty to control the conduct of another for the benefit of third persons when one is in a "special relationship" to either a potential perpetrator or a potential victim of harm. Therefore, a psychotherapist is liable for damages if he has reason to believe that his patient is a danger to another yet fails to warn the intended victim or notify anyone who is likely to warn the intended victim. The psychotherapist-patient relationship is a "special relationship" that carries with it a duty to warn of threatened danger. *Tarasoff* is a landmark decision because it expands the "special relationship" category to include psychotherapists and their patients. It is also a landmark because it broadens the duty of care previously associated with "special relationships" under California law, which required a warning to an intended victim only by one who has a "special relationship" to the likely perpetrator *and* the intended victim. After *Tarasoff*, one who has a "special relationship" to the likely perpetrator *or* the intended victim is obligated to warn of threatened danger.

Tarasoff also illustrates the implications of common-law decision making. It shows that judges must choose between competing values such as public safety and the confidentiality of therapist-patient communications, even when no statutory or constitutional language exists to guide their reasoning. It also shows that the common law responds to modern societal conditions, such as urbanization, technological sophistication, and human interdependence, by expanding our legal responsibility for the safety of others.

Administrative regulation requires courts to resolve disputes arising out of decisions by state and federal agencies that regulate all aspects of life, from delivering babies to operating schools to licensing professionals to ensuring retirement security to maintaining sanitary standards for funeral homes. Judicial review of agency action aims to ensure that agencies do not exceed the rule-making and rule-adjudication authority that statutes and the Constitution, respectively, give to them. That is, judicial review seeks to hold agencies accountable to the constitutional principles of separated powers and due process of law. Toward that end, courts that must resolve challenges to agency actions examine *what* actions an agency is authorized to take, *why* an agency acted or failed to act in a certain way, and *how* an agency acted in reaching the challenged decision.

Courts consider *what* actions an agency is authorized to take when plaintiffs contend that rule making either occurred pursuant to an unconstitutional delegation of legislative power by Congress or exceeded the statutory authority that Congress conferred upon the defendant agency. In *Mistretta v. United States,* the plaintiff alleged an unconstitutional delegation of legislative power to the United States Sentencing Commission, whereas in *the benzene case*, the plaintiff alleged that the secretary of labor exceeded his authority under the Occupational Safety and Health Act to establish workplace health standards. Courts consider *why* an agency acted or failed to act when plaintiffs charge that the agency refused to explain its reason(s) for rejecting alternatives and/or departing from prior policies. In *Pacific Legal Foundation v. Department of Transportation,* the foundation argued that Secretary Adams ignored public opposition to passive restraints and the dangers that airbags pose when he announced Motor Vehicle Safety Standard 208.

Courts consider *how* an agency acted when plaintiffs allege that an agency (1) employed faulty procedures for gathering and analyzing data during rule making, and/or notifying interested parties about its conclusions; or (2) deprived an individual of a liberty or property interest without due process of law during adjudication of a dispute. In *Pacific Legal Foundation,* the foundation charged that the Department of Transportation's tests did not establish that airbags are effective in preventing injuries and deaths from automobile accidents. In *Goldberg v. Kelly* and *Mathews v. Eldridge,* the plaintiffs maintained that government agencies deprived them of property interests in welfare benefits and social security disability benefits, respectively, without the pretermination hearing that due process of law requires.

Courts consider the what, why, and how of agency action in order to reconcile the need for regulation in a technological, interdependent, and dangerous society with Americans' passionate devotion to individual freedom and the rule of law. In reconciling those values, courts exercise discretion and make difficult choices, as the divergent outcomes in *Goldberg* and *Mathews* illustrate.

CONCLUSION

The divergent outcomes in cases like *Goldberg v. Kelly* and *Mathews v. Eldridge,* or *McCollum v. Board of Education* and *Zorach v. Clausen,* illustrate more than just the power of judicial discretion. They illustrate that courts are important public policy makers in the American political system. American courts are important public policy makers not only because they exercise discretion but because Americans expect them to decide what the law is and routinely ask them to use their analogies, linguistic analyses, and discretion to resolve thorny legal and political controversies.

Admittedly, judicial decision making, especially by appellate courts, is less publicized and less overtly partisan than legislative and executive decision making. Judicial decision making is also subject to procedural constraints that legislative and executive decision making are not. For example, legislators, governors, and presidents can investigate issues that interest them; courts can only decide issues that come to them in the form of lawsuits.[3] Court decisions are just as "political," though, as legislative and executive decisions because they allocate power among the branches of government, distribute wealth among competing groups and individuals, and determine the boundaries between individual freedom and governmental authority. Courts' political power is limited but, nevertheless, significant.

Courts cannot make foreign policy, but they can influence it by affirming the president's power to cancel a defense treaty without Congressional approval.[4] Courts cannot appropriate money to improve public mental-health facilities, but they can decide that unsafe and unsanitary conditions in those facilities violate the residents' constitutional rights, thereby forcing legislators to improve conditions.[5] Courts cannot increase property taxes in order to finance a public-school desegregation plan, but they can authorize a school district to levy property taxes at a rate sufficient to finance the plan.[6] Courts cannot replace the local property tax with an alternative means of funding public schools in order to ensure equality of funding between property-rich and property-poor school districts. They can decide, though, that the property tax–based funding mechanism violates the state constitution and thereby force the state legislature to devise an alternative.[7]

[3] Article III, section 2, clause 1 of the United States Constitution empowers the federal courts to decide "cases" and "controversies," which the Supreme Court interprets as prohibiting federal courts from issuing advisory opinions to the president or the Congress concerning the constitutionality of proposed presidential or Congressional actions. In other words, federal courts can only decide lawsuits that are actual, not hypothetical, disputes between two or more parties. State courts in thirty-eight states are subject to the same limitation. In the other twelve states, the supreme courts have authority, pursuant to their state constitutions, or to statutes, to issue advisory opinions about proposed actions in response to formal requests from the governor or the legislature.

[4] *Goldwater v. Carter,* 444 U.S. 996 (1979).

[5] See, for example, *Wyatt v. Stickney,* 344 F. Supp. 387 (M.D. Ala. 1972).

[6] *Missouri v. Jenkins,* 495 U.S. 33 (1990).

[7] State supreme courts in more than half of the fifty states have held that the property tax–based system for funding public schools violates the right

Such "policy-making" decisions place courts in the center of the political process and regularly spawn critiques by legislators and scholars that courts have exceeded their constitutional authority in making those decisions. The courts' supporters respond that raising taxes to improve mental-health facilities or to make school funding more equitable is often so politically unpopular or divisive that legislators procrastinate until courts force them to act. Therefore, legislators should not criticize courts for addressing the difficult issues that legislators are afraid to address. This debate is continuous and intense, and it reflects the importance of courts in contemporary American life. The importance of courts makes the craft of legal reasoning well worth studying.

Having studied the craft, you can now dissect appellate opinions and identify the elements of law and policy contained therein. The next challenge is to anticipate the alternative paths a court *could* take in resolving a hypothetical case and then predict the path the court *would* take. Both tasks become easier as you read more cases and learn more legal principles and rules. To return to the metaphor of this book's introduction, then, it is fair to say at this point that you have learned to "walk," and can now begin learning to "dance." Enjoy!

---

to a free public education contained in their respective state constitutions. The most recent example of this type of decision is *Brigham v. State,* No. 96-502 (February 5, 1997), in which the Vermont Supreme Court invalidated that state's property tax–based school funding mechanism. Other recent examples include *Roosevelt Elementary School District No. 66 v. Bishop,* 877 P.2d 806 (Ariz. 1994); *Tennessee Small School Systems v. McWherter,* 851 S.W.2d 139 (Tenn. 1993); and *Edgewood Independent School District v. Kirby,* 777 S.W.2d 391 (Tex. 1989).

APPENDIX A

American Courts: Organization and Jurisdiction

Table A.1   The Federal Courts

Court	Organization/Procedure
United States Supreme Court	Comprised of a chief justice and 8 associate justices, all appointed by president to hold office during "good behavior", and removable by impeachment (House of Representatives impeaches, Senate tries and removes). Annual term begins on first Monday in October, concludes in early July. Term divided into sittings of two weeks each, when Court hears oral arguments, and recesses, when justices write opinions. Court decides 100–150 cases per term by full written opinion. Unsuccessful parties in Court of Appeals seek Supreme Court review by filing *writs of certiorari;* if 4 justices vote to "grant cert", Court hears the case. Court rejects vast majority of petitions for cert.
United States Courts of Appeals	Includes 11 numbered circuits plus District of Columbia Circuit, Federal Circuit (also located in Washington, D.C.), and Court of Military Appeals. Several states in each numbered Circuit; judges have offices in separate cities, but gather monthly to hear oral arguments and decide cases (see Appendix B). Three-judge panels decide most cases; judges rotate so same three do not sit together permanently. Occasionally hear case *en banc,* which means all judges on court hear case, except on Ninth Circuit Court of Appeals, where *en banc* means 11 judges hear case. Judges appointed by president to hold office during "good behavior;" removable by impeachment.
United States District Courts	Ninety-four courts, at least 1 per state. Range in size from District of Wyoming (2 district judges) to Southern District of New York (37 judges). President appoints district court judges to hold office during "good behavior;" they are removable by impeachment. District courts are the trial courts of the federal system, and the only federal courts in which attorneys question witnesses, and juries decide cases. In non-jury, or "bench" trial, 1 judge decides the case. District Courts include bankruptcy courts. District court judges appoint "magistrate judges" to 8-year terms to assist with workload.
Specialized Federal Courts	These federal courts possess specialized jurisdiction. They include the Tax Court, Court of International Trade (reviews rulings and appraisals made by customs officials on imported goods), Court of Federal Claims (rules on damage claims brought against the federal government for negligence, unlawful taking of private property, breaches of contracts), Court of Veterans' Appeals (reviews decisions on benefits by Veterans' Administration), and Court of Military Appeals (reviews decisions of military courts).

The table above depicts the ways in which the federal courts are organized and the jurisdiction that each court possesses. "Jurisdiction" includes the persons and the types of disputes subject to a particular court's authority.

Table A.1 *Continued*

Court	Jurisdiction
United States Supreme Court	(1) *Original and exclusive:* (Supreme Court first and only Court to hear case) disputes between 2 or more states. (2) *Original, but not exclusive:* (usually delegated to District Courts) disputes to which ambassador or consul from foreign country is party; disputes between United States and a state, or between a state and citizens of another state or aliens. (3) *Appellate:* appeals from Courts of Appeals in civil and criminal cases; appeals from special 3-judge district courts; appeals from state courts of last resort, (conflicts between state and federal law), appeals from Court of Military Appeals.
United States Courts of Appeals	Civil and criminal appeals from final decisions of district courts. Appeals from interlocutory orders of district courts (e.g., non-final order admitting or rejecting certain potential evidence). Appeals from Tax Court. Only the Court of Appeals for the Federal Circuit hears appeals from the Court of International Trade, Court of Federal Claims, and Court of Veterans' Appeals.
United States District Courts	Original jurisdiction of all civil cases arising under Constitution, federal statutes, and treaties; admiralty or maritime cases; civil suits against foreign countries; civil suits between citizens of different states ("diversity of citizenship" suits) in which amount in controversy exceeds $50,000; civil suits in which United States is plaintiff or defendant. Original jurisdiction of all criminal offenses against federal law. Bankruptcy courts hear individual and corporate bankruptcy cases. Magistrate judges conduct pretrial proceedings in civil and criminal cases, and decide misdemeanor criminal cases.
Specialized Federal Courts	*See previous page.*

Sources: (1) Kamla J. King & Judith Springberg. *D.N.A.'s Directory of State and Federal Courts, Judges, and Clerks, 1994–95* (Washington, D.C.: Bureau of National Affairs, 1994) p. 1. (2) 28 U.S.C.A. 1–500; 1251–1259; 1291–1295; 1330–1367. (3) 18 U.S.C.A. 3231.

Table A.2. A Composite State-Court System

Court	Organization/Procedure	Jurisdiction
Court of Last Resort: Usually called Supreme Court (42 states)	Five-nine judges (or justices) who sit *en banc*, usually in state capital. Judges may be appointed by governor, elected, or a combination of the two. Most common method is combination of gubernatorial appointment, followed by "retention election" after 1–3 year probationary term. Most common method of removal is impeachment. Decide cases on written briefs and oral argument.	Usually, civil and criminal jurisdiction (48 states) of state law matters. Hear appeals from intermediate *appellate* courts where they exist. In states without intermediate *appellate* courts, court of last resort hears civil and criminal appeals from trial court of general jurisdiction on a mandatory basis. Presence of intermediate *appellate* court gives court of last resort some discretion over which cases to hear.
Intermediate Appellate Court: Usually called Court of Appeals. Thirty-five states have 1 intermediate appellate court; four states have 2 intermediate *appellate* courts.	Range in size from 3 judges (Alaska) to 88 judges (Texas). Most common methods of selection are election (17 states) and combination of appointment/election (13 states). Most common method of removal is impeachment (lower house of legislature impeaches, upper house tries and removes) (30 states). Decide cases on written briefs and oral argument.	Appeals from trial court of general jurisdiction in civil and criminal matters in which trial court has made a final decision. May also hear interlocutory appeals from non-final decisions of trial court. Usually hear appeals of final decisions on a mandatory basis. May also have discretionary jurisdiction on some subjects. Tennessee and Alabama have separate courts for criminal and civil appeals, respectively.
Trial Courts of General Jurisdiction: Different states use different names for this court. May be called Circuit Court, Supreme Court, District Court, County Court, Chancery Court, Court of Common Pleas, or even Supreme Court, (New York State only).	Range in size from 17-member Wyoming District Court to 820-member Illinois Circuit Court. Judges may be elected, appointed, or appointed to probationary term, followed by "retention election". Election is the most commonly used method (18 states). Usually divided into "districts" or "circuits" of 1 or more counties. These are trial courts that hear major civil and criminal cases; usually 1 judge hears case. Typically removable by impeachment.	Felony criminal cases; criminal appeals from trial court of limited jurisdiction. Civil cases without a maximum amount in controversy, but there may be a minimum amount necessary for this court to have jurisdiction. Civil appeals from trial court of limited jurisdiction. This is the court in which civil and criminal jury trials occur.
Trial Courts of Limited Jurisdiction: Constitute 90% of America's courts, and handle the bulk of litigation in this country. Have different names in different states. May be called Justice of the Peace Court, Magistrate's Court, Municipal Court, City Court, Juvenile Court, Family Court, Probate Court, or Metropolitan Court.	Election and appointment followed by "retention election" after probationary term are most commonly used means of selection. Most commonly used method of removal is impeachment. Trials are rare; less formal "hearings" are the norm. A state may have several of these courts, each with its own limited jurisdiction.	Criminal infractions and misdemeanors; fines usually $1,000 or less, and jail terms less than 1 year. Civil disputes may have maximum dollar amount. Often, these courts are limited to hearing traffic, family, or juvenile matters. May conduct pretrial proceedings in felony criminal cases (e.g., preliminary hearings; arraignments).

The names and the jurisdiction assigned to state courts vary considerably from state to state. Therefore, it is necessary to illustrate state-court organization and jurisdiction by means of a composite court system, which the table above presents. Every state contains at least one appellate court, trial court of general jurisdiction, and trial court of limited jurisdiction.

Sources: Council of State Governments. *The Book of the States, 1996–97* (Lexington, KY: Council of State Governments, 1996), pp. 127–130; 133–143. David B. Rottman et. al. *State Court Organization, 1993* (Washington, D.C.: Bureau of Justice Statistics, 1995), p. 5.

APPENDIX B

The Federal Appellate Circuits

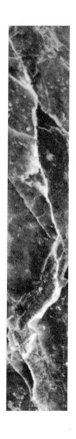

The **First Circuit** includes Maine, Massachusetts, New Hampshire, Rhode Island, and Puerto Rico. It sits at Boston, San Juan, and at other locations as ordered by the court.

The **Second Circuit** includes Connecticut, New York, and Vermont. It sits at New York City and at other locations as ordered by the court.

The **Third Circuit** includes Delaware, New Jersey, Pennsylvania, and the Virgin Islands. It sits at Philadelphia, Charlotte Amalie in the Virgin Islands, and at other locations as ordered by the court.

The **Fourth Circuit** includes Maryland, North Carolina, South Carolina, Virginia, and West Virginia. It sits at Baltimore, Richmond, and at other locations as ordered by the court.

The **Fifth Circuit** includes Louisiana, Mississippi, Texas, and the Panama Canal Zone. It sits at New Orleans, and at other locations as ordered by the court.

The **Sixth Circuit** includes Kentucky, Michigan, Ohio, and Tennessee. It sits at Cincinnati, and at other locations as ordered by the court.

The **Seventh Circuit** includes Illinois, Indiana, and Wisconsin. It sits at Chicago and at other locations as ordered by the court.

The **Eighth Circuit** includes Arkansas, Iowa, Minnesota, Missouri, Nebraska, North Dakota, and South Dakota. It sits at St. Paul, St. Louis, and at other locations as ordered by the court.

The **Ninth Circuit** includes Alaska, California, Guam, Hawaii, Idaho, Montana, the Northern Mariana Islands, Nevada, Oregon, and Washington. It sits at Juneau, San Francisco, Pasadena, Honolulu, Portland, Seattle, and at other locations as ordered by the court.

The **Tenth Circuit** includes Colorado, Kansas, New Mexico, Oklahoma, Utah, and Wyoming. It sits at Denver, Wichita, Oklahoma City, and at other locations as ordered by the court.

The **Eleventh Circuit** includes Alabama, Florida, and Georgia. It sits at Montgomery, Jacksonville, Atlanta, and at other locations as ordered by the court.

The **District of Columbia Circuit** includes the District of Columbia. It sits at Washington, D.C.

The **Federal Circuit** includes all federal judicial districts. It sits at Washington, D.C.

Source: *The American Bench: Judges of the Nation*, sixth edition (Sacramento: Forster-Long, 1991–1992), pp. 1–4.

APPENDIX C

Finding Legal Sources

This appendix identifies the various legal sources that this book cites and explains how to find them. It does not explain how to use them because that is a book-length subject in itself. Consult a reference librarian at your college library; a city, county, or state law library; or a law school library for instruction in using a specific source. Read William P. Statsky, *Legal Research and Writing: Some Starting Points,* fourth edition (Minneapolis/St. Paul: West, 1993) for a clear and concise explanation of how to conduct research using multiple legal sources.

In the past, the sources discussed below were available only in bound form in libraries. They still are available in bound form in libraries, but they are now also available through on-line legal-research services, which operate by a hookup between your computer and another computer, often through a telephone line. The best known of those services are WESTLAW, a product of West Publishing Company, and LEXIS, a product of the Mead Data Company. Both services enable you to find and read cases, statutes, and other legal materials without traveling to a law library. They are available to anyone who is interested in using them and willing to pay for them. Law school libraries typically offer both services, and your college library may offer one of them. Do not neglect the bound volumes, though; you can research the law just as effectively in its bound form as in its electronic form. Using the bound materials is slower, but it usually is cheaper, too.

UNITED STATES SUPREME COURT DECISIONS

Supreme Court opinions appear in the *United States Reports,* published by the Government Printing Office, and in two privately published volumes, the *United States Supreme Court Reports, Lawyers' Edition,* and the *Supreme Court Reporter.* The latter two volumes print exactly the same opinion as appears in the *U.S. Reports,* so feel free to use whichever of the three volumes is available. Every Supreme Court decision contains a three-part citation that indicates where the decision appears in each volume. For example, *United States v. Eichman,* 496 U.S. 310, 110 L.Ed.2d 287, 110 S.Ct. 2404 (1990) appears in volume 496 of the *U.S. Reports,* beginning on page 310; in volume 110 of the *Lawyers' Edition,* second series, beginning on page 287; and in volume 110 of the *Supreme Court Reporter,* beginning on page 2404. New cases appear in the *Lawyers' Edition* and the *Supreme Court Reporter* more quickly than in the *U.S. Reports,* so do not give up if you cannot find a one or two-year-old decision in the *U.S. Reports.* College libraries usually contain the *U.S. Reports;* city, county, or state law libraries may have all three publications; law school libraries usually have all three. The most recent opinions appear in *United States Law Week,* a loose-leaf volume that is published each week. For example, *Vacco v. Quill* appeared in print the week after the Court's decision, at 65 L.W. 4669. *United States Law Week* is available in all law libraries, and in many college libraries.

UNITED STATES COURTS OF APPEALS DECISIONS

United States Courts of Appeals decisions appear in the *Federal Reporter.* The citation for a Court of Appeals decision contains a *Federal Reporter* volume number followed by either "F.," F.2d," or "F.3d" and then a page number. That means, for example, that *United States v. Sheek,* 990 F.2d 150 (4th Cir. 1993), appears in volume 990 of the *Federal Reporter,* second series, beginning at page 150. The citation also indicates that the United States Court of Appeals for the Fourth Circuit decided the case in 1993. The volume and series numbers ("F." indicates first series) appear on the spine of each *Federal Reporter,* making it easy to find the correct one. Many college libraries and all law libraries—whether city, county, state, or law-school based—contain the *Federal Reporter.*

UNITED STATES DISTRICT COURT OPINIONS

District Court opinions appear in the *Federal Supplement.* The citation for a District Court decision contains a *Federal Supplement* volume number followed by "F. Supp." followed by a page number. That means, for example, that *Crockett v. Reagan,* 558 F. Supp. 893 (D.D.C. 1982), appears in volume 558 of the *Federal Supplement,* beginning at page 893. The citation also indicates that the United States District Court for the District of Columbia decided the case in 1982. Many college libraries and all law libraries contain the *Federal Supplement.*

STATE COURT DECISIONS

Decisions of state appellate courts may appear in both an official state reporter and a regional reporter, or if a state does not publish an official reporter, in a regional reporter only. For example, New Hampshire Supreme Court opinions appear in an official reporter, the *New Hampshire Reports*, and in a regional reporter, the *Atlantic Reporter*. Therefore, *New Hampshire Donuts, Inc. v. Skipitaris*, 129 N.H. 774, 533 A.2d 351 (1987), has **parallel citations;** it appears in volume 129 of the *New Hampshire Reports*, beginning on page 774, and in volume 533 of the *Atlantic Reporter*, beginning on page 351. Indiana, however, does not publish an official state reporter, so decisions of the Indiana Court of Appeals and the Indiana Supreme Court appear only in the *Northeastern Reporter*. Therefore, the citation for *Isom v. Isom*, 538 N.E.2d 261 (Ind. App. 1989) means that the case, which the Indiana Court of Appeals decided in 1989, appears in volume 538 of the *Northeastern Reporter*, second series, beginning on page 261.

California appellate court decisions appear in three separate reporters, two of which contain only California cases and one of which is a regional reporter. Therefore, the citation for *Tarasoff v. Regents of University of California*, 17 Cal.3d 425, 131 Cal. Rptr. 14, 551 P.2d 334 (1976), means that the case appears in volume 17 of the California Reports, beginning on page 425; volume 131 of the *California Reporter*, beginning on page 14; and volume 551 of the regional *Pacific Reporter*, beginning on page 334. College libraries sometimes contain the official reporters of the states in which they are located. State law libraries usually have all seven regional reporters, and law school libraries always do.

STATUTES

Federal statutes appear in the *United States Code*, published by the Government Printing Office, and in two privately published volumes, the *United States Code Annotated* and the *United States Code Service*. Statutes retain the same title and section numbers in each volume, therefore the citation for the Flag Protection Act of 1989 is 18 U.S.C. section 700, 18 U.S.C.A. section 700, or 18 U.S.C.S. section 700, depending on which volume one uses to research that statute. The Flag Protection Act appears in the volume of the U.S.C., U.S.C.A., or

U.S.C.S. that contains Title 18 and section (designated by the symbol {) 700 of the United States Code. College libraries often contain the *United States Code*, but it is usually necessary to visit a law library to find the *United States Code Annotated* or the *United States Code Service;* that may be wise because those two volumes contain helpful notes and commentaries about the statutes.

State statutes appear in bound volumes containing the respective state codes. For example, the Texas law against flag desecration at issue in *Texas v. Johnson* appeared at section 42.09(a)(3) of the *Texas Penal Code Annotated* before the Supreme Court invalidated it. College libraries, and local law libraries outside of Texas are unlikely to contain the *Texas Penal Code Annotated,* but state law libraries everywhere probably have it, and law school libraries certainly have it.

LEGISLATIVE HISTORY MATERIALS

Legislative history materials, including committee reports, are available in the *U.S. Code Congressional and Administrative News,* in the volumes with the words "Legislative History" printed on their spines. If you know the title (or at least the subject) and the year of a statute, you can locate legislative history materials pertaining to it by searching the index of the "Legislative History" volume for that year. For example, the legislative history for the National Traffic and Motor Vehicle Safety Act of 1966, including committee reports and agency comments, appears in volume 2 of the *U.S. Code Congressional and Administrative News* for 1966, beginning at page 2709. Many college libraries and many local law libraries contain the *U.S. Code Congressional and Administrative News;* state law libraries and law school libraries are sure to have it.

UNITED STATES CONSTITUTION

The Constitution often appears at the end of constitutional law textbooks that undergraduates and law students use. It also appears in the first five volumes of the *United States Code Annotated* and in the first ten volumes of the *United States Code Service,* complete with commentaries and lists of related cases and scholarly writings.

ADMINISTRATIVE RULES

Administrative rules appear in the *Federal Register,* which is available at some college libraries, and most, if not all, law libraries. Issues that are more than six months to a year old may only be available on microfiche or microfilm, so it is wise to consult a reference librarian for assistance. It is necessary to know the volume and page numbers or the relevant volume number and the date of a *Federal Register* entry in order to find it without a laborious search.

EXECUTIVE ORDERS

Like administrative rules, executive orders appear in the *Federal Register* and are accessible if the researcher knows the volume and page numbers at which the order appears or knows the relevant volume number and the date of the order. Executive orders also appear in the *Public Papers of the Presidents,* which are commonly available in college libraries, state law libraries, and law school libraries. For example, Executive Order 12,866, entitled "Regulatory Planning and Review," appears in *Public Papers Of The President—William J. Clinton* for 1993, beginning at page 1633. It is easily accessible if the researcher knows its number or subject matter and the year President Clinton issued it, because each volume of the Clinton Papers contains a list of executive orders issued during the year that volume covers. Finally, executive orders appear in volumes of the *U.S. Code Congressional and Administrative News* that have the words "Executive Orders" printed on their spines. Each volume contains the orders issued during a particular year.

LAW REVIEW COMMENTARIES

"Law reviews," or "law journals," as they are sometimes called, are periodicals, usually published by law schools, that contain scholarly writings on a wide variety of legal subjects. Law professors, judges, and practicing lawyers write "articles" that appear in the front of law reviews, and law students write "notes" or "comments" that appear in the back, with the student author's name printed at the end of the note or comment. Some law reviews are available in local law libraries, more are usually available in state law libraries, and all or almost all of them are available in law school libraries. An example of a law review article is Judge Patricia Wald's piece, "Thoughts On Decisionmaking," cited in Chapter One, which appears in volume 81 of the *West Virginia Law Review*, beginning on page 11.

BOOKS AND TREATISES

Law-related books intended for a general audience, such as Benjamin Cardozo's *The Nature of the Judicial Process*, Arthur Hogue's *Origins of the Common Law*, and F. T. Plucknett's *A Concise History of the Common Law*, are available in many college libraries and most, if not all, law school libraries. **Treatises** are books devoted to technical discussions of particular fields of law; law professors write them for the use of lawyers and law students. There are one-volume treatises such as Aman Jr. and Mayton, *Administrative Law*, and multivolume treatises such as *Moore's Federal Practice* and *Anderson's The American Law of Zoning*. Treatises are available in law libraries, especially in law school libraries.

BRITISH CASE REPORTS

It is sometimes helpful to consult British case reports, especially to read old cases that influenced the development of American common law. The *English Reports* and *Meeson's and Welsby's Reports* are useful for that purpose. For example, *Longmeid v. Holliday*, 155 Eng. Rep. 752 (1851), cited in Chapter Four, appears in volume 155 of the *English Reports*, beginning on page 752. *Winterbottom v. Wright*, 10 Meeson & Welsby 109 (1842), also cited in Chapter Four, appears in volume 10 of *Meeson's and Welsby's Reports*, beginning on page 109. Some college libraries contain at least partial sets of these volumes and most law school libraries do too, on microfiche or microfilm if not in bound form. Complete sets are difficult to find, so consult a reference librarian before using these reports in order to determine what is available.

INDEX

Abortion, constitutional right to, 4
  prohibition of undue burdens
    on, 4
  use of public funds for, 47
Abraham, Henry, 66n
Adams, Brock, 146, 168
Adaptability, law's need for, 98–99,
  123
Administrative fine, 139
Administrative Law Judge (ALJ),
  139–140
Administrative Procedure Act
  (APA), 134, 140–141, 150
Administrative regulation, 19–20,
  153, 167–168
Advisory opinions
  by administrative agencies, 139
  by state supreme courts, 169n
Age Discrimination in Employment
  Act (ADEA), 117n
*Akron v. Akron Center for Reproductive
  Health,* 17
Aleinikoff, T. Alexander, 82n
Aman, Alfred, 131n, 132n, 140n
Ambiguity, statutory, 30, 96
*American Power and Light Company v.
  Securities and Exchange Com-
  mission,* 142n
Arbitrary or capricious test, 145–
  149
Arbitrator, 140n
Arnett v. Kennedy, 153n
Articles of Confederation, 61
Asbestos, withdrawal of rules on
  production and use of, 138
Assumption of the risk, 106, 107
Ayres, B. Drummond, 106n

Baer, Judith, 71n
Baker v. Carr, 62
Baker v. Jacobs, 31–32, 37
Balancing (see constitutional
  interpretation-prudential
  method)
Bank of the United States, 76–77
Barr, Stephen, 130n
Bassham, Gregory, 71n, 72n, 74n
Befort, Stephen, 116n, 118n
Bell v. Burson, 153n
Benoir v. Ethan Allen, Inc., 120–122
Benzene case (see Industrial Union
  Department, *AFL-CIO v.
  American Petroleum Institute*)
Berger, Raoul, 71n
Berman, Harold, 101n
Bernal, Marie-Louise, 101n
Bill of Rights, 65, 165
Binding and mandatory arbitration,
  140n
Black, Hugo, 14, 15n, 72–73,
  164
Blackmun, Harry, 5, 45, 86, 142–
  143
Block grants, 150n
Board of Education v. Allen, 79
Bob Jones University v. United States,
  38–40, 52, 139n
Bobbitt, Philip, 68n, 69n
Bonfield, Arthur, 131n
Bork, Robert, 69, 72, 165
Bowers, James, 131n
Bowers v Hardwick, 17, 85
Brennan, William, 4, 8, 70, 82–83,
  92, 150–151, 165
Brigham v. State, 170n

Brown v. Board of Education, 71–72
Brown v. Duchesne, 39
*Browner v. Holmes Transportation,
    Inc.,* 117
Bruno, Philippe, 102n
Bureau of Commercial Fisheries,
    149
Burger, Warren, 39, 45, 79–80, 83
*Burlington Truck Lines, Inc. v. United
    States,* 147n, 148n
Bush, George, 69
Byrne v. Boadle, 108n

Calabresi, Guido, 28n
Canons of statutory construc-
    tion, (see statutory
    construction)
Cannon, Bradley, 69n
Cardozo, Benjamin, 87, 96, 98
Carter, Lief, 11n, 12, 18n, 31n, 50,
    87
Cases or controversies, requirement
    of (see Constitution of the
    United States)
Charitable organizations, legal
    definition of, 39
Child custody, modification of, 7
Chisholm v. Georgia, 78n
Civil law systems, 101
Civil liberties, 60, 65
Civil Rights Restoration Act, 51–52
Claremont School District v. Governor,
    67
Clinton, Robert Lowery, 77n
Clinton, William, 130, 138, 150n
Coffin, Frank, 18, 19n, 164n
Colegrove v. Green, 62n
Collective bargaining agreements,
    118
Common-law decision making
    generally, 96–97, 123, 166,167
    in relationship to statutory and

    constitutional provi-
        sions, 96
    reasoning process, 97–99
    history of, 99–100
    principles of, 100–101
    in tort law, 109–116
    in employment law, 116–123
Commonwealth v. Tilley, 37, 40, 52
Compensatory damages, 105n
Conclusions of law, 141
Concurring opinion, 35
Conference committees, 41–42
Congressional investigative power,
    62
Congressional oversight (of rule
    making), 136
Consent settlement, 139
Constitution of the United States
    preamble, 63
    art. I, section 8, cl. 3 (commerce
        clause), 76
    art. I, section 8, cl. 18 (necessary
        and proper clause), 76
    art. II, section 1, cl. 4 (presiden-
        tial eligibility clause), 74
    art. II, section 2, cl. 1 (pardon
        power), 61
    art. II, section 3, (duty to faith-
        fully execute laws), 137
    art. III, section 2, cl. 1 (cases or
        controversies), 169n
    supremacy clause, 75–76
    first amendment, 4, 8, 14, 21, 73,
        75, 163
    third amendment, 8
    fourth amendment, 8, 10, 69,
        78
    fifth amendment, 8, 150, 152
    ninth amendment, 8, 85
    tenth amendment, 63
    eleventh amendment, 78n
    thirteenth amendment, 78n
    fourteenth amendment

equal protection clause of, 8,
163–164
due process clause of, 150n
liberty, protection of, 153
property, protection of, 152–
153
sixteenth amendment, 78n
twenty-sixth amendment, 78n
Constitutional interpretation
generally, 60, 165–166
context, importance of, 74
double standard, development of,
66
equal protection analysis, 9
incorporation of Bill of Rights,
67
methods of,
generally, 68
historical, 68–73
textual, 73–75
structural, 75–77
doctrinal, 77–80
prudential, 80–83
ethical, 83–86, 165
Continental Congress, 61
Contracts, 96, 123
Contributory negligence, 106
Cooper, Joseph, 138n
Corpus Juris Civilis, 101
Corwin, Edward, 71
County of Allegheny v. A.C.L.U., 4
Court functions
dispute resolution, 6
norm enforcement, 6
Crockett v. Reagan, 5n
Cruel and unusual punishment,
prohibition of 67
*Cruzan v. Director, Missouri Dep't. of
Health*, 5–6

Danner, Richard, 101n
Davis, Kenneth Culp, 131n

Debt, writ of, 100
Deductive reasoning, (see legal
reasoning)
Delegation of legislative power,
132, 142–143, 145, 167
Devlin v. Smith, 112
Dickerson, F. Reed, 29, 36, 52, 96n
Doctrinal method, (see constitu-
tional interpretation)
Dorf, Michael, 85
Double standard, (see constitu-
tional interpretation)
Douglas, William, 8, 14–15, 83
Dred Scott v. Sandford, 78n
Due process, 100, 150–151, 153
Dunne, Gerald, 15n
Duty of care
generally, 104
breach of, 104

Eisenberg, Melvin, 112n
Eisenstadt v. Baird, 8–9, 13, 17n, 47
Ejusdem generis, 48
Ely, John Hart, 77n
Employment-at-will
generally, 116
implied contract exception to,
116–123
public policy exception to, 117
*Englewood Independent School District
v. Kirby*, 170n
Environmental Protection Agency
(EPA), 138
Equal protection clause, (see Con-
stitution of the United
States)
Establishment of religion, 14, 78,
80
Ethical method, (see constitutional
interpretation)
Exclusionary rule, 78, 82
good faith exception to, 81

Executive order (EO)
  generally, 137
  EO 12, 291, 137
  EO 12, 498, 138
  EO 12, 866, 138
Expressio unius est, exclusio
      alterius, (see statutory
      construction)

Fact freedom, 11–12, 16, 99, 163
Farnsworth, E. Allen, 96n
Federal Kidnapping Act, 53, 163,
      165
Federalism, 60, 62–64
  nationalist view of, 63
  states' rights view of, 63
*Federal Power Commission v. Hope
      Natural Gas Company*, 142n
Federal Register, 134–136
Fellow-servant rule, 106–107
Fifth Amendment, (see Constitu-
      tion of the United States)
Final rule, 135
Findings of fact, 141
Finkelman, Paul, 106n
First Amendment, (see Constitution
      of the United States)
Fisher, Louis, 61n, 137n
Flag desecration, constitutionality
      of, 4, 60
Flag Protection Act, 60
Floor debates, (see statutory con-
      struction)
Floor managers, legislative, 42
Food and Drug Administration,
      130, 148–149
Food, Drug and Cosmetic Act, 130,
      149
Foote v. Simmonds Precision Products,
      120–122
Fourth Amendment, (see Constitu-
      tion of the United States)

Fox v. Snow, 18n
Frankfurter, Felix, 33
Freedom of speech, 20
Friedman, Lawrence, 103n, 106n,
      107n

Gans, Alfred, 105n
*Garcia v. San Antonio Metropolitan
      Transit Authority*, 64
Garrard, William, 6n
Garvey, John, 82n
General Accounting Office (GAO),
      136
Goldberg v. Kelley, 150–153, 168
Goldman, Ronald, 105n
Goldwater v. Carter, 5n, 169n
Gray, Horace, 47
*Green v. Bock Laundry Machine Com-
      pany*, 35
Greiner, William, 101n
Griswold v. Connecticut, 7, 9, 13, 17n,
      47, 84–85, 163
Grove City College v. Bell, 51–52
Gun Free School Zones Act, 64

Hall, Kermit, 106n
Hamilton, Martha, 130n
Hammer, 136
*Hampton and Company v. United
      States*, 142n
Hanly v. Mitchell, 149n
Harlan, John Marshall, II., 75
Harrington, Christine, 131n, 139n
Heirs, 103
Historical method, (see constitu-
      tional interpretation)
Hogue, Arthur, 99n, 100n
Holmes, Oliver Wendell Jr., 33
Homosexuals, privacy rights of,
      86
Hurst, James Willard, 38n

Immediate purchaser, 109
Immigration and Naturalization Service v. Chadha, 136
Indian Gaming Regulation Act, 64n
Indiana Court of Appeals, 6–7
Inductive reasoning, (see legal reasoning)
Industrial Union Department, AFL-CIO v. American Petroleum Institute (benzene case), 144–145, 167
Industry guides, agency publication of, 139
Inherently dangerous products, 109
Initial decision, 140
Intelligible principle, 142
Internal Revenue Service, 38–39
Internal Revenue Code
section 170, 39
section 501(c)(3), 39–40
International Union, U.A.W. v. Johnson Controls, Inc., 5
Interpretivism, (see constitutional interpretation-historical method)
Isom v. Isom, 7

Jackson, Robert, 42, 72
Jehovah's Witnesses, 72
Jensen, Merrill, 61n, 63n, 65n
Johnson, William, 6n
Joint tenancy, common law presumption of, 103
Jones v. Keough, 117
Judicial discretion, (see legal reasoning)
Judicial review, 60
of administrative agency actions, 141, 153, 167

Kennedy, Anthony, 4, 17, 18n
Kerwin, Cornelius, 132n, 138n
Krause, Charles, 105n, 106n
Konigsberg v. State Bar, 74–75

LaRose v. Agway, 119–120, 122
Last clear chance doctrine, 108
Legal reasoning
defined, 2
generally, 19–20
components,
reasoning by analogy, 2, 8–9, 77, 163
linguistic analysis, 2, 28, 163–164
of constitutional provisions, 60
judicial discretion, 3, 19–20, 164
interaction between components, 3
explained, 7–19
deductive reasoning, as part of, 8, 98, 163
inductive reasoning, as part of, 13, 163
relationship to stare decisis, 9, 12–13
relationship to fact freedom, 11–12, 16
summarized, 19–20, 163–164
contexts of, (see statutory construction, constitutional interpretation, common-law decision making, administrative regulation)
Legislative history, (see statutory construction)
Legislative supremacy, doctrine of, 29
Legislative veto, 136

Lemon test, 79–80
Lemon v. Kurtzman, 78–79
Levi, Edward, 9n
Lewis, Drew, 146
Liability, 105
Liberty, protection of, (see Constitution of the United States)
License, agency revocation of, 139
Litigiousness in America, roots of, 123
Llewellyn, Karl, 10n, 49
Lochner v. New York
  generally, 84–85, 116n
  evaluation of, 88
  as example of Puritan legal ethic, 104n
Longmeid v. Holliday, 110–111
Loop v. Litchfield, 111
Losee v. Clute, 111

MacCormick, D. Neil, 30, 34
MacPherson v. Buick Motor Company, 113–115
Madison, James, 65
Madole, Juanita, 106n
Maher v. Roe, 47–48, 52
Mapp v. Ohio, 78, 85n
Markup session, 41
Marshall, John, 76
Massachusetts Supreme Judicial Court, 38
Mathews v. Eldridge, 152–153, 168
Mayton, William, 131n, 132n, 140n
McCollum v. Board of Education, 14–16, 18, 163, 168
McCulloch v. Maryland, 76–77
Meaning of the words, (see constitutional interpretation-textual method)
Mediator, function of, 140n

Meese, Edwin, 68, 71–72
Merit Systems Protection Board, 140n
Miranda v. Arizona, 67, 85n
Missouri v. Jenkins, 169n
Mistretta v. United States, 141–143, 167
Moment of silence, constitutionality of, 80
Motor Vehicle Manufacturers' Association v. State Farm Mutual Insurance Company, 146
Motor Vehicle Safety Standard 208, 146–148, 154, 168
Mullaney v. Goss Company, 116–120
Murder, effect of premeditation on, 7

Necessity, principle of, 97–98
Negligence
  generally, 104, 107
  proof of, 104n–105n
New Hampshire Donuts, Inc. v. Skipitaris, 6
New Hampshire Supreme Court, 6–7
New York Times Co. v. United States, 72
Ninth Amendment, (see Constitution of the United States)
Nix v. Hedden, 46–47, 52
Nixon, Richard, 73, 82
Noninterpretivism, (see constitutional interpretation-ethical method)
North Haven Board of Education v. Bell, 44–45, 51–52
Noscitur a sociis, (see statutory construction)
Notice of final rule making, 135
Notice of proposed rule making, 134

Nuclear Regulatory Commission, 139

O'Brien, David, 69n
O'Connor, Sandra Day, 4, 17, 18n
Occupational Safety and Health Act
  generally, 144
  construction of, 144–145, 167
Office of Management and Budget
  (OMB), 134, 137–138
Office of Personnel Management,
  140n
Olmstead v. United States, 86n
Oregon v. Mitchell, 78
Original intent, 68–73
Originalists, 68–73, 165
Owens v. Owens, 32

*Pacific Legal Foundation v. Department
  of Transportation,* 154–157,
  168
Passive restraints, 146
Payne v. Rozendaal, 117
Peltason, Jack, 63n
Pentagon Papers, 72
*Personnel Administrator of Massachu-
  setts v. Feeney,* 89–93, 163,
  166
Personnel policy manual, legal sig-
  nificance of, 119–122
Perry, Barbara, 66n
Pfeffer, Leo, 15n
Pildes, Richard, 138n
Pierce, Richard Jr., 131n
Plain-meaning rule, (see statutory
  construction)
*Planned Parenthood of Southeastern
  Pennsylvania v. Casey,* 4,
  17–18
Ploof v. Putnam, 97–98
Plucknett, Theodore, 100n

Pollock v. Farmers' Loan & Trust Co.,
  78n
Popkin, William, 42n
Pound, Roscoe, 102n
Powell, Lewis, 45, 48, 152
Power of the purse, 136
Preamble
  to Constitution, (see Constitution
    of the United States)
  to administrative rule, (see rule
    making, process of; see
    also statement of basis and
    purpose)
Precedent, role of, (see common-
  law decision making)
Predictability, law's need for, 98–
  99, 123
Preferred freedoms, 66
Preponderance of the evidence,
  requirement of, 140
Presentment, 137
Presidential oversight (of rule mak-
  ing), 137
Presumptions
  in statutory construction (see
    statutory construction)
  in common law of land, 103
Principles, (see common-law deci-
  sion making)
Privacy, right of, 69, 85
Privity of contract, 109, 116
Products liability, 114
Program evaluation, 136
Progressive movement, 28
Promissory estoppel, 121n
Property, protection of (see Con-
  stitution of the United
  States)
Prudential method (see constitu-
  tional interpretation)
Public Citizen, 154
Punitive damages, 105n
Puritans, legal ethic of, 104, 123

Rakove, Jack, 70n
Reagan, Ronald, 34, 137–138, 146
Reasoned analysis, requirement of, 145
Reasoning by analogy, (see legal reasoning)
Recommended decision, 140
Record (of a rule making), 135
Regulatory impact analysis, 137
Rehnquist, William, 5, 17n, 45, 64, 80
Replevin, writ of, 100
Res ipsa loquitur, 108
Restrictive covenant, 6n
Riggs v. Palmer, 31–32, 37, 51, 96
Right to die, 5
Roe v. Wade, 4, 16, 17n, 18, 47, 69, 84–85
  trimester analysis as part of, 16–17
Roosevelt Elementary School District No. 66 v. Bishop, 170n
Rule adjudication
  generally, 132, 139
  informal, meaning of, 139
    process of, 139–140
  formal, meaning of, 140
    notification requirements of, 140
    process of, 141
Rule enforcement, 131
Rule making (administrative)
  meaning of, 131–132
  functions of, 132–133
  process of, 133–136
  informal, 135, 146
  formal, 135
Rules, (see common-law decision making)
Ryegate v. Wardsboro, 31

Satter, Robert, 9n, 10, 19
Scalia, Antonin
  views on statutory construction generally, 34–36
  views on use of legislative history to construe statutes, 42
Schuck, Peter, 131n
Schultz, David, 35n
Schwartz, Bernard, 131n
Schwartz, John, 130n
Sentencing guidelines, 141–142
Sentencing ranges, 143
Sentencing Reform Act
  generally, 141
  construction of, 142–143
Separation of church and state, 4, 14
Separation of powers, 60–61
Seminole Tribe of Florida v. Florida, 64n–65n
Shapiro, Martin, 101n
Shapiro, Sidney, 131n
Sherbert v. Verner, 151n
Sherman v. Rutland Hospital, Inc., 118–119, 121–122
Simpson, Nicole Brown, 105n
Simpson, O.J., 105n
Sixteenth Amendment, (see Constitution of the United States)
Slochower v. Board of Education, 151n
Smith, Christopher, 35n, 69n
Social Security Act, 152
Souter, David, 4, 17, 18n
South Dakota v. Dole, 64
Speiser, Stuart, 105n, 106n
Speiser v. Randall, 151n
Stare decisis
  generally, 9, 20, 99
  reasons for prominence of, 10–11
  relationship to fact freedom, 12–13

State courts, common-law decision making by, 97
State v. Kirchoff, 67
State v. Sullivan, 7
Statement of basis and purpose, 149 (see also rule making, process of)
States' rights theory, (see federalism)
Statler v. Ray Manufacturing Company, 113
Statutes
    generally, 96, 131
    increased importance of, 28
Statutes in pari materia, (see statutory construction)
Statutory construction
    generally, 28, 50–53, 164–165
    cognitive component of, 29
    creative component, necessity for, 29
    relationship to doctrine of legislative supremacy, 29
    limitations on, 29–30
    examples of, 31–32
    techniques of
        plain-meaning rule, 32–33
        context, 36–37
        statutory purpose, 35, 37–40
        legislative history, 35, 40–46
        post-enactment legislative action, 43
        post-enactment legislative inaction, 43–44
        presumptions, 46–48
        canons
            generally, 48
            ejusdem generis, 48
            expressio unius est, exclusio alterius, 48
            noscitur a sociis, 49
            statutes in pari materia, 49
            critiques of, 49–50

Statutory entitlement, 150–153
Stevens, John Paul, 80, 144–145
Strict liability, 115n
Structural method, (see constitutional interpretation)
Substantial evidence in the record, requirement of, 141, 145
Summers, Robert, 30, 34
Sunset, statutory provisions for, 136
Sunstein, Cass, 37n, 138n
Supermajority, 70
Supremacy clause, (see Constitution of the United States)
Supremacy of law, principle of, 100
Survival action, 105n
Symbolic expression, 73

Tarasoff v. Regents of the University of California, 122n, 124–127, 166–167
Taylor v. National Life Insurance Company, 122, 123n
Tenancy in common, 103
Tennessee Small School Systems v. McWherter, 170n
Texas v. Johnson, 67
Textual method, (see constitutional interpretation)
Thirteenth amendment, (see Constitution of the United States)
Thomas, Clarence, 69, 165
Thomas v. Winchester, 110–111, 113, 115
Tinker v. Des Moines Independent Community School District, 21–25, 73, 163–164
Title VII, Civil Rights Act of 1964, 5, 117n

Title IX, Education Amendments of 1972, 44–45, 51–52
Torgesen v. Schultz, 112–113
Torts
  generally, 96
  in nineteenth century America, 104–109
  intentional, 105n, 123
Towne v. Eisner, 33n
Toussaint v. Blue Cross and Blue Shield of Michigan, 122
Travers, Timothy, 115n
Trespass, writ of, 100
Tribe, Lawrence, 85n
Trimester analysis, (see *Roe v. Wade*)
Twenty-sixth amendment (see Constitution of the United States)

Undue burden, (see abortion)
United States Department of Health, Education, and Welfare, 44
United States Department of Transportation, 146
United States Sentencing Commission, 141–142
United States v. Butler, 63n
United States v. Carolene Products Co., 66n
United States v. Darby, 66n
United States v. Eichman, 3, 60, 67
United States v. Leon, 81, 85n
United States v. Lopez, 64
United States v. Mania, 33n
United States v. Nixon, 62, 82
United States v. Nova Scotia Food Products Corporation, 148–149

United States v. Public Utility Commission of California, 42
United States v. Sheek, 53–56, 163, 165
Unreasonable searches and seizures, 67, 78

Vacco v. Quill, 162n–163n
Vagueness, statutory, 30, 96
Vanderbilt, Arthur, 18
Van Geel, T.R., 82
Verkuil, Paul, 131n
Vermont Fair Employment Practices Act, 117n

Wald, Patricia, 12, 13n, 32, 41n
Wallace, J. Clifford, 70
Wallace v. Jaffree, 79
Walz v. Tax Commission, 79
Warranty, 115n
Washington v. Glucksberg, 162n–163n
Watkins v. United States, 62
Watson, Alan, 102n
Webster v. Reproductive Health Services, 17
Weeks v. United States, 78
West Virginia Board of Education v. Barnette, 72
West, William, 138n
White, Byron, 81, 85, 147
White, G. Edward, 3, 11n, 19
Wiecek, William, 106n
William the Conqueror, 99
Winterbottom v. Wright, 110
Wiretapping, 69
Wisconsin Public Intervenor v. Mortier, 42
Writs, 100

Wrongful-death suits
  generally, 105
  common-law prohibition of,
    106–107
Wyatt v. Stickney, 169n

Zaphiriou, George, 101n, 102n
Zone of privacy, 8, 13
Zorach v. Clausen, 14–16, 18, 163,
  168

Yakus v. United States, 142n, 143n